THE TOUR

Best Wishes,
Bill Staines

THE TOUR

A Life Between the Lines

Bill Staines

Library of Congress Number: 2003093194
ISBN : Hardcover 1-4134-0965-2
Softcover 1-4134-0964-4

This book was printed in the United States of America.

To order additional copies of this book, contact:
Xlibris Corporation
1-888-795-4274
www.Xlibris.com
Orders@Xlibris.com

19098

CONTENTS

Dedication

For all of the Troubadours Past, Present, and Future

ACKNOWLEDGMENTS

How can one tell the story of a life in so few pages? Many of my dearest friends are not mentioned here. To those, and you know who you are, I thank you for being my friends and for making the journey with me.

To Lynn Damme: thank you for the editing, and the reassurance that I was not flailing around in the ozone.

To my son Bowen: thank you for the cover art, and all of the help when I had no idea what happened to this file or that when they disappeared on the computer.

To my wife Karen: thank you for your patience, and for knowing that a book cannot be written unless one takes the time to do so. And to all who take the time to read this narrative: thank you, thank you, thank you.

AUTHOR'S NOTE

It is three years later, or five, or twenty. Some things have changed; some things will never change. A tour comes to an end; a tour begins anew. So shall it be, on and on, until infinity.

CHAPTER 1

The Beginning

I have never been a person with great lifelong goals. Perhaps that is a bad thing. I don't think so. Perhaps not having great goals is the only way I could have survived, for 35 years, the craziness and uncertainty of life as a road musician. Without goals to channel my direction, I have always been free to wonder at the experiences of life as they have come my way in their own time. I have been able to explore the paths and the open doors, and I've sometimes taken opportunities without the fear that they might lead to dead ends or result in time wasted. I have sometimes thought of myself as a ship out on the vast ocean, steaming toward some distant horizon. I know not where I am going, but I do know that as long as I can look behind me and see a wake strung out in a straight line, I am on my way to somewhere, and all is well. I must always see that wake, for its presence reassures me that my life is in motion.

A life of music is a life driven by the heart and fired by deep emotion. It is of subtle dangers, little victories, and great rewards. In that sense, I suppose, it is not unlike many other lives—but then again, it is a life of music, and that is special. It is perhaps not the one I would have chosen for myself had I been driven by goals, but it is a life that has brought me everything that I know in this world.

I have always loved music: my mother, the piano player, and the duets at the kitchen table with my father the violinist. Neither of my parents were professional musicians, but in the 1930s, my mother had been a dancer in some of the stage shows at the hotels in Boston. My father was a civilian mechanic for the Air Force, working at Hanscom Field in Bedford. He had been a member of the ground crews that repaired and refitted the fighter planes in Iceland during World War II. Although music was not their profession, it was in their blood, and it was a great joy for them.

In the fourth grade, I took up the clarinet. With my lips drooping at the sides and my cheeks bulging and turning blue, I struggled up and down the scales while my father softly supported my efforts with simple but beautiful harmonies. I loved listening to him play and desperately questioned whether my musical output would ever be as true or as effortless as his. It is quite possible that he may have been asking himself the same question. Now and then, as a relief from my barrage of squeaks and squawks, he would simply lean back in his chair, close his eyes, and play a passage from his favorite melody, "Lieberstraum." After a short time, he would return to my world, and we would go through the lesson again. Up and down the scales, "Minuet in G," "March Slav," over and over. I never minded those lapses. They were my first sense of how much music could mean to a person and what an incredibly powerful force it is. Years later, it became the one voice by which I was able to convey my innermost feelings to others. I suppose that when I was so very young it was never in my mind that I would make my living as a musician, but certainly somewhere a greater being had different plans.

I gave up any thought of being a serious clarinetist when I was 12 years old and taught myself how to play the guitar. Because I am left-handed, my inclination was to turn the guitar over so that I fretted with my right hand and strummed with my left. I learned the chords by putting my fingers where the dots were in a guitar music book and played for two years before someone informed me that I was not playing left-handed, but, indeed, I was playing upside down. By then, I had already learned to play and was not about to be persuaded to change my ways. After all, Jimmy Hendrix and Elizabeth Cotton played upside down. Over the years, I've met many other upside-down guitar players, and when it comes to how they learned to play the guitar, they all tell the same story.

My father and mother separated, and he moved away. One day my younger brother Steve came running to me while I was involved in a neighborhood baseball game. He informed me that my father needed me to help him pack his car because he was leaving home. It was one of the most difficult things I have ever had to do. I swore at that moment that I would never do this thing to a child of mine. Perhaps there were too many squeaks and squawks in their marriage for him. Perhaps it was one too many nights out with his National Guard buddies for her. I really don't know. We communicated over the years, but over time those communications became shorter and fewer, and those duets with him that I remember so well were never played again.

Somewhere along the way it came to pass that the wonderfully undeniable moving force of music within me prevailed over all others, and I became a musician. I don't think that it was meant to have happened any other way.

CHAPTER 2

The Fall Tour

At the beginning of each October, I leave home for what has become known as "the fall tour." It is the longest road trip of the year for me, and over the course of five weeks it takes me from my home in New England to Alaska and back. During this time, I perform almost every night and log about 14,000 miles on my car. October of 1999 marked the 20th anniversary of the tour, and although I return to many of the same places each fall, I had a sense that this year would be special. Perhaps it was because it was the 20th year, or perhaps it was because we were approaching the end of the millennium. Whatever the case, I decided that I should chronicle the tour and mark the passing of all these miles in my life. This narrative is the result.

Fall is my favorite season. It is a time of great color in New England. It is the time of fresh apple cider and old cheese, of wood smoke and wooly coats. Fall marks the return of the students along the Charles River in Boston, the moving in, the vans along the streets of the city, the laughing excitement of youth. I have always looked forward to fall. Some people consider the season the winding down of the old year, the closing out of what is old and gone by, but for me it is surely the bright beginning of something new. It is the busy time, the time of the music.

The minstrel takes to the road, and what the road has in store is nothing less than the great unknown. Each morning, that highway opens a new door, an untraveled trail, a chance to do something with the gifts that have been given. If someone were to ask me what the great secret of life might be, I think that I would have to respond that it is always having something to look forward to. I look forward to that great unknown. In fact, I look forward to looking forward to each day. Perhaps before sundown a tragedy awaits, or perhaps the finding of a new friend. What will be given? What will be taken away? Will I see the next dawn? I hope so, for I am certainly looking forward to it.

* * *

After 20 years, the preparations for the tour are pretty well defined. It takes a day or so to get all of the recordings and books loaded into my van. I usually travel with about 1,500 pieces, so positioning each box in the van is important. There is the weight distribution factor, and the availability of each title. The last thing I want is to have to unload half of the recordings into the street on a rainy day to get at a submerged box of books. There is the paperwork, the inventories, and all of the business paraphernalia that goes along with the traveling. There are the airline tickets, itineraries, maps, and hotel directories. Then there is the packing. I sometimes have to laugh at the things that I take along with me in the fall. There is clothing for the warm weather of southern California as well as emergency gear for the surprise blizzard in Fairbanks, Alaska. This includes my L.L. Bean footwear. In Alaska, they call these boots "tundra tennies." Considering the size of the boots that I've seen some people wear in the far north, this term seems to be right on target. I have always carried a sleeping bag in my van, but the packing of extra warm clothing has stood me well more than a time or two in my travels. The fall tour involves doing a bit of commercial flying, so my "flying guitar," as well as my everyday guitar, makes the journey. I made up my mind long ago that I would not fly with my everyday instrument, a Martin D-18 that I have had for 34 years. Even though the guitar looks as if it was used as a weapon in the Crimean War, the wear and tear comes from years of loving use—not from some inept baggage handler. Once after a show a member of the audience commented that my guitar looked like what must be "the Velveteen Guitar." I guess I would tend to agree. It does indeed have that look about it; what is more, it has been a long-time, true, and real friend.

All preparations are completed and the day of departure arrives. What is most difficult about this time is saying goodbye to my family. I think that each year there is a different reason that those goodbyes are rough. In the early years, it was simply the time apart. Now that I have a son, perhaps I wonder whether I will make it back home again. I have always been mindful of Harry Chapin's song, "The Cat's in the Cradle," in which the traveling father, because he is gone so much, misses out on the years that his son is growing. A life on the road, no matter how rewarding, will never be easy on a marriage or a family. The time apart breeds spaces and is one of those subtle dangers. The responsibilities remain, however, and when music is all that you know, you simply do the best that you can and hope that things work out well in the end.

My family has a small tradition. Just before I leave, all of us, including the dog, gather in what looks like a football huddle and hug each other. All that remains after this is for me to climb behind the wheel of my van and leave. There is a country road that runs for about a mile between my house and the highway. It is lined with magnificent white pines and is surrounded by farm fields. I have come to know these beautiful trees as my friends, and they are the last to whisper their goodbyes before I turn onto the larger road that leads to the interstate.

CHAPTER 3

Where Have All the Flowers Gone?

I grew up in the town of Lexington, Massachusetts, then a sleepy little suburb of Boston, best known, I suppose, as one-half of the famous Lexington and Concord of Paul Revere fame. April 19th is called Patriots Day in Massachusetts, and it was always a day of great goings-on around the town. The battle of Lexington and Concord, which kicked off the American Revolution, was fought on that day in April 1775. Paul Revere's ride, and the battles on Lexington Green and at Concord Bridge, are staged year after year, punctuated by parades and ceremonies. I marched in those parades with the junior high school band. There I was, happily tooting away on my clarinet, making up my own parts, not paying any attention to the music written in the band books, and loving the whole experience—all under the watchful and not-so-impressed eye of the band leader. Having already fallen in love with the guitar, I knew that my days in the marching band were nearly over and that my lack of a future as a clarinetist was pretty much decided. I also loved to sing—and singing and playing the clarinet at the same time was a challenge I was not about to tackle. The guitar certainly seemed to be the answer to my musical dreams.

In 1960, John and Dick Curtis and I formed the first and last rock-and-roll band of my career. The Curtis brothers lived a few houses away, and their mother Louise was the youth choir director at our church. It was Dick, after showing up at my house one day with a new guitar, who convinced me that I really should give the instrument a try. Having limited funds, I ended up buying a three-quarter-size Silvertone guitar from Sears. The guitar had a picture of a cowboy riding a horse on the front of it. I immediately got a block of sandpaper and liberated the guitar out from under the painting. With a few upside-down guitar chords under my belt, I was soon on my way to perceived stardom. There was another problem, however. In order to have a successful rock-and-roll band, to be able to play at the school dances, and to be cool at all, one should have an electric guitar. My guitar was not electric, and I had no money to upgrade to a fancy model. Enter Dick, the electronics whiz.

There was an old television set sitting around my house. The television contained a tuner and an amplifier. By hooking some dohickey up with a plodgett and rewiring one wire into this hole or that, and investing seven dollars into a microphone that clipped into the sound hole of the instrument, lo and behold, when I played my guitar, the sound came out through the television set! Oh happy day! Now that I was with it, it was time to experiment with some additional effects. The first idea that I had was to introduce a small circuit breaker similar to the kind that one finds in blinking Christmas tree lights into the power chord of the television set. The resulting sound produced by the power to the television being turned off and on by the breaker was something akin to a tremolo effect. This was a sound used by many of the rock-and-roll bands of the era, and I loved it. My mother did not. The experiment not only produced the sound, it produced a plethora of blown fuses and sparking wall fixtures. The house survived, but my experiments were short-lived.

Buddy Holly was gone but still very popular. Instrumental

groups like The Ventures, The Fendermen, and The Stringalongs were the rage, and I was in hog heaven playing rock-and-roll.

One afternoon, perhaps early in 1961, I was hanging around with Dick in the basement of the Curtis' home when his mother suggested that we listen to an LP that she had come across. It was a recording of a group called The Weavers doing a concert at Carnegie Hall in New York. That recording, and that afternoon, set the life's course of a young guitar player.

It was the beginning of the "folk years," the rise in popularity of a music style that spoke to me like no other music ever had. The Weavers had made the pop charts with "Goodnight Irene" in the early 1950s, and The Kingston Trio made the charts in the late 1950s with "Tom Dooley," but there was something deep in this music, with its powerful simplicity, that could not be denied now, and the public seemed ready. It was the kind of music that belonged to the people. It was about the people. It was a music devoid of effects and noise and yet so very rich in the human spirit. Little did anyone know at the time just how inspirational some of these songs would become—and just how deep a few of them would make their way into history.

* * *

Boston is a city of culture. It is a community that abounds with colleges and universities, and with the energy of youth. It has always had a wonderful music scene, and growing up around this music was a real blessing. Not only was there the world-renowned symphony orchestra and all of the classical music available, there was a great jazz scene. There were also a number of small coffeehouses around town, and on most nights poets could be seen and heard holding court with their recitations. With the rise in the popularity of folk music, many of the coffeehouses became havens for young singers and songwriters, and it was here in these coffeehouses that I began to make my musical way in the world.

There were actually two separate music scenes in the area. There was the Boston scene, and there was an emerging musical community across the Charles River in Cambridge. It was here, on one of the streets just outside of Harvard Square, that the Club 47 Mount Auburn came into existence. The address was 47 Mount Auburn Street, and eventually the place came to be called The Club 47. During the ten-year period that it was open, The Club 47 became one of the premiere folk venues in the country—the place where many of the future folk music greats began their careers.

The Club 47 is where I saw my first coffeehouse performance. There were three acts scheduled for that evening in 1962: Tom Rush; Frank Hamilton (formally of The Weavers); and a country-bluegrass trio which consisted of Jim Rooney, Joe Val, and Herb Applen. I was enthralled. The place was jammed with people, and even though I was only a sophomore in high school, I knew that spending nights like this, listening to this kind of music, was all that I wanted to do for the rest of my life. There was one more event which would be as important to me as a musician, but that was not to come for another few years during the 1965 Newport Folk Festival.

My rock-and-roll band was defunct, but my friendship with the Curtis brothers wasn't. They had also become interested in folk music, and before long we had traded in our electric guitars for acoustic instruments and put together a group called The Green Mountain Boys. I have no idea why we picked that name. I don't think that any one of us at the time had ever seen, much less knew anything about, the Green Mountains. We played some small shows around Lexington, and before long we had even made a couple of appearances at the Sunday night hootenannies at The 47. All one had to do was to show up early at the club, sign up on a list of performers, and play a tune or two for the audience. The "hoots" were the precursor to the contemporary "open mike."

In my scheme of life, schoolwork became secondary. I managed to get by with a B average in my classes, but what I really wanted to do was to spend time in the evenings at the coffeehouses. My mother tried to limit that time to the weekends, to no avail. As long as I finished my schoolwork and got decent grades, I figured that my time was my own, and that meant listening to and playing music.

I spent a good deal of time at the Cambridge Folklore Center. The center was a small storefront operation managed by guitarist Peter Walker. It was also located on Mount Auburn Street, and many of the local musicians either gave guitar lessons there or just dropped in to talk or play some of the instruments that hung on the walls. Every summer, the Folklore Center obtained a permit from the city of Cambridge to close Mount Auburn Street and present a music marathon. The music lasted from Friday noon until sometime Sunday evening. Groups like The Holy Modal Rounders, The Charles River Valley Boys, and members of the Jim Kweskin Jug Band performed at an area facing the street inside the front window of the center. Others, including Tim Hardin, Tom Rush, and Jackie Washington, also played while the audience gathered in the street to listen. From time to time, someone from the Folklore Center would pass among the people in the street and collect donations for a local charity. This was the official reason for the marathon and the understanding under which the permit to close the street was issued.

I graduated from school in the spring of 1964 with no particular goals or prospects for work. I knew that by the fall I would need a job, but that summer was going to be my first taste of total freedom, and I was going to make the best of it. The Curtis boys had become interested in string-band music and I had gravitated toward slower ballads, so although we remained friends, The Green Mountain Boys gradually faded into oblivion, and I began singing as a solo.

For the summer of 1964, the Folklore Center had managed to convince the city of Boston that the Hatch Shell, on the banks of the Charles River, would be a good place to hold a marathon mini-folk festival. With donations once again slated for a local charity, the dates were determined and the event was set to go. Other forces were at work, however—far away, and yet not so far away in the South.

It was June of the Freedom Summer, and it was a summer of tragic violence. Three civil rights workers had disappeared in

Mississippi, and a few days before the festival at the Hatch Shell, the bodies of the murdered—Ben Chaney, Andrew Goodman, and Mickey Schwerner—were located. It was a sad day in our history. Although I was never really involved as an activist in the Civil Rights movement, I supported the cause, and those events in Mississippi that June touched and angered me deeply.

Given the turn of events, The Folklore Center decided that the money collected at the festival would be donated to the Student Nonviolent Coordinating Committee (SNCC). The city revoked the permit, and the festival was moved into a space operated by the Unitarian Church in Kenmore Square. It was a small area on the second floor of a building on Boylston Street, and for three days and nights musicians, poets, and speakers of all sorts made their way up the crowded staircase and onto the makeshift stage. I was there for the duration, filling in onstage whenever there was a space in the list of performers, and often catching a nap on one of the couches in the room. I remember once, sometime around two in the morning, being disturbed by Jim Kweskin, who was busily sweeping up the place with a push broom. The crowd had thinned out a bit, given the hour, and it just seemed to him as if it were the thing to do. The news of the murders in Mississippi spawned a great deal of media coverage, and toward the end of the weekend a few of the performers, myself included, loaded their instruments into a van and headed over to one of the local radio stations to do an interview with talk-show host Jerry Williams. His interview centered around our views on civil rights and our thoughts about what had happened in Mississippi. I let it be known, as all of the other performers did, that I was angry and ashamed that something like this, that any killing or beating, should be happening to people who were simply trying to bring us all closer together.

Late that last evening of the weekend, I took the subway home feeling as if I had truly started to become a member of the folk music community, and that these songs—songs like "We Shall Not Be Moved" and "Where Have All the Flowers Gone?," simple songs of great dignity and rich in the human spirit—would come to have a lasting effect on me and ultimately become the measures by which I would judge my own writing. When I arrived at the front door, my mother met me with a concerned and somewhat frightened look on her face. Soon after the radio show had been broadcast, she had received a number of threatening phone calls.

CHAPTER 4

The Fall Tour, Day 1

The first day of this fall tour is to be a 500-mile run from my home in New Hampshire, over the backbone of New York state and into Buffalo for an evening concert. This particular morning, the fully loaded van feels a little sluggish as I pull onto Interstate 95 at Kittery, Maine, climb up over the Piscataqua River Bridge, and enter New Hampshire at Portsmouth. It amazes me to travel through Portsmouth nowadays. I played here in the late 1960s at a café called The New World Gallery when the town was nothing more than a stopover for travelers on their way to Maine. It was a town of corner taverns and 20¢ beers. It was a town of sailors' clubs and, here and there, a decent restaurant. It was Gilley's town. Gilley sold hotdogs, hamburgers, and chili out of what amounted to a diner on wheels. Each afternoon since what seemed like the beginning of time, he towed the wagon, using an old Chevy truck, from an empty side street lot out into the middle of Market Square and set up shop. He even had his own designated, although illegal, parking space and was served each day with a parking ticket. Pretty cheap rent, all things considered. Business hours were from four or five in the afternoon until the wee hours of the morning. Gilley's was usually my final stop on the nights that I played at The New World Gallery before the 70-mile drive back to Boston. Gilley retired in the early 1990s and sold his wagon and truck. The truck had recorded a grand total of 52 original miles. The whole rig was moved by the new owner back to one of the side streets and still operates until those early morning hours when the customers leave and wander off back home.

Today, Portsmouth is a place with a new heartbeat. It abounds with restaurants and has a great jazz and blues scene. Once just a stopover, this seaside community has become a popular destination.

Just south of Portsmouth, the morning traffic starts to get heavy as the commuters make their way toward the big city. I turn on the radio to check the morning news and then switch to Channel 19 on the CB to hear what the truckers have to say about road conditions and the location of police radar traps in the area. Immediately, my senses are leveled by a blast of profanity and crude jokes. Most of the CB conversations are informative and interesting, but now and again someone decides to saturate the airways with this lowlife drivel. Fortunately, this morning the perpetrator is traveling in the opposite direction, and he is soon out of range.

About 20 miles farther south, I take the turnoff for Interstate 495, the outer beltway around Boston, and cross over the Merrimack River at Lawrence. Off to my right on the banks of the river stand the huge red brick textile mills. These buildings, many of which are now being restored, are enduring monuments to the workers of the 19th and early 20th Centuries when textiles from the cities of Lawrence and nearby Lowell were marketed around the nation and the world. To these mills came the families of French Canada, the blood of Quebec; the men found jobs, and the women and children worked these mills for long noisy hours and short pay. Some stayed and settled here, and their strong French-Canadian heritage remains. It was at these mills in 1912 that 23,000 workers, led by the mill women, took to the streets demanding better pay and working hours in what became known as the Bread and Roses strike.

Out of these mills and marches came not only textiles, but a wealth of music and a legacy of songs about the common working people living their lives out along these rivers. Each Labor Day, this legacy is celebrated as part of the Lowell Folk Festival, a festival of music, history, crafts, and community.

I tune in to one of the area radio stations that offers nothing but folk and acoustic music. I have traveled all over this country, and I must say that the Northeast has always had the greatest media support for this type of music. Living in New England, I have always been grateful for that. If each radio station that offered folk music and each folk performance venue were beacons of light shining up toward the sky, and if you observed the scene from space, this corner of the world would truly shine like no other.

I follow Interstate 495 until it intersects with the Massachusetts Turnpike and, for the first time on this tour, point my van due west.

I believe we are the sum total of every experience we have ever had, every person we have ever known, and every action that we have ever taken or has been enacted upon us. It strikes me that everything I have known in my life, all of these ingredients, has now come together, and the result is this being whose physical presence occupies this current place in time and space. I think to myself as the hours pass and the highway slowly ascends into and over the Berkshires, "So it has come to this: I am this moment, this musician alone on his way westward across a great continent." I ask myself, "Am I a worthy result, given the friends, loved ones, and experiences that have all contributed to my makeup?" Sometimes the answer is yes, and if it is, I am glad. Sometimes the answer is no; but if it is no, I understand that there is always the possibility of change, for who I am is only momentary, and what I can still be is always waiting around the bend in the road before me.

* * *

Descending out of the russets, yellows, and smoky oranges of the Berkshires, I enter New York and cross the Hudson River at its capital of Albany. I look north up the splendid river valley and ponder its history. There is the racing town of Saratoga Springs, where early one misty morning I saw the big red horse Secretariat run a few warm-up laps before his final race. A few miles farther north is the resort town of Lake George and the string of forts: Fort Edward, Fort Ann, Fort William Henry, and the supposedly invulnerable Fort Carillon. Fort Carillon was the original French name for Fort Ticonderoga. One night Ethan Allen and his crew put the kibosh on the supposition of invulnerability by slipping through an open and unguarded door in the fort's wall and wresting the fort from the British forces.

These places came to life for me through the writings of James Fennimore Cooper and his *Leather Stocking Tales*. How well I came to know Cap Huff, Steven Nason, and so many of the characters in the writings of Kenneth Roberts. I traveled with Robert Rogers in *Northwest Passage* and got to know Benedict Arnold in *Rabble in Arms*.

Who was this Benedict Arnold, undeniably known to everyone as a traitor? He was a truly gifted and brilliant American general, without whom we probably would have lost the Revolution. It was Arnold who commanded the small fleet of bateaux with names like *Resolute, Defiant,* and *Vigilant*, that halted the British ships heading south on Lake Champlain in support of British General John Burgoyne in 1777. It was the very first engagement of the fledgling American Navy. All of Arnold's bateaux were lost, but this action ultimately forced Burgoyne to stand and fight at Saratoga. This time, the colonial forces, with Arnold riding his horse at the lead, were victorious, and the Battle of Saratoga eventually came to be considered the turning point of the war and one of the more important battles in history.

So why did Arnold switch his loyalties? The simple truth is that he was frustrated by the lack of recognition and cooperation shown to him by the American military leaders at the time.

How often in life we are met with what seem like insurmountable obstacles. Arnold, perhaps, took the easy way out, and that's how we have come to remember him as the traitor. Yet there are so many others, people who every day face their own hardships and somehow endure. Whether it be disease or personal tragedy, bad luck, or the uncertainty of survival itself, there are those who know of nothing else to do other than to keep pushing on, and again, just keep on pushing on.

West of Albany, the highway parallels the Mohawk River Barge Canal. I pass Johnstown, Herkimer, Utica, Rome, and Syracuse. The road continues west, running just north of the Finger Lakes with their lovely names: Owasco, Cayuga, Seneca, Keuka, and Canandaigua, and then passes just south of the city of Rochester. Finally, at Mile Yardstick 425 as the truckers would say, I enter the Buffalo area.

Once in town, I head over to the home of an old friend. I have known Jim Dombrowski for close to 30 years. When we were both younger, he used to come to hear me perform at the University of Buffalo when they had their coffeehouse there in the early 1970s. Over the years, Jim and I had become good friends, and he has always had an open door and a cold beer waiting for me when I pull into town. In the fall of 1989, I stopped by his place to spend the night on the first leg of my annual tour. At some point in our conversations during the evening, the talk turned to my itinerary for that season. I recited a list of all of the usual places that I was headed that year, including Alaska, and I noticed a sort of wistful look come into Jim's eyes. He slowly leaned back in his chair and sadly informed me that he had never been west of some place like Kalamazoo, Michigan. It was not long before I ended up convincing him that he should fly out to San Francisco the following week, where we could meet up and finish the rest of my tour together. Late in the afternoon of the appointed day, I picked him up at the airport in San Francisco and off we went over the Bay Bridge, headed for Oregon and points north. As we were crossing the bridge, I remembered a bit of information that I thought might be timely and related it to Jim.

A good friend of mine, Martha Pike, and her husband, Dabris, had lived in San Francisco for a number of years. Marty was a nurse at Saint Mary's Hospital in the Bay Area. As a part of her job, she was routinely briefed on procedures to follow in case of an earthquake. She had been told that there was a four-day window on either side of the full moon in October when, because of the Earth's position around the sun, the stresses on the planet's crust were at their greatest. That was not to say that a quake would happen, it was just that this particular period of the year was a prime time for such an event.

I jokingly mentioned this story to Jim and proffered the fact that it was probably a good thing that we were leaving town, as it was the fourth day after the full moon in October. There was a World Series game between San Francisco and Oakland being played that day, so we decided to tune in to pass the time on the road. I don't think that either of us will ever forget what we did hear on the radio that day. A major earthquake, with reports of severe damage and loss of life, had just struck the area. There were also reports that a section of the Bay Bridge had collapsed. We never felt the tremors. We never heard the rumble. We just looked at each other, and I think that down deep inside we were both thanking our lucky stars that we hadn't left town a few minutes later.

Occasionally someone will ask what my favorite places are around the country. There are certainly many beautiful spots all over this land, but truly it is the people that I've met along the way who have become friends, wherever they may be, that determine the answer to that question. Buffalo is not the most picturesque city on the map, but friends like Jim will always keep me looking forward to my returns.

I see no need to describe each of the concert dates along the tour in this narrative. I hope that it will suffice to say that I love playing my music for people. Music is the purpose for the tour. It is why I am on the road in the first place. Of course, there are moments during many of the performances that are simply magical, and in some cases I will try to describe that concert and that magic, but for now I will only write that I look forward to each and every show.

And so at the end of that evening in Buffalo, the first concert of the tour is history, and Jim and I head off to a local pub for a few beers before we head back to his place. Once there, I crawl into my sleeping bag, feel its surrounding warmth, and drop immediately off to sleep.

CHAPTER 5

Early Morning Rain

Late in the summer of 1964, I went to work for Sears & Roebuck at their catalogue store in Lexington. There I was a "jack of all trades," doing everything from unloading trucks to fixing lawnmowers. I worked during the day, and when the evening came, I was off to the Club 47. The years between 1964 and 1967 were the richest in my early musical life. On Mondays I went to see Tom Rush, and on Tuesdays I went to see Jackie Washington. Jackie was one of the local balladeers who could fingerpick the guitar. His first recording was for Vanguard Records and was simply entitled *Jackie Washington.* I was amazed at how someone could play a lead part on the guitar while at the same time picking out a rhythm part. I bought the album and after much frustration learned three of the cuts: "Little Brown Dog, " a traditional song; "Freight Train," by Elizabeth Cotton; and "The Blackfly Song," by Wade Hemsworth. Jackie Washington at that time was my favorite singer and ultimately one of my biggest influences.

On Wednesdays I would go to The 47 to see the Tim Hardin Trio. The trio consisted of Tim on the electric guitar, a sax player, and a fellow playing the piano who called himself Taj Mahal. Tim Hardin lived a life of fire. He was too quickly consumed by that fire, but not before leaving us with songs like "If I Were a Carpenter," "Reason to Believe," and "Blacksheep Boy."

Thursdays were bluegrass nights at The 47, and groups like The Greenbriar Boys, The Charles River Valley Boys, and The Lilly Brothers broadened my musical roots and gave me a real sense of the old musical traditions.

Fridays and Saturdays at the club were generally reserved for out-of-town players. Performers on tour, including Judy Collins, Joni Mitchell, and Jesse Colin Young, held down those weekend slots. I went to see the great blues players Jesse Fuller, Son House, and Mississippi John Hurt, and I sat and listened to the new writers Martin Mull, the Fariñas, and Jerry Corbitt, who later teamed up with Jesse Colin Young and started The Youngbloods.

Eventually, because I was at the club so much, some of the performers even began to remember my first name. At that time, the club was managed by Byron Lord Linardos, and at one point he asked me if I would mind filling in as the emcee for the Sunday night hoots. This was a big boost, because now I got to meet and talk with so many more of the performers that I looked up to and respected. Phil Ochs, if he was in town, would occasionally drop by to do a song or two; so would Eric Andersen or Paul Arnoldi.

Paul Arnoldi was a happy-go-lucky sort of person who played in an easy ragtime style. He recorded his first album with Kapp Records, and Dick Fariña penned the liner notes. Contained in these notes was one of my all-time favorite descriptions of someone. I don't recall the words exactly, but they were something to the effect that " . . . when Paul cries, even his tears fall up."

Musically, it was a wonderful time. Radio station WBZ in Boston had a three-hour Sunday evening "Hootenanny" show hosted by Jefferson Kaye, and on WCRB every Friday evening after the 11:00 news, you could tune in to "Folk City, USA" hosted by Bob Lurtsema. These two people not only played folk music on their radio shows, but each was truly interested in the performers and were frequently found at the clubs or attending concerts in the area. Bob Lurtsema eventually became known as Robert J. Lurtsema, the host of the popular National Public Radio show "Morning Pro Musica."

The Unicorn, the largest of the Boston clubs, was located downstairs at 825 Boylston Street. Each of the city's folk venues seemed to have their own musical families, and those headliners who seemed to return on a regular basis to The Unicorn included Dave Van Ronk, The Irish Rovers, Ian and Sylvia, and Jose Feliciano. Now and again, a writer from New York with a big, bushy head of hair and a beautiful voice would show up at the Unicorn hoots. His name was Art Garfunkel. There was no shortage of talent to be found in this music scene.

So there it was, The Club 47 and The Unicorn both in full swing, the coffeehouses on Charles Street presenting the best of the local pickers; it seemed as if the music would live forever.

In the fall of 1964, I bought my first car for $75. It was a 1959 Hillman Husky. I loved that car, even though it was barely big enough to seat three people. It was to be my chariot, my key to the rest of the world. On the weekends that fall, if there wasn't anyone I wanted to hear at The Club 47, I would take little solo sojourns around New England in my Hillman. I loved driving down the tiny country roads lined with the red, yellow, and orange maples. I was discovering places that I had never seen before, and it was exciting. In hindsight, these trips were great practice for all of the driving that was to come.

During the Christmas season of that year, I was assigned by my boss to manage an overflow warehouse that Sears operated in Lexington. This was fine with me; the only drawback was that I had to unload trucks that arrived at the warehouse at 5:00 in the morning. My trips into Cambridge that winter to hear music were somewhat reduced, given that now and then a person needs to get some sleep.

With the arrival of the spring of 1965, I was out of the warehouse and back to my old routine. I worked during the weekdays, listened to music at night and, on the weekends, traveled all over New England in my Hillman. Often on these weekend trips I was accompanied by some of my old high school friends—Roger Holman, Jesse Ennis, Dick LaRose, and Dan Jellis. What a band of crazies! On Friday afternoons after I finished work, we would all hop into a car and drive to Hoosick, New York. The drinking age in New York at the time was 18, and we could spend those nights partying the time away at a dance hall called The Three Way. At the end of the evenings, we would camp somewhere out in a farm field; we would make our way back home by Sunday night via a Canadian route through Montreal or Quebec City and down through Maine. They were wild trips, and yet we never did any mischief that was serious enough to warrant any run-in with the law.

That spring, I heard a song that would forever have an effect on me. It was a Gordon Lightfoot tune entitled "Early Morning Rain" and was the title song on the latest Ian and Sylvia recording. When I heard the song, something inside of me began to burn, a wanderlust that would come to guide my whole life and remains with me to this day. The song spoke to me of all the far-off horizons imaginable, and of all the places I had never been.

It got to the point where I would drive my Hillman to Logan Airport in Boston, sit at the terminal gates, and listen as the Air Canada flights came in from Winnipeg, Calgary, and Vancouver—places I knew nothing about, places that, because of the song, I was bound and determined to see someday. I studied road maps and set up hypothetical tours that I would make when the time was right to the far west and the vast Pacific. How that fire burned inside of me! How I longed to be the traveler in that song!

In order to keep up with happenings in the world of folk music around the New England area at the time, one would pick up a copy of *The Broadside*. It was a biweekly journal of approximately a dozen pages that contained reviews of the latest folk recordings, concert and club listings, and all of the folky news and gossip around the town. For more than a year I had subscribed to *The Broadside*, and that June I received the latest issue in the mail. I was reading through the pages of the issue when I happened upon a schedule for the 1965 Newport Folk Festival. I was particularly attracted to the schedule for the Sunday afternoon concert. Among those performers who appear that day were Mimi and Dick Fariña; Kathy and Carol, two young women from California who were receiving rave reviews for their first, and I believe only, album on Elecktra Records; the Chambers Brothers; and—could it be?—the Canadian singer Gordon Lightfoot. Ian and Sylvia; Peter, Paul and Mary; and Pete Seeger were also scheduled to appear that weekend.

There would be no keeping me from this festival. I also felt sure that Roger and Jesse, my weekend traveling amigos, would want to come along on the trip. I was right, and when the time came, we packed all of our gear into my Hillman and headed for Newport, Rhode Island, festival-bound, singing at the top of our lungs.

We arrived in Newport early that Friday evening, purchased tickets at the gate, and headed off into town looking for a camping area that might have room for us. It was not surprising that every campground was full, but we were not the least bit deterred. Finding a spot just off the road on the edge of a swamp near the festival site, we set up our camp. I had brought only the necessities for the trip: my guitar, a Harmony Sovereign Jumbo Model, one of the classic guitars of the time; my autoharp, which I had taken up playing because I was secretly in love with Mimi Fariña; one change of clothes; a sleeping bag; and a pup tent that I had owned since I was in Cub Scouts. I think we also managed to stow away a few six-packs of beer in hopeful anticipation of whatever activities might arise.

The next morning we left our little camp on the banks of the swamp and headed for the festival grounds. That day I felt as if I were in another universe. Here were all of the people who until now I had only heard on recordings. The Saturday night concert: Bill Monroe, Theodore Bikel, Odetta, and finally Ian and Sylvia. I sat up and closed my eyes as they sang "Un Canadien Errant." The feelings inside me almost could not be harnessed. I looked across at Roger and knew that he felt the same way.

After the concert, we returned to camp and opened the beer. It did not take very much to drink in those days to reach some sort of altered state, and the next thing I remembered was waking up the following morning, lying under some bushes with both of my feet submerged in swamp water.

As much as I was there to see all of the performers at the festival, it would still be that Sunday afternoon show that would direct my destiny. It was very hot, and the people waited outside the entrance gates until they opened at noon. Quite a crowd had amassed, and as the barricades were moved to the side and the people started filing in, a few of the folks began to make sounds like cattle on the move. In a few moments, the whole mass of us responded with similar snorts and moos.

* * *

Slowly the grounds filled for the afternoon concert. I really don't know how to describe my feelings that day as artist after artist made their way to the stage. Mark Spoelstra played "Just a Hand to Hold," the Chambers Brothers sang "People Get Ready," Kathy and Carol sang "Gold Watch and Chain," and throughout the performances something inside of me kept saying, "Bill, you will do this; you will be a singer and a writer; you will be a vehicle that will bring these same feelings to others."

Gordon Lightfoot took the stage and began with "Steel Rail Blues." He followed with "Long River" and "That's What You Get for Loving Me," and that same voice spoke again to me and said, "You already know that you will be a musician, now observe and listen, for it is in this next moment that you will come to know your style and who you are as a performer." Lightfoot began singing "Early Morning Rain," and I knew that the voice inside me was right. I knew that I would grow and leave these beginnings behind, but I also knew that on that afternoon I had chosen the path along which I would travel as an artist.

At the conclusion of the concert that evening we all made our way back to the camp packed up our belongings—now wet because it had started to rain—and headed for home. I may have been a little withdrawn on the drive. Maybe it was because I was tired, or maybe it was because I had just been born. I still have that autoharp, and there is still rust on its tuning pins from that soft and gentle rain.

Some years later, a documentary film chronicling that weekend in 1965 at Newport was produced. The film is called *Festival.* I saw it only once. The opening shot is of a mass of people filing through the entrance gates. On the soundtrack, Peter, Paul, and Mary sing "If I Had a Hammer." Somewhere under their voices, I can still hear the moos.

Shortly after that festival, I wrote my first "keeper" song. It was entitled "That's the Way It's Happened All the Time." It was written for a girl named Janet. I was madly in love with her. It was really an innocent romance, but still, that romance was all that my heart needed to first make its feelings known through my own music.

During the Christmas season of 1965, I was again put in charge of the Sears warehouse, so it was back to getting up at 4:30 in the morning to be at work by 5:00. There was no time to travel; there was no time for the person that I really wanted to be. There was one saving grace however, and that was called The Barn.

There was a small barn located behind the house adjacent to the Curtis' house in Lexington. The house belonged to the Broderick family; Mrs. Broderick was a policewoman in the town. The Curtis brothers, along with the Broderick's son Dave, and I decided in the late summer of 1965 that we should transform the old barn into a coffeehouse. Mrs. Broderick thought that having a place to go would keep many of the kids off the street and under some sort of supervision on weekends, so she gave us the okay to use the barn. We all went to work clearing the place out, building a stage, wiring in sound and lights, and putting in a makeshift kitchen on the second floor. The Barn Coffeehouse opened early that fall. We had a seating capacity of about 80 and became an instant success. Every Saturday we attracted not only the high school folkies, but also many of the adult members of the community. The Barn operated for about a year with performances by Carl Watanabe, "Ragtime" Eliot Kenin, The Charles River Valley Boys, and a host of young local performers just starting to sing out, including myself who, with a performance at The Barn, chalked up my first truly professional gig.

I recall one snowy night at The Barn. The place was filled to capacity, as the Fariñas were performing that evening. The kitchen, run by Joy Curtis, sister of John and Dick, was in full swing, serving up coffee and all kinds of pastries.

The lights dimmed, there was an introduction, and Dick and Mimi took the stage. It was about halfway through the first set when Dick announced that they were going to try doing a new song. He wasn't so sure that he could remember all of the lyrics without a little help, and so he had written the words on the knees of his jeans and would just read them as he sat and played his dulcimer. The new song was "Pack Up Your Sorrows." There they were, the Fariñas, onstage at our little coffeehouse, playing this beautiful new song on guitar and dulcimer, with Dick reading the words from his pants leg. I think that we paid them the unheard-of sum of $25 that night. To this day, that memory is priceless.

When the night was over, the Fariñas, along with their German Shepherd, Lush, and all of their instruments, piled into my tiny Hillman, and I drove them back to their place on Putnam Street in Cambridge.

The Barn continued to operate until late in 1966 when, one evening in the middle of the week when no one was there, it was totally destroyed by fire.

* * *

I received a letter from the local draft board early in 1966. Things were heating up in Vietnam. Being from Lexington, and having been indoctrinated with the spirit of patriotism since I was a child, I simply felt that it had come my time to put my life on hold and answer the call. I can't say that I was very happy about it, but I guessed that it was just the way it was going to have to be.

For three or four years, I had been bothered by a lump at the base of my spine. It was not really troublesome, but it could be uncomfortable if I sat still for long periods of time. All of my friends seemed to have been called for their physicals at the same time. We showed up at the local draft board and were bused to the South Boston Naval Shipyard for the ordeal. There I was in my underwear and cowboy boots (I could always relate to Arlo Guthrie's "Alice's Restaurant"), standing in line. I passed all the tests with flying colors until I got to Station 12, which was the general practitioner's post. Whatever wasn't poked or in some way tested at any of the other stations was dealt with at Station 12. I was instructed to place a thumb over one of my nostrils and inhale. The procedure was repeated for the other nostril. The examiner hemmed and hawed, made some strange noises, and then instructed me to bend at the waist for the other appropriate exams. After making a few notes, he informed me that I was suffering with a pilonidal sinus. Well, to tell the truth, I wasn't painfully suffering with anything at all, and I had no idea what this malady might be.

The examiner asked whether this sinus ever bothered me. Thinking back to when I had to place my thumbs on my nostrils, I answered yes, I sometimes had difficulties with a runny nose. It all seemed very logical to me. With a look of consternation, he glanced up from his cluttered desk and asked me if I had any idea what this problem was. I responded with an obvious and truthful "no." He proceeded to tell me, in great detail, what the lump on my spine was all about. I had been classified IY, a temporary deferment, and that was it. They would be in touch, and I would be reexamined in six months.

To say the least, I was relieved at my draft classification. Because I was finished with my physical early, I skipped the draft board bus and walked the 18 miles back to Lexington.

Roger and Dick were classified IA. Roger joined the Marines, and Dick went into the Army. Jesse and Dan were temporarily deferred as they were headed for college.

I have struggled for years with my feelings about Vietnam. I came to see the fruitlessness of the conflict and the resulting waste of human life, and I came to oppose the war. I was, at the same time, someone who truly loved this country and the principles on which I believe it stands. I did not understand how so many of us could come to be so divided and torn apart when we had always had basically so many common ideals. These questions came to a head some three years later as I stood on Lexington Green, "the Birthplace of American Liberty."

I showed up at Sears one day wearing a black armband, which signified an anti-war sentiment, and asked my boss, who had been a bomber pilot in World War II, whether he would allow me an extended lunch hour so I could attend an anti-war rally on the Battle Green. He responded by telling me that one of the reasons he flew his missions in the war was ultimately to enable me and all others like me to be free to express feelings about issues like Vietnam in a responsible manner at any time. He certainly did not agree with my views, but he would grant the extra time that I may attend the rally.

I arrived at the Battle Green at noon, and already the rally was well underway. The featured speaker was Francis Sargent, the governor of Massachusetts. Sargent was late, so other speakers filled in until he arrived.

What followed I will never forget. It was a profane parade of speakers cursing the country and flag in a manner I could not imagine. "F—the flag this!" and "F—the flag that!" I could not believe what I was hearing. I thought, "Here I am, on the Battle Green in Lexington, Massachusetts, listening to these people run the country into the ground." I had to sit down. How had it come to this? Why in the world was I here? The governor finally arrived, and a saner decorum prevailed, but by that time I was genuinely shaken.

Some years after that rally, it dawned on me that those people who stood on Lexington Green and fired those first shots in 1775 could quite possibly have had the same feelings toward the British king as these protesters did for the administration in 1969. If one could not stand on the ground that spawned a revolution in order to speak his or her free mind, then where, indeed, was there a place more fitting?

I think of this country as a boat filled with people, traversing a sea of constant chaos. The boat is leaky, worn, and sometimes pointed in the wrong direction, but dare anyone take out an auger, with no better craft in sight in which to transport their dreams, and drill holes in the bottom of that boat? I think not.

CHAPTER 6

The Fall Tour, Day 2

Interstate 90 is one of the busiest roads in the country, and it lives up to its reputation as I depart Buffalo early the next morning. There is a steady rain, and the reflection of the headlights from the wet pavement produces the illusion of an even greater volume of traffic. To compound the lack of visibility, the rainwater settles as a milky residue on the surface of the road, and it coats the windshield of my van when any one of an endless line of tractor-trailers passes by. My destination is Ann Arbor, Michigan, and a concert at The Ark, but for now I'll just be happy to make it out of Buffalo.

I believe that when a windshield wiper blade is designed, it is mandatory that the designer include a flaw in the blade. This flaw must manifest itself no later than two weeks after the blade is purchased, and it must be located approximately two-thirds of way to the end of the blade. The resulting streak must occur exactly at the driver's eye level and be wide enough to cause profound aggravation. I have never had a set of windshield wiper blades that did not contain this flaw.

This oily, white residue settling on the highway is perplexing. So this must be the stuff produced by the industries of the Midwest that is carried by the prevailing winds, washed out of the air by the cleansing rains, and dumped on the states of the Northeast to wreak havoc on the forests and streams. This is the toxic milk that pits the marble of monuments and, on this morning, is just too visible to ignore.

The weather forecast is for clearing from the west, and I am hoping that in a few hours I will leave this rain behind. White Rain used to be a brand name for a cleansing shampoo. How sad that it has come to this.

I pass the town of Fredonia, and when I enter Pennsylvania, I stop to have a late breakfast at the truck stop at State Line. The coffee is rich and strong, and the biscuits that I order are smothered with a creamy gravy, heavily endowed with chunks of sausage. The meat has a spicy flavor of sage to it. I have always loved sage. When I was very young, my father was always in charge of the Thanksgiving meal, and he used a lot of sage in the bread stuffing that he made for the turkey. As he filled the bird, he would always give me a tiny amount of the stuffing in a spoon. To this day, I can still recall the taste of that wonderful mixture.

The clouds thin and the sky brightens just west of Erie. I pass a tie-dyed 1970 Volkswagen bus. I do a double-take, because I notice that the driver looks a lot like me. He glances over, smiles, and then waves. I get the feeling that he has no schedule to follow, no place to be, no time constrictions, and I wonder at his life. Is it he who is the enduring free spirit?

My gas gauge chimes at me, indicating that my engine will soon be getting very thirsty, so I pull off at the first exit ramp to refuel and attend to some "technical difficulties." I notice that the VW follows me in, and I am tempted to strike up a conversation with the driver. The brightly painted VW slows at the entrance to the fuel pumps, but then does this kind of automotive "touch and go" and heads back out onto the highway. With my pit stop completed, I too rejoin the traffic, hoping to catch up with this spirit, but, alas, there is not a trace of him to be found anywhere.

It crosses my mind that perhaps I have come in contact with some sort of parallel universe offering me a glimpse of myself having traveled another path in life. I am also reminded of a line penned by Willa Cather in her novel *Oh, Pioneer:* " . . . freedom so often means one isn't needed anywhere . . . ." What is really more important, to be free or to be needed? I suppose that the obvious answer is a little of both.

With the northeast coast of Pennsylvania in my rearview mirror, I enter Ohio. In a little over an hour, I find myself on the outskirts of Cleveland.

It seems to me that cities nowadays are a lot like the contemporary automobile. It used to be that you could tell the difference between a '57 Chevy and a '57 Ford a mile away. Now no matter what make the car, with a few exceptions, they all look alike. It used to be that cities were different. There was a signature in the skyline, a building or landmark that made a skyline unique. Now the cities all look the same. There are, as with the cars, a few exceptions—San Francisco, with its architecture and the Transamerica Building; or St. Louis, with its Gateway Arch—but if you're not a resident, try and tell the skyline of St. Paul, Minnesota, from that of Oklahoma City, or the skyline of Houston from that of Dallas, and I think you will have a tough time of it.

Cleveland is the only city that I know of in the country where the main interstate artery takes a 90-degree turn in the middle of downtown. Approaching the bend, you cross one of the rumble strips which are designed to make your dentures dance, make your turn, and come flying out on the other side. The scuff marks on the cement barriers attest to the warnings that have gone unheeded.

It is only another 110 miles to Toledo, and then north for another 50 until you get to the college town of Ann Arbor, home to the University of Michigan.

My second concert of the tour is at The Ark, founded in 1965 by Dave and Linda Siglin. They still run the place with a host of volunteers. The original performance space was on the first floor of a large Victorian house on Hill Street, and about every touring musician on the folk circuit has played The Ark at one time or another. David and Linda have never forgotten their roots, and even though they're in their third building, and the new Ark is a pretty fancy club that can seat 400, they still make space among the new, young, and popular performers for those whose music is steeped in the old folk traditions.

Perhaps this a good time for me to get up on my soapbox. I find that I frequently do nowadays when it comes to describing the music of contemporary writers who consider themselves—and are considered by many—to be "folksingers."

I am well aware of how easy it could be to get involved with simple semantics by saying that all music is music of the people and therefore "folk" music, but many of the songs being written today are, rather than songs of the people, songs of the individual performer. They do not have the depth or the universality to make their way in the world much beyond that writer.

I wrote earlier that folk music is a music rich in the human experience and spirit. I cannot stress how important this is, because what is generated out of this source determines how many people can relate to a song and how this song will affect them enough so that it may endure. This depth of spirit springs, and is nourished by, the roots of the living of life. There are those who live to write; and there are those who live to live, and then write about it.

Take, for example, Woody Guthrie and Pete Seeger, considered by all to be two of the quintessential folksingers. Why do people accept this? Where did their songs come from? Who are they?

Woody and Pete are two very extraordinary people who lived two very extraordinary lives, traveling and meeting people all over the country and the world. They took the time to get know how these people felt about their families, their hopes, their frustrations, their homes, and their everyday lives. Pete and Woody were organizers, unionists, miners searching for the spiritual mother lode of humanity and what it takes to be a human being. In the beginning they weren't folksingers, although they were versed in the folk traditions. That did not happen until later. They were simply living their own lives in search of everything, in search of what we all are, and what we could be. Now and then, along the road, Woody or Pete would be extremely moved by these living experiences. They recognized what was common in us all, and because they were extraordinary people, they wrote extraordinary songs about that human experience. These songs not only reached the ears, but also reached into the hearts of all who would listen. They sang those songs to us, and those songs showed us something about not only our own lives, but the lives of others. That is when they became folksingers.

Theirs were not songs just about Woody or Pete, but songs about all people. They were songs that had the depth and spirit that it takes to survive over the passage of time. Theirs were songs forged from the same fire that gives the starving mother the will to struggle day after day to feed her children, or the young soldier or civil rights worker the resolve to hold a position against all odds.

I think of Woody's song "The Plane Wreck at Los Gatos," where he describes the plight of migrant workers, unnoticed and unknown. Is this not also a song of so many others, the working person who tolls their whole life unnoticed and unknown, unappreciated, and yet so important in the foundation of humanity?

Listen to Pete's "Oh, Had I a Golden Thread," a song which celebrates the whole fabric of life—the bravery of a new mother, the wonder of a child.

Can anyone listen to Stan Rogers' "The Mary Ellen Carter" and not be moved? The song is an anthem of hope for everyone.

To me, that is why the songs of Woody and Pete, or Stan Rogers, or Phil Ochs, or Malvina Reynolds, will endure, and why they will be remembered as artists.

Folk music will never remain static, and one should not think that "Barb'ry Allen," "The Greenland Whale Fisheries," or "The Cruel Mother," will always be in the repertoire of those who perform folk music. But in the creation of contemporary songs in the folk genre, one should at least feel the deep roots of these songs and recognize that they sprang from love, work, death, and all of the other great facets of life.

There is also what I refer to as the "acoustic pop" music scene—contemporary songs performed on acoustic instruments, but in content geared to what the current pop culture demands. Because they are performed on acoustic, or "folky," instruments, many consider these songs as part of the folk genre, but my feeling is that these songs lack the depth in spirit and heart that it takes to rise above what is simple entertainment. Is there a place for these songs? Of course there is. There has always been a need for all kinds of music. Will they endure? That remains to be seen, but I rather doubt it. As a test, try to remember the lyrics to the number one song on the Hit Parade in, say, April of 1956. Now, sing a few lines from Woody Guthrie's "This Land Is Your Land." Which song has truly survived?

Perhaps these acoustic pop pieces are what amount to the highest tops of the new growth on the musical family tree. They are certainly in the fullest of limelight but so very far from the roots. They sway, as blow the popular winds, and derive their nourishment from only what is left after it has traveled from those roots through the rest of the branches.

Perhaps the true continuation of the folk music genre will depend upon the contemporary songs which have sprung from the fallen seeds of that tree, now growing on their own, and once again taking nourishment from the old, good earth.

As the music endures, so shall places like The Ark, and at the end of the concert that evening, I bid a "goodbye for now" to David and Linda, pack up my van, and head out of Ann Arbor. My plan is to get a few hours of driving done before I get too sleepy. I pass the University of Michigan stadium, dark now and asleep, waiting for the arrival in a few days of 104,000 screaming football fans. Traditions come in all shapes and sizes.

CHAPTER 7

Farewell, Silver Love Line

One Sunday evening early in February of 1966, Renee Boghosian walked into my life. Renee was a pretty, dark-haired Armenian girl with flashing eyes and a personality that could bring a circus to its knees. She had just moved to Boston from Maine in order to make her own way in the world, and on this particular night, she and her friend Vicky had decided to come to one of the hoots at The Club 47. It just so happened that it was one of the nights that I was running the stage. I don't remember the dance; I don't recall the dynamics, but by the end of the following week, I was calling on Renee at the Franklin Square House, a women's boarding establishment in Boston's South End.

We began to see more and more of each other, and before long I was helping Renee and another of her friends, Lynn Buntin, move into an apartment on Buswell Street near Boston University. Renee and I had begun a relationship that would last, off and on, for four years.

That April I was booked into a coffeehouse in Ipswich, Massachusetts, called the King's Rook. The original King's Rook was located in Marblehead, Massachusetts, and still operates today. The owner of the Marblehead club, Gardner Damon, wanted to offer music in the place, but the zoning in Marblehead at the time did not allow entertainment, so a second Rook was opened in Ipswich. Damon called on a fellow by the name of Frank Reardon to manage the place, and before long the King's Rook became the premiere folk music club on the North Shore of Massachusetts. On the weekends, one would enter the place (which on the inside had the appearance of a colonial tavern, with its posts and beams and heavy wooden tables) and listen to the likes of Richie Havens, or Jesse Colin Young and Jerry Corbitt, who later became the founders of the Youngbloods. On Mondays there was a hootenanny, and Thursdays and Sundays were reserved for the local talent. My spot was usually every other Sunday. The Sunday night that I did not play was taken by either Peter Childs or a new face in the Boston area, bluesman Chris Smither.

If those years between 1959 and 1966 were the golden years of music for me, then the late 1960s and early 1970s must have been the silver years. Not only was I still occasionally running The Club 47 hoots, I was playing at most of the coffeehouses in the New England area.

On the Sunday afternoons that I wasn't in Ipswich getting ready to perform at the King's Rook, I would be hanging out for the hoots at the Café Yana. The Yana was located in an old building adjacent to Fenway Park, and on those afternoons, a long line of pickers showed up for the music. The building was eventually torn down to make way for the construction of the Massachusetts Turnpike, but to this day as I cross the bridge between Kenmore Square and the ballpark to see the Red Sox play, I can just hear, a little above my head, the smoky, musical echoes of the Yana.

In Boston, there were three coffeehouses on Charles Street alone. The Loft, a dark, woody, room on the second floor above one of the many shops on the street; The Orleans, which later became The Sword in the Stone; and The Turk's Head.

One would enter The Turk's Head from the sidewalk through a small stone portal, descend three or four steps into a narrow, sloping passageway, follow the passage, and finally make a left turn through a door and into the coffeehouse. The Turk's Head was a dimly lit room with red brick walls and a seating capacity of about 50. A light would shine from the kitchen at the end of the room, and inevitably one could find sitting at one of the 20 or so tables, engaged in deep conversation, the owner, Arnold Cummins, medical doctor and philosopher at heart. There was no issue large or small that "Doc" Cummins could not or would not comment upon. He was a formidable adversary in debate, and should you think that perhaps you might have him cornered in a discussion, he would simply lower his eyeglasses over his nose and stare at you until you would begin to doubt your own hypothesis. One of the doctor's favorite partners in conversation was a brilliant blues guitarist by the name of Ralph Cahn. Occasionally, upon entering the place, one would stumble into a heated discussion about Vietnam, the beginnings of the universe, or the true elements of jazz.

A conversation with Arnold Cummins was mandatory before a performer could consider himself worth his salt in the world of The Turk's Head.

The late spring of 1966 brought about the completion of one of the turns in the great musical wheel. The era seemed to end with a crash, in the form of a violent motorcycle accident that claimed the life of Richard Fariña, on his way from a release party for his new novel *Been Down So Long, It Looks Like Up to Me.* The musical world had lost an innovative and gifted voice.

Inasmuch as it was, to me, the end of one time, it surely was the beginning of another. I was still working for Sears, spending time with Renee, and singing regularly at night in all of the coffeehouses. On the weekends, if I wasn't singing, I still enjoyed driving out into the country or taking a jaunt up to Quebec City.

By now, the coffeehouse scene in Boston and Cambridge had begun to draw a number of musicians from out of the area. This group included Paul Geremia, Bill Madison, Ken Girard, Pam and Ray Clayton, and Robin Batteau. They would intermingle with all of the Boston regulars including Paul McNeil, Leonda, Nancy

Michaels, Carl Watanabe, and so many others, to become the core of the Charles Street music scene for the next eight years.

And so to me these were the silver years—the time, beginning in the fall of 1966, when the music ruled and the musicians moved into apartments adjacent to Charles Street, on the down side of Beacon Hill, and the late night parties would go on and on until early morning would find a group of bleary-eyed pickers huddled around a large table in the window of Haskell's, the local Charles Street greasy spoon deli, staring at the breakfast special in front of them and wondering what in the world had happened to their minds and bodies since the previous setting of the sun.

Renee and I began singing together. She was a fine singer in her own right, and after a few guest sets with me at The Turk's Head and some encouragement from some music friends of ours, we decided to try it as a duo. We sang as a couple for almost a year, playing the circuit and doing pretty well.

It was with Renee that I had my first recording experience. She introduced me to John Synnott, a family friend and musician she had known growing up on Cape Cod in the summers. Although a chemist by profession, John had played many of the clubs in the Boston area.

The three of us decided to pool our resources and record an album, with John on one side and Bill & Renee on the other. We got together one weekend in the summer of 1967 in an apartment in Allston that belonged to an acquaintance who had some recording equipment and took up the task. It was the ultimate in home recording. We would have to stop in the middle of a take if the kids playing baseball in the street started to get too noisy.

The album contained a few traditional pieces, as well as a number of songs by local writers. We even included a few original tunes by either John or me. By the end of the weekend, we had a finished master tape. It was less than ideal sound quality, but it was the best that we could do at the time, and it *was* finished. We called the project "A Bag of Rainbows." John sent the tape off to a local pressing plant, and before long we expected to have 250 LPs in our hands.

We knew that the albums would come in blank white jackets, so the next step was to get some cover slicks with photos on them printed up and pasted to the fronts. Rick Sullo, a photographer for *The Broadside*, took the cover photographs; we arranged them in a montage and had the cover art printed, and the slicks were ready to be attached to the jackets.

Soon after the arrival of the albums and their jackets, four of us, me, Renee, John, and John's girlfriend, Lois, had a party at John's apartment on Commonwealth Avenue in Boston. Supplies for the evening included a dozen bottles of mucilage glue, one bottle of gin, a few limes, and three quarts of tonic. We finished all the pasting over the course of the evening. That night was the last time I ever had a drink of gin.

Late in July of 1967, my friend Roger was home on leave from the Marine Corps, and the two of us decided to take a trip to Innis Lake, just outside of Toronto, to see the Mariposa Folk Festival. I had a vacation week coming to me from Sears, so the timing seemed perfect. We even had a plan.

Roger and I would drive up to Toronto the weekend before the festival and take a few days to camp and explore the country along the shores of Georgian Bay. Renee would fly into Toronto on the Friday of the festival. Upon our return to the city, we would pick her up at the airport, and the three of us would spend the weekend camping at Innis Lake and listening to the music. When the festival was over we would all drive home together. It was on this trip that we met the Turner family of Brampton, Ontario.

Roger and I had driven that first weekend as far north as Parry Sound on Georgian Bay. He and I had decided that, rather than traveling any farther from Toronto, we would find a good place to set up a camp and spend the few days that we had in one area. We found what seemed like an ideal location at a secluded spot on the side of a small country road about 20 miles north of Parry Sound. The road abutted a lake, so we backed the car off under the trees and set up our camp at the edge of the water. We started a small fire, cooked a meal, and when we had finished eating broke out our guitars to sing a few quiet songs. It was only a few minutes later that we heard footsteps and voices coming at us along the road. Cal Turner and a group of eight or ten children had come to call.

Cal was a tall, thin man, perhaps in his early 40s, with a passion for music, beer, and life in general. He informed us that he and his brother owned all of the land along this part of the road and asked us in a kind yet sincere way what our intentions might be. We told him who we were and about our plans to see the festival outside of Toronto the following weekend. He had already noticed our guitars. I remember that moment when he stared directly at us and a softness came into his eyes. Perhaps what I saw was an understanding or a patience that only a parent with so many children at his heels could have. He sat down by the fire, asked if he could play a tune on my guitar, and before another bullfrog on the lake could croak, started up with what might be the wildest version of "The Wreck of the Old '97" anyone has ever heard. It must have been one of those old family favorites, for no sooner had he started to sing than most all of the small fry joined right in.

When he had finished, he laid the guitar gently aside, stood up, and brightly announced that his family and his brother's family were getting together the following evening for a barbecue and that they would be mighty pleased to have us come by for dinner. Of course there would be some music after the meal and, if we might just have an inclination, they'd love to hear a tune or two, or perhaps a dozen.

The Turner's place was a small barn that had been converted into a cabin. It was situated halfway up the side of a small hill and overlooked a meadow brimming with yellow, white, and pale blue wildflowers. All of Canada seemed visible in the distance. That weekend, the old barn-turned-cabin was filled to the brim with kinfolk, all running this way and that, playing games and preparing for the evening's festivities. Between the two families, there were at least 16 children, 2 dogs, and 4 adults. We all ate, drank, and sang our way through that evening, and when it was finally time for me and Roger to make our way back to the camp by the lake, Cal took us aside and made us an offer that we just could not refuse.

Although he had not mentioned this before, Cal now told us that their home near Toronto was only about two miles from the festival site at Innis Lake. They were all leaving the next day to drive back, and it seemed only logical to him that Roger and I should spend the rest of our time in the north at their cabin. When it came time for us to leave and drive back, we would simply close up the cabin, gather some things that they would leave behind, and rejoin them at their home near Innis Lake. We could even set up our camp in their backyard. Feeling a little uncomfortable, I told Cal that we would be picking up Renee at the airport. His answer to this was something to the effect of "the more, the merrier!".

On that Friday morning, Roger and I arrived back in Toronto with all of the stuff we had been instructed to bring down from the cabin, picked up Renee at the airport, traveled out to Innis Lake, and set up camp in the Turner's backyard. The first evening concert of the festival was due to start at 7:00 that night. Before the three of us could leave for the site, the Turners let it be known that they were planning on having us join them for nothing less than a late afternoon feast of lobster, corn, and baked potatoes. How could we refuse?

The Mariposa Folk Festival was, at the time, the Canadian equivalent of the Newport Folk Festival, and over the weekend we listened to concerts and workshops by Joni Mitchell, Doc Watson, Gordon Lightfoot, Reverend Gary Davis, and Pete Seeger, among others. We left early each morning for the festival and did not return to our camp at the Turner's until very late at night. It mattered not how late we arrived at the house, Cal was always at the back door, inviting us in for eggs, bacon, and juice.

And so the weekend passed, filled with music and the friendship bestowed upon us by a family we would probably never see again. They had adopted first two, and then three total strangers, invited us into their lives, trusted us with their cabin, and taken care of us as if we were their own. I mentioned this to Cal as we packed up our camp for the drive back to Boston, and I thanked him as best I could for his family's hospitality. He placed one of his hands on my shoulder and with the other, pointed toward his two oldest boys, now approaching their late teens.

"Bill, look at those two boys over there. Hell, look at this whole raft of kids." He called them "Turner's Army." "Before long, they'll be out doing exactly what the three of you are doing, discovering their own worlds, following their own roads, and just finding out who they are in the great scheme of things. Well, I'll tell you, I'd like to think that maybe there will be somebody out in that world to offer them a place to stay or to help them if trouble should cross their paths. I won't be there. I can't be there, so if there's anything I can do for someone else's family, should they pass my door, then maybe somewhere or somehow down the line, it will go easier on my own."

The three of us corresponded with the Turners for a few years, but as it happens so often, we eventually lost touch. I have always hoped that the roads that the Turners traveled would be smooth, and that the fair winds would find them to keep them happy and safe.

Shortly after that trip, Roger returned to the Marines and was eventually shipped over to Vietnam. Renee had an apartment on Park Drive, near Fenway Park, and that year she and I went to most of the home games. I guess that I was never truly comfortable being anything but a solo performer, so after some months Renee and I stopped singing together. She moved to San Francisco and got a job working as a waitress on Fisherman's Wharf. Eventually she would return, and for a while we would resume our relationship, but it was never the same.

The Red Sox won the pennant in 1967, but true to form, they lost the World Series.

CHAPTER 8

The Fall Tour, Day 3

The parking lot at the local market in Middlebury Indiana, is about the same as every other parking lot in the country, except that along with the usual parking spaces, there is a hitching rail standing right in the center of the lot. The rail, made of iron, is about 30 feet long, and on this day there are 5 horse-drawn wagons tethered to it. The local industries include tourism and the manufacture of house and recreational trailers of all sizes and designs. Yet alongside this world of providing for people constantly on the move, one discovers the world of the Amish, the patient people.

These are the descendents of the original German and Dutch Amish invited in 1743 by William Penn to come to America and settle in Pennsylvania. Moving toward the West, many of this group originated settlements in Ohio and Indiana.

The Amish way of life is founded on a belief in hard work, harmony with the soil, family, and the fear of God. It is a simple and plain life of perseverance.

It is this community of farms and crafts, horse-drawn wagons, and a people with a gentle and yet deliberate demeanor that gives this part of the country its quiet charm and beauty.

It is the middle of the afternoon on the third day of my tour, and it is a relief to leave the trucks and traffic of the Indiana Tollway to make my way the dozen or so miles south into Middlebury. I turn onto a narrow country road on the outskirts of town. It is a warm sunny day, and the air is filled with the lingering scent of horses and the rich earth of farm country.

I pass an Amish school with the young girls dressed in long gray skirts and white bonnets. The boys are wearing dark gray trousers with suspenders, collar-less white shirts, and wide-brimmed hats. They are playing a game of what looks like tag, their laughter mixing with the bird songs in the surrounding trees.

A left turn onto a long dirt driveway brings me to the home of Elva Miller and LVD's

Concert Hall, the third stop on the tour. Once upon a time, Elva decided that the area around Middlebury needed a place where people could come and hear good down-home music. Gathering together some friends to help, he refurbished his barn and turned it into a concert space in the middle of the farm fields of Indiana. It is one of my favorite places to perform, and people will drive 50 or 60 miles to hear the music that is offered at Elva's barn.

It is encouraging to see people turn out and drive these distances to hear live music. It can be so tempting nowadays to just stay at home and rent a video, as so many do. I have often wondered about the future of live, small-scale performances, the future of the single musician traveling about the land just to sing a song or two for people in a church basement or Grange hall.

In the late 1950s, when I was 10 or 11 years old, I saw a one-hour television drama that truly scared me. I don't remember all of the details, but the general story I will never forget.

The time is the near future. In 1958, that would be around the turn of the century, say the year 2000. Humans have overpopulated Earth, and they have honeycombed the planet. There are around 20 people living in each of the cells. The population is required to remain constant, so a child cannot be conceived until someone in the cell has died.

Each morning the inhabitants awaken and line up for a daily routine. First, each member is allowed a few breaths of fresh air from the surface by way of a tube extending from a wall in the cell. Each inhabitant is then allowed a glimpse of sunlight from the surface of the planet through what amounts to a periscope type of device, also mounted on the function wall of the cell. A drawer opens on the wall, and each occupant is issued a morning meal of dehydrated food on a plastic tray. There is an exercise period, and at the conclusion of a few calisthenics, it is time to go to work. Once again, a drawer in the great function wall opens, and the leader of the cell extracts a three-ring binder which contains some problem pertaining to the operation of the society. It is now the responsibility of the people in the cell to solve the problem. This is their vocation, their life's work, problem after problem, no incentive, no reward other than the continuation of the cell.

The chaos in the drama comes when someone in an adjoining cell kills a fellow inhabitant and breaks through the wall between the two cells. This forces an interaction between the two groups of people, and the result is far from successful.

This drama scared me as a ten-year-old, and as time passes, what I see happening to our society scares me for the same reason.

I believe that the computer and the advent of the Internet are profound tools—tools that open the door to vast stores of knowledge—but consider this: we can order everything from CDs to celery and have it appear promptly at our door. We stay at home more and watch video machines as an easy form of entertainment. Many of us sit at home at a workstation, do our jobs at a terminal, and send it in to the office, having never set foot out of the door of our home.

As new technology allows us to cocoon more and more, I can't help but be reminded of that television production of more than 40 years ago, and sometimes I want to scream out an alarm to all, saying "Don't you see what is happening? Be careful that you don't lose your identity as a mobile human being; spend at least some amount of energy to explore the world outside your door!".

So I am pleased as the barn fills up this evening, here amongst the simple farms of Indiana, not only because the people are coming to hear my performance, but because they are coming to hear the music at all. And what of my fears for our society? Time will be the judge, and 50 years from now, we shall see.

The stars are brilliant, and there is a bright moon overhead as once again I pack up the van after the concert. It is an old routine. My 14-year-old boy recently traveled with me over a weekend of performances, and when we returned home, I asked him what he thought about being on the road as a musician. His only comment was, "It seems like it's pretty much the same night after night." I don't think that it takes a lot of insight to see that much of what comes to pass *is* pretty much the same: the sound checks, changing guitar strings, hauling CDs in and out of the hall. Some of it does get to be old hat, but the fact of the matter is that each night, it is the people that make the experience new. No audience is ever the same. Even if the exact same people were to show up for three nights in a row, the energy would be different each time.

There are a number of charming bed and breakfast homes around Middlebury, but most of the performers stay at Bontrager's. Tom and Ruby have been avid supporters of LVD's, and their home will be my last stop for the night. With the van once again all packed, and with the Indiana moon and stars above me, I follow my headlight beams down the driveway, past the school, and make it the short distance into town. It is October, and there is a reminder of that fact in the brisk night air.

CHAPTER 9

Oh, Freedom

In March of 1968, I made my first musical trip out of the Boston area to Saratoga Springs, New York. I had heard of a place called the Caffé Lena, contacted Lena Spencer who operated the club, and arranged for an audition. I was still working for Sears, so my time to travel and sing was pretty limited. My plan was to audition on Saturday, stay at Lena's—her place was always a haven for musicians, actors, and transient souls—and drive back to Boston the next day.

It just so happened that Mother Nature had different plans for me. A blizzard struck the northeast, and rather than spending one day, I spent four days at the café visiting Lena. We got to be good friends and remained so until her death in 1987.

Lena, along with her husband, Bill Spencer, opened the café in 1960. Soon after the club opened, Bill went his separate way, but Lena continued to operate the place. The list of musicians who have appeared onstage at Lena's reads like a Who's Who of folk music. Bob Dylan, Arlo Guthrie, Hedy West, Peggy Seeger, Logan English, Nanci Griffith, Dave Van Ronk, Pete Seeger, Rosalie

Sorrels, and hundreds more have passed through the doors of the café. It has attained legendary status.

Because the scheduled performer could not make it through the storm, I began playing at the café the night that I auditioned for Lena, and I think that I've sung there a couple of times a year ever since.

When Lena passed away in 1987, the café became a nonprofit organization. Recently the Caffé Lena received a grant from the state of New York to buy the building in which it has been housed since Lena and Bill opened it so many years ago.

The snowstorm of 1968 subsided and I finally made it back home.

* * *

Later that spring, I started what would become a lifelong friendship with a partner and traveling companion that continues, and hopefully will continue as long as I play the guitar.

I was singing at The Turk's Head one evening when the roommate of one of the local musicians came hurriedly through the door with a guitar case in his hands. During the break, he asked me if I knew of anybody who might want to buy a used Martin D-18 guitar. He needed the money and would take what he could get for the instrument. I remembered when he had bought the guitar, so I knew that it wasn't stolen. I asked him if I could take a look at it. I was playing an Epiphone guitar at the time and I loved it, but I had always dreamed of owning a Martin. As it happened, I was scheduled to buy a car the next morning, and that night I had $125 in my pocket. The opportunity was just too much. I bought the Martin on the spot. The case, and the electric pickup that was installed on the guitar, were not part of the deal, so the pickup was taken off, and that night I returned home with the Martin over my shoulder.

Immediately I felt guilty about not playing the Epiphone, and I was literally losing sleep over which guitar I would play at my gigs. The situation was soon resolved when I traded the Epiphone for a small Martin 0-18 and gave the 0-18 to Renee.

That was the last guitar I would acquire for many years, until a friend gave me a classical guitar that he never used. Eventually I would acquire a Guild that I would take with me when I had to fly somewhere, but the Martin D-18 that I bought that night at The Turk's Head instead of a car would come to have a lasting place in my heart. I have played many other guitars in passing, some very expensive, but they have never sounded as sweet or felt as good to play as my friend.

The Club 47 closed down in the late spring of 1968. Although there was still an abundance of coffeehouses in the Boston area, the passing of The Club 47 left a big hole in the music scene. I was playing at all of the clubs around town, but now I was beginning to travel out of the area on the weekends. Not only was I playing at Lena's, I was also playing in Timonium, Maryland, at a place called Patches 15 Below. It was one of the premiere clubs in the Baltimore area, and I had done a few openers with Emmylou Harris and John Denver. Now I was playing there as a headliner and developing my own audience.

After one of my shows at The Sword in the Stone in Boston, I was approached by a fellow by the name of Chuck Baker. Chuck lived in Montreal and ran a coffeehouse called The Yellow Door. He invited me to perform at the place, we set a date, and a few weeks later he sent me a letter with all of the particulars and directions to the club.

At this point, in the late spring of 1968, the Vietnam War was in full swing, and many Americans were headed for Canada to avoid or protest the conflict. The border agents between the United States and Canada had their hands full with the flow of these people. Also, there was another problem. The French separatist movement, FLQ, was active in Quebec and determined that the province should secede from the rest of Canada. There had been political kidnappings and bombings around Montreal, so on the whole, everybody was pretty tense.

In the middle of all of this, up to the border I came with my guitar player, Kenny Girard, to play at a club that we had never been to before and for a person that I had only met once. We crossed out of the United States but were informed at the Canadian border point that we would need working papers to get into Canada, and we were denied entry. Turning back to reenter the United States, Kenny informed the border agent that he did not have any identification, and we were stopped again. There we sat for most of the day between countries, wondering what was to become of us. Fortunately Chuck Baker came to the rescue with the appropriate documents, and the gig was on. The weekend went very well at the club and we stayed at the apartment Chuck was sharing with Jesse Winchester. For many years, The Yellow Door became a frequent stop on my touring schedule.

With my performance area rapidly expanding, I began to feel restless working for Sears. In the summer of 1968, I took a leave of absence from the job to play music full time. During my leave, I took a part-time job working at a recording studio in Dorchester, Massachusetts, called AAA Recordings. It was run by a fellow by the name of Joe Saia, and my job was to sweep up the place, answer the phones, and move the microphones around for the recording sessions. Not only was I learning about the recording business, but when I wrote a song, I would come into the studio with my guitar player and record the song for free.

The recording engineer at AAA at the time was Don Felder. Don had just moved to Boston from Florida and was working temporarily at the studio. During his spare time he was also laying down tracks of his own original music, and frequently we would play on each other's sessions. His plan was to eventually move to California and rejoin some of his Florida friends who were putting together a band on the West Coast.

In the fall of 1968 and the early spring of 1969, I edited together all of the recordings that I had done at AAA and released them on my own label, Champlain Records, as the album *Somebody Blue*, which I sold exclusively from the stage at my gigs.

Don moved to California to join up with his friend, Bernie Leadon, and became one of the members of The Eagles.

By this time, I was back working for Sears; however, in the fall of 1969, my back began to bother me, the condition worsened, and I recognized that I would soon have to have the problem resolved. In January of 1970, I entered the hospital for surgery.

The procedure itself was not all that serious, but it was of the type that would take a long time to heal. In fact, it would take almost two years for my back to mend properly. I collected my half pay from Sears for 16 weeks, and in April of 1970 informed my boss that I would not be returning to the job.

I was free, still recovering from surgery, but free at last to play my music on a full-time basis. I was now truly a professional musician. The road was waiting for me, and I was ready to take it wherever it might lead.

CHAPTER 10

The Fall Tour, Day 4

The next morning is the brightest and sunniest of Saturdays. I descend the narrow flight of stairs from my room, suitcase in hand, and enter the bright, glassed-in back porch of Bontrager's Bed and Breakfast. There is a table set for me, complete with cereal, muffins, coffee, fresh juice, and the morning newspaper. A note from Tom and Ruby, the innkeepers, informs me that they are sorry to have missed me that morning as they had errands to do. I should help myself to anything in the refrigerator, and they would see me the next time that I came to Middlebury.

I take my time over breakfast. I relish the coffee, read the news, and do the crossword puzzle. I am in no hurry to leave, and the crosswords have always been an addiction. My next concert is in Park Forest, Illinois, only a few hours away, so it seems as if it will be a lazy day. I retrieve my journal from the van and spend an hour or so chronicling the tour so far. It is the fifth volume of a journal that I started in 1978. At one time, I was religious about making an entry every day, but for the last few years those entries have not been as regular as they should be. I make a mental note to change that situation.

The Indiana sun is warm, and it seems to me a good time to do a little tidying up in the van before I leave town. I am always amazed at how, after only a few days of traveling, the van's interior takes on this appearance of having just been attacked by aliens.

With a little rearranging here and there, I am once again ready to take to the road. Now, with most of the morning gone, I leave a note thanking my hosts, head north out of town, and jump back onto Interstates 80 & 90, the Indiana Tollway, for a straight shot due west across the rest of Indiana and a late afternoon arrival in Park Forest, just south of Chicago. East of Portage, I hop off onto State Route 49 and drop down to pick up U.S. Route 30.

U.S. Route 30 is called the Lincoln Highway. Prior to its completion in 1915, there was no surfaced, transcontinental highway in the United States. In fact, most all of the roads in the country were little more than two ruts in a muddy dirt bed, hard to travel at best, and sometimes totally impassable when wet.

The idea of an "improved" highway from coast to coast was the brainchild of one Carl Fisher, president of the Prest-O-Lite Company, developer, automotive enthusiast, and builder of the Indianapolis Motor Speedway. His vision in 1912 called for the construction of a gravel highway, coast to coast between New York and San Francisco, to be completed by 1915, in time for the Panama-Pacific Exposition. Fisher expected to raise much of the cash for the ten-million-dollar project by convincing the automobile manufacturers to donate one percent of their assets to the construction fund. The rest of the capital would be paid by the public in the form of five-dollar memberships to what was then called the Coast-to-Coast Rock Highway Organization. Communities along the route would be expected to supply men and machinery for the project, and Fisher's people would supply the materials.

Henry Ford immediately rejected the proposal, claiming that the public would never fund future roads if the auto manufacturers did that for them now. Fisher, however, found two enthusiastic allies in Frank Seiberling of the Goodyear Company, who immediately forked over $150,000; and Henry Joy of the Packard Motor Company.

Joy suggested that the road be called the Lincoln Highway in honor of the fallen president. He felt that it would be a fitting tribute to old Abe's memory, and that the patriotic element would fire the emotions of the public and energize support for the project.

Just as the completion of the railroad in 1867 had made transcontinental travel relatively easy, so would the completion in 1915 of the Lincoln Highway pave the way for the new and accepted mode of family travel, the automobile. America would never look back. We would become a people on the move. Whether out of pleasure or necessity, out of commerce or war, from New York to San Francisco (or later, from Chicago to Los Angeles along Route 66), the throbbing pulse of a nation quickened, and the energy of a population was set in motion.

From this first "improved" road, U.S. Route 30, the Lincoln Highway, now stretching out before me this sunny morning in Indiana, conceived and constructed during the Woodrow Wilson years, came the great interstates of today, conceived and begun in the Eisenhower years.

I may complain about the increase in traffic and the attitudes of some drivers nowadays, but I have come to love these roads. They excite me, and I feel as if they are a part of my being. The thumping beneath these wheels becomes my heartbeat; the hissing of the painted, broken lines beneath the tires becomes the blood sound as it courses through my veins. The whole country is my backyard. It is familiar to me. I know its seasons and moods, and deep inside I will forever feel its interminable fire.

Indiana is behind me now, and I enter Illinois, the "Land of Lincoln," and certainly more of his highway. I pass the fancy hotels and sprawling malls, franchise steakhouses, hospitals, and seedy neighborhoods. Study the personality of the roadsides and you will discover a microcosm of what we are as a society. The pride, and the problems with the lack of pride, are all there.

At 5:00 in the afternoon, I meet up with the people who are

promoting the evening concert and we have dinner together at a nearby restaurant. The performance is for a local folksong society, and the show will be held in the basement of a neighborhood church.

How many songs have been sung by traveling troubadours in church basements, community centers, and the back rooms of country style restaurants? No matter how small the audience, wherever there are people willing to listen, music will find its way to them. Far from the music business, the glitter, and the pyrotechnics meant to wow that money heavy monster of the masses, the simple music still survives.

If you listen carefully, you can hear the sound of the mountain dulcimer as it wafts across the hills and valleys of the land. Listen carefully, and you will hear the song of the high and lonesome fiddle carried to you on an Appalachian wind. Be gone dull care! I can hear the melody of the mandolin. Be gone dull care! You are nothing against the simple music in my heart.

At each concert, I ask the people to sing with me on many of the songs, and they usually do. On this night in Park Forest, their voices come back to me as a breath of exquisite air, laden with life-giving energy. There are some audiences who are at the outset a little timid when it comes to singing, and then there are some audiences who sing a song as if they have lived their lives for that musical moment. It is very special to stand in front of a group of people and hear them singing one of your songs. It is a confirmation of the fact that you, as a musician, are able to reach into another person's heart. Let the music play on and the people will lift their voices to the song.

The concert is over and it is close to midnight. I have been on Interstate 57 out of Park Forest for most of an hour, and now I am bathed within the Saturday night lights of Chicago on a journey through the center of a giant, translucent, black opal. Every colored light seems to be in motion. Their myriad shining numbers surround me. I pass the projects on the south side with their stark fortress walls, then Comisky Park, and I race with one of the metro trains as it makes its way, station to station, toward downtown.

Interstate 57 ends at a merge with Interstates 90 and 94. From this point, where the two interstates pass the Sears Tower, it is exactly 1,000 miles east to the entrance of my driveway. I have measured it many times. My journey, however, is in the other direction, and I know that it will take me over a month and a distance of more than 13,000 miles before I see my home again.

Pushing on to the north and west, the energy is still with me, and I find myself singing out loud. It is an old song.

> *"Oh, the fox went out on a chilly night,*
> *He prayed for the moon to give him light,*
> *He had many a mile to go that night,*
> *Before he reached the Town-o, Town-o, Town-o*
> *He had many a mile to go that night,*
> *Before he reached the Town-o . . . ."*

The interstates split up, and I take the Eisenhower Expressway, Interstate 90 west, the Town-O, Chi-Town, Old Windy gradually releasing its grip on me. Out past O'Hare Airport, where the landing lights of the planes on final approach, one behind the other, five, ten of them, look like new and brilliant constellations in the night sky. Slowly descending, ever so deliberately, we pass each other going in opposite directions. Now I am on my own final approach to some hotel parking lot in Rockford. Perhaps the Clock Tower Inn, where in the basement at one time one could have experienced (for that's what it was—an experience) one of the finest time museums in the world. I always arrived there at 11:45 A.M. and planned to stay for at least half an hour, for all of the clocks were set to celebrate noon over a 30-minute period. From early sundials to one of the three atomic clocks in existence, the museum was a marvelous experience.

The young woman at the front desk inks an X onto the map of the hotel, indicating where my room is located. I tramp the hallways, lugging two guitars, a suitcase, and a satchel, until finally my room number appears on a door in front of me. I know that I should get some sleep. If one loses too much sleep early in a tour, there will be hell to pay as the days press on. I open a book and lie back on the bed. Since my late 20s, I don't think that there has been a period in my life when I haven't had one or two books going at the same time. At this point, one of two things happens. Either the whole blasted volume falls on the bridge of my nose, or as I am about to fall asleep, I jump and hurl the book across the room. At 1:45 this morning, it is the bridge of my nose.

Lights out now. Wisconsin is but a few miles away, and then the Mississippi, and then the seemingly endless expanse of the great West.

CHAPTER 11

Down Mexico Way

April of 1970 not only marked my permanent separation from Sears, it was also the month that Roger was mustered out of the Marine Corps. His first stop after receiving his discharge was Houston, Texas, where he spent a few weeks visiting with George Harper, one of his Marine Corps friends.

I had been dating a woman named Cynthia who had an apartment on Phillips Street at the base of Beacon Hill in Boston. My friends Jesse Ennis and Lee Martin had a place on Russell Street, just a few blocks away. Jesse and Lee were studying at Northeastern University, but I think that we all spent most of our time brewing beer in plastic garbage cans in their apartment.

Late that month, Jesse received a phone call from Texas. It was Roger saying that he would be arriving back in town by train later that week and needed a place to stay. It would only be for a few days, because he needed to return to Texas to retrieve his belongings, which now included a 1953 Ford pickup truck. The truck needed a good deal of repair, but the price had been right. Roger's plan was to go back to Texas, load up the back of the truck with his gear, and drive the thing back to New England.

Sometime during the last few days of April, Roger's train pulled into South Station in Boston and we all got together for a grand party on "the hill." As I recall, it was a two—or three-day affair, during which we drank up most of the beer that we had brewed. The celebration was progressing rather well. Only a few bottles of our beer, "Old Shnitzenpoogle," had blown up in our hands, and nobody had gone blind drinking the stuff. In the excitement, somebody came up with an intriguing idea: Jesse, Lee, and I would drive Roger back to Texas in Jesse's car. Jesse and Lee had a little time before taking finals, and they would have to return home early, but I could stay on to help Roger repair the truck and eventually drive north with him. None of us, with the exception of Roger, had been south before, and it would be like old times when we used to spend the weekends driving around New England together.

Roger told me about a coffeehouse in Houston called Sand Mountain. He had been to the place a couple of times, and it seemed to him that I might be able to get a gig there while we were in town. I called Sand Mountain and spoke with Mrs. Carrick, the woman who owned the place; she said by all means, drop in and at least do a guest set. If the audition worked out, she might be able to find a spot for me while I was in Houston as the third act on a triple bill.

The date for the grand departure was set for Monday, May 4th, 1970. I had one concert to play on the Sunday before we left at the University of Massachusetts. I was to be part of a day-long festival. My spot on the bill had been arranged by Mark Edwards, who ran The Sword in the Stone coffeehouse in Boston at the time. I knew nothing about the festival program until I arrived in Amherst that Sunday morning. It had been raining, and so the event had been moved into the field house. I parked my car, and as I headed for the site, I passed a poster advertising the days' events. I must admit, I had to pause.

Today in Concert at the UMass Fieldhouse
Noon until 8PM

James Taylor	*Sonny Terry & Brownie McGhee*
Bonnie Raitt	*The Blues Project*
Seatrain	*Doc Watson*
Tim Buckley	*Bill Staines*
The Pentangle	*Odetta*

I was on at noon, the first act, but I confess I spent the rest of the afternoon feeling pretty good about myself. That concert, in retrospect, seems to have been the perfect springboard into the next phase of my traveling and performing life.

* * *

Monday, May 4th, 1970, began as a beautiful spring day in New England. It would end as a tragic day for a nation.

Jesse's car was a bright red 1962 Chevy Nova convertible. It always struck me that whoever managed to come up with that name for a car model must have been nuts, considering the fact that "*no va*" in Spanish means "no go." In any case, on that Monday morning, the four of us deposited our packs in the trunk of the Nova, climbed in, and headed for New York City on the first leg of our marathon trip to Texas. We figured that the sooner we arrived in Houston, the more time Jesse and Lee would have before they had to return for their final exams. If we took turns driving and continued straight through Monday night, our expectation was that we would arrive in Texas early on Tuesday evening. The four of us would rotate counterclockwise every two to three hours with the two in back resting, and the two in front driving and navigating.

At noon that day, we were speeding across the Hudson River on the George Washington Bridge. At noon that day, tear gas canisters were exploding amidst students and protesters at Kent State University in Ohio. At 12:25 P.M that day, we were headed west along Interstate 80, where in Pennsylvania we would pick up Interstate 81 and turn south. Four friends on an adventure, we were probably laughing and joking about some inane subject. At 12:25 P.M that day, at Kent State, after two days of rioting and protests, Ohio National Guard troops retreating up a hill suddenly whirled and opened fire on the crowd, killing four students and injuring nine others.

The radio in Jesse's car didn't work, so we continued on our way, oblivious to the series of events that would shock and disturb a nation for years to come.

For me, once more, there were those far off names: Richmond, Roanoke, and Bristol. As we drove, I remembered listening to the planes landing at Logan Airport six years earlier and how I had dreamed of these far-off places. Now here they were, just outside the open car window, visions in the warm southern night. At 1:00 A.M, we entered Knoxville, and then it was the long climb over the Cumberland Plateau, where you could look back across the dark valleys of Tennessee and catch the glimmering firefly lights of the towns. I should have been resting in the back, but to miss any moment or any mile of road would have been an abomination. We drove through Nashville as the first hint of light touched the eastern sky, and we stopped outside Ryman Auditorium, home to "The Grand Ol' Opry," perhaps just to stare at the place, or perhaps to catch a glimpse of some ghost as it strummed a guitar beneath the corner street lamp and softly sang:

"Oh, come Angel Band
Come and around me stand,
Bear me away on your snowy wings,
To my immortal home,
Bear me away on your snowy wings,
To my immortal home."

There will always be ghosts in Nashville, for not only are there the dreams that come true, there are also those that have been left by the side of the road, abandoned, to wander forever in the night.

Just west of town, we stopped for fuel. The sky had brightened enough now so that we could see all of the changes that had taken place in the landscape. The trees were different than those of the Northeast: yellow poplar; catawba; and, close to the ground, sassafras. I started singing to myself "Cornbread, Molasses, and Sassafras Tea," an old song that I had heard the Lilly Brothers sing one night at The Club 47. The highway ran through great cuts in wooded, limestone hills, cuts gouged out by the big machines of the road builders. On toward Memphis we traveled, over the Buffalo River, and the Tennessee, and then across the Natchez Trace.

One of the oldest travel ways in the world, the Natchez Trace was used by native peoples as long ago as 8000 B.C. Stretching across Tennessee, Alabama, and Mississippi, the road was continually used by pioneers, settlers, traders, outlaws, traveling preachers, and just about any other person on the go, until river traffic on the Mississippi took over and passage on the road died out.

It's 225 miles from Nashville to Memphis, the river city, the city with its own kind of blues, the city that has felt the music of W.C. Handy; John Lee Hooker; and, of course, Elvis Presley, the Mississippi boy who traveled so far and became a king.

At 10:00 on Tuesday morning, May 5th, we crossed the Mississippi River on the old steel girder bridge that looked as if it had been constructed out of a giant Erector Set. I looked down at the muddy river water and a barge passing under us. I looked north toward St. Louis and the states of the northern Midwest. Would I ever get to see them? I looked to the south, and wondered how this immense waterway looked as it passed into the Gulf of Mexico at New Orleans. I looked through the windshield of the Nova as we reached the opposite shore of the river and thought to myself, "Now, for the first time in my life, I am truly passing into the West."

Entering West Memphis, we came upon a sign welcoming us to Arkansas and warning us that there would be no tolerance when it came to exceeding the speed limit. We stopped to refuel again at a gas station/liquor store and decided that a celebration was in order. After all, we were two-thirds of the way to Texas; not only that, we were still alive. There must be something in this to celebrate. Jesse bought two six packs of beer and a straw cowboy hat. Passing by the newspaper stands that were crying out their headline news from Ohio, we roared out of the parking lot of the store proclaiming, "We are bound for Texas and nothing can stop us now!".

At Texarkana, we entered Texas and headed straight down Stateline Avenue. The west side of this thoroughfare belongs to Texas and the opposite side to Arkansas. It just so happened at the time that the adjoining county in Texas was a dry county, so needless to say the Arkansas side of the street featured all of the bars and liquor stores. We stopped for another celebratory drink and headed south out of town on Route 59, the East Texas Highway. We were on the final leg of the trip, passing through pine forests, rolling hills, and pasture land, and making our way out onto the flat, wooded plains that mark the outskirts of Houston. We had made it!

George Harper's house was a modest place, one of many like it on the north side of the city, and Harper and his wife were there to meet us when we pulled into the driveway. Not only were we greeted by the Harpers, but there, sitting at the other end of the driveway with a front end that appeared to be smiling at us, was Roger's truck. It was a pretty pitiful looking piece of machinery, but Roger assured us that it would be ready to travel with "just a little work." I thought to myself, "Yeah, like a new engine, transmission, and anything else that moves on the thing." At that time of night, however, none of us really felt like examining the truck. That would be something for another day. Right now, it was time for reunion and the celebration of arrival. It seems as if we were always celebrating something in those days. Harper's younger brother Bill dropped by with his girlfriend Carol, and we all talked and drank until early in the morning. The conversation was centered on the state of the country and the events in Ohio, but as we all finally faded and slipped toward our assigned sleeping quarters, as terrible as those events were, we were just glad to be in Texas.

The next day we were up relatively early and decided to do

some sightseeing. None of us had been to Galveston before, so we decided that we would spend the day on the Gulf of Mexico, visiting the island. It was at Galveston on September 8, 1900, that the worst natural disaster in U.S. history occurred. More than 6,000 people lost their lives when a hurricane out of the Gulf, with winds of over 200 miles per hour, rampaged the area, totally flooding the island with a 20-foot wall of water, destroying the entire town. Subsequently, a seawall was built to protect the island from future storms. With modern forecasting and weather prediction, the likelihood of a disaster such as the one that occurred in 1900, at least as far as loss of life, is almost negligible.

We drove down Broadway through the center of the town, past the Bishop's Palace, and out onto the seawall, right to the very end, where we discovered a little place called the Tidelands Bar. The place seemed as if it had emerged right out of an Ernest Hemingway novel. The stools along the bar were occupied with a collection of regulars including old salts, fishermen, pool players, and just plain characters. With as much as we could have been doing with our time that day, what we did do was spend the whole afternoon playing pool at the Tidelands and getting a feel for the locals. On each of my future trips to Texas, I would always put aside a little time for a visit to Galveston and the Tidelands, until one trip when I returned to the end of the seawall only to find a burnt-out shell.

After a few days, Jesse and Lee returned to Boston, only to find that because of the shootings at Kent State, their finals had been postponed. Roger and I stayed on in Houston to repair his truck, and after a short audition one afternoon with Mrs. Carrick, I was booked into Sand Mountain.

Sand Mountain was located on Richmond Avenue, a few blocks west of Montrose. The interior of the club was lit by black lights, and the décor was dominated by a 12-foot papier-mâché dragon painted in day-glow green, yellow, and orange. The dragon was positioned right above the stage and looked as if it was ready to pounce on any performer or audience member at will. The black walls sported larger-than-life portraits of Jerry Jeff Walker, Guy

Clark, and Townes Van Zandt, also done in day-glow colors, for it was out of Sand Mountain that many of the well-known Texas musicians made their way into the world.

My gig at Sand Mountain was for two nights as part of a weekend show with two other acts: Don Sanders, a Houston songwriter; and Bill and Lucille Cade, a husband and wife duo. Bill and Lucille rented an apartment upstairs at Sand Mountain from Mrs. Carrick and were regulars at the place. Bill, Lucille, and Don were the first musicians from Texas that I came to know; 30 years later they would remain dear friends.

In the passing days, Roger and I patched up his truck, and the time soon came to make the drive back to Boston. Our final night in Houston was a wild affair. Bill Harper showed up with a bunch of friends, and after eating some rather strange-tasting brownies, we all ended up swimming in an old stone quarry somewhere on the outskirts of town at midnight. Whether or not I realized it at the time, I would be leaving a big piece of my heart in this hot, wild, and wonderful place called Texas. I knew that it would not be long before I would be back. One of the points of the Lone Star had already pierced me, and we had become one in some sort of crazy spirit, a spirit that would not only influence my music, but become yet another force that would alter the course of my life.

There were two tired and trampled cowpokes driving north the next morning. It was doggedly slow-going, but the truck seemed almost excited about venturing out to some new horizons. It felt as if you could let go of the steering wheel, and like some old horse, the truck would lead you home. We crossed the Trinity River, the Neches, and then the Angelina. Roger played his harmonica and I sang a song about the rivers of Texas:

"Oh, we crossed the broad Pecos,
And we crossed the Nueces,
Swam the Guadalupe, and we followed the Brazos,
Red River runs rusty, the Wichita clear,
But down by the Brazos, I courted my dear."

Five days later, Roger and I showed up at Jesse's apartment, a little road weary, but none the worse for the wear. Cynthia decided that it must have been some sort of divine intervention that got us back safely. I wonder now whether perhaps that one trip hadn't instilled within me a kind of bizarre faith in all vehicles that would, throughout my life, allow me to take the most decrepit mechanical objects on four wheels out onto the highway and drive great distances with a trust that I would somehow reach my destination on time and without trouble.

It was in my 1959 Volkswagen Beetle that I returned to Texas two more times before the close of 1970, playing at Sand Mountain each time, and staying with Bill and Lucille in their apartment upstairs. I was developing my own set of friends in Houston. I had discovered there was a plethora of fine musicians around town and a real and vibrant folk scene existed, albeit unknown around the rest of the country. That, of course, would change in a few years when Jerry Jeff, Willie Nelson, Waylon Jennings, and the Outlaw/Cosmic Cowboy scene made itself known all over the land. People would soon open their eyes to Texas, but in 1970, there remained that quiet scene that included Eric Taylor, Guy Clark, Vince Bell, Peter Gorish, Lucinda Williams, Rex Bell, Blaze Foley, Lynne Langham, Mickey White, and so many others.

In Boston, the holiday season had settled about Beacon Hill, the city lamp lights illuminating the great mounds of snow between the sidewalks and the street. Louisburg Square sparkled with the decorative candles adorning each of the windows of the old brick townhouses. It was a happy time. There were parties with hot, mulled merlot and brandy mixed together, and we all, musicians and friends, went caroling up and down the narrow streets. Once, someone opened a third-floor window and lowered a basket of warm cookies and a bottle of wine on a brightly colored ribbon to us; we sang a few extra songs for them. We were good. The harmonies were there and oh so close, and we laughed; the time passed much slower then, because we were very young.

In the spring of 1971, I once again headed south. Texas was nearly becoming my second home. It was not only the music, but the personality of the people. Everybody, each person, seemed to bring something to the scene. Everybody was a character. There was Roger, the roller-blading taxi driver who had a folk music program on Pacifica Radio; Lisey, the champion cowgirl who raised chimpanzees; Sally, one of the waitresses at Sand Mountain who trained horses and taught me how to ride (although I never became a rider); and Reb Smith, the young, long-haired mandolin player who never wore shoes, even in the winter, and bicycled everywhere he went. Time would not slow down for Rebel, and so one day he took a gun and desperately fired at the future.

My musical world was expanding. Driving long distances seemed like nothing to me anymore. I was performing all over the Northeast, and now when I took my trips to Texas, I would schedule stops along the way to play in New Jersey, or Baltimore, or at the Prism in Charlottesville, Virginia. My performing circle in Texas had also broadened to include shows at The Rubyiat in Dallas with Bill and Bonnie Hearne, and Guy Clark. In Houston, Sand Mountain's days seemed numbered, but in the heart of downtown, Rex Bell and Dale Sofar opened another place called The Old Quarter. It was the only place that I ever played where they collected the door admissions in an old hospital bed pan. Many of the musicians were beginning to play at The Old Quarter, and it was there that Townes recorded his classic album, *Townes Van Zandt Live at The Old Quarter.*

I was finding it harder and harder to leave Houston and make the drive back home again. Of course, most of my work was in the Northeast and my roots were in the Boston area, but something inside of me constantly longed for the South. I think that Cynthia could feel what was happening to me, and she sensed the competition. We began to slowly drift apart, and in the summer of 1971 we split up.

I moved to Marblehead, Massachusetts, for the summer to spend time with some friends who had opened The Me & Thee Coffeehouse there. The coffeehouse was located in the community hall of the Unitarian Church in the old section of town and quickly became the premiere folk music venue on the north shore of Boston. During my stay that summer, I was also invited to compose the incidental music and the songs for an adaptation of the Tolkein story "Farmer Giles of Hamm" being performed by a theatre group in the area. It was my first attempt at writing for a theatre production, and I loved spending afternoons creating music by the ocean. It was only a small production but it was a great deal of fun.

Early in the fall, I received a phone call from a fellow by the name of Bruce Patch. Bruce was a record producer living in the area and had worked with many of the bands in the Boston music scene. He had either heard me in concert or heard about me by reputation and said that he was interested in working with me on a recording project. We talked at length, and he offered me a deal whereby he would front the money to do an album at one of the local studios, and then he would try to shop the tape to a major label. Bruce would co-produce the recording with his partner, Harry Bee.

We worked throughout the fall months on the project and used some of the best musicians available on the recording sessions. The recording engineer and bass player was John Nagy. I had known John through his work as the sole backup guitarist with The Mandrel Singers. The group performed regularly at The Unicorn, and I had been to hear them many times. He had also recently been a member of one of the successful area rock groups called Earth Opera. I respected John and knew that he would be an important addition to the record. There were two other guitar players besides me: Greg Prestopino and Jeff "Skunk" Baxter, who later went on to work with the Doobie Brothers. On one of the cuts, "Mexico Way," he played the pedal steel guitar. It was his first gig on that instrument, and he did an impressive job. Rick Nelson (not Ricky Nelson) played percussion, Jeff Lass played piano, my younger brother Steve played the harmonica, and the violin player was Richard Greene, who at the time was with the group Seatrain. Two of the songs were written by Martin Mull, so even Marty dropped by and played some backup parts on a session, although his name never appeared on the credits.

The album, which was entitled *Bill Staines,* was eventually released on Evolution Records. Evolution was the "pop" label subsidiary of the classical music mail-order giant Longinnes Symphonette. Unfortunately, about six weeks after the record was released, Longinnes decided to discontinue Evolution, and all of their artists were let go. My album was immediately sent to the "rackers," which meant that it was bound for the cutout bins in the music stores—a sort of musical purgatory—and was never seen, and as far as I know, never heard of again. Once in a great while, someone will approach me with a copy of the album to have it signed, but that is a rare occurrence.

That year, Bruce and Harry became involved in an interesting project. They had heard of a sculptor traveling around the country who had been erecting large and unusual pieces of art in various places from Hawaii to New England. At the crest of a hill just outside of Chelsea, Vermont, the sculptor had put up a 17-foot Aeolian harp, strung the thing with aircraft cables, and left it there throughout the seasons to sing out its spiraling songs as the wind rose and fell across the hills. It was a beautiful and haunting sound, so Bruce and Harry decided to spend a bit of each season recording the sounds of the "Wind Harp." The project would be released late in the summer of 1972 as a two-album set on United Artists. The album's moment in the sun came a short time after the release, when much of it was used in the soundtrack for the film *The Exorcist.*

Cynthia and I began seeing each other once again in the spring of 1972. She had moved to a bright, sunny apartment on the top floor of a house on Linden Street near Brookline Village, and I spent most of my time there when I wasn't on the road. It was a spring of wine and neighborhood softball games, music and walks through the fragrant, flowering parks of the city. It was a good time once again, the way it had been when we caroled up and down the streets of Beacon Hill during what seemed like that long-ago Christmas.

CHAPTER 12

The Fall Tour, Day 5

When I was in the fourth grade, our class devoted a period of time to studying the states that make up this country of ours. There were only 48 states then, and each child in the class was assigned 2 states on which to report. Along with the report, each of us was to take two shoeboxes, one for each of our states, put wheels on them, and paint or decorate the boxes with pictures or items appropriate to the state. The class would then connect the boxes into a long train, and we would parade this project up and down the corridors of the school in a profound display of the knowledge that we had of our country.

Being an Erector Set whiz, I suggested to the teacher that she permit me to build a large wind-up locomotive to tow the whole rigmarole. My responsibility then, would be for only one of the states plus the locomotive. That state was Wisconsin.

The project was a grand success, with my float being adorned with pictures of farmers and cows, and complete with small chunks of cheese. Even the engine provided enough power to pull the whole train—except that, after every ten feet, the thing needed to be rewound.

It was early on then that I developed an affinity for Wisconsin—although, needless to say, I never expected that someday I would get there during football season to find people walking around with large foam slices of cheese perched upon their heads, and nearly every car adorned with a Green Bay Packers bumper sticker or flag.

I must admit that in an world of corporate takeovers and big-money sports, and with teams leaving town in the middle of the night for perceived greener pastures, it is comforting to find one place in the country where the team is actually owned by the city in which it is located, and that the civic and statewide pride in that team can bring a pride in one's self. We are from Wisconsin! We wear cheese on top of our heads, and we are proud of it!

It is Sunday morning, the fifth day of the fall tour. I cross the Wisconsin state line and pass Beloit. A friend of mine once joked that the name of this town sounds like somebody dropping a quarter into a toilet bowl. Scattered billboard signs begin to appear at the side of the road, beckoning travelers to "*Visit Wisconsin Dells!,*" or "*Win BIG at the Ho-Chunk Casino!,*" or "*Stay at the Arrowhead Lodge!*".

I pass the town of Janesville, home to Parker Pens, and then the capitol city of Madison. Every other spring I do a concert in Madison at the Old Music Hall, one of the most beautiful venues in the country, with its wonderful acoustics and ornamentation of dark wood and brass.

Forty five miles northwest of Madison, the billboards abound as I approach Wisconsin Dells. The Dells are a collection of chasms carved into the local sandstone by the Wisconsin River. The sheer walls of the canyons rise up from the river as much as 150 feet, and over the years a number of natural rock formations have been created. Early on they were given names like "Black Hawk's Head," "Chimney Rock," or "Standing Rock." A dam along the river has divided the area into the Upper Dells and the Lower Dells, and the whole area has become a kind of Midwestern tourism version of Niagara Falls, without the falls.

Continuing past the Dells, I stop for fuel across the highway from the Camp Douglas Military Reservation. There are two fighter planes on pedestals positioned by the front gates of the camp; one is a P51 Mustang, the Cadillac of fighters from the World War II era; the other is an F86 Sabre Jet, the workhorse of the Korean Conflict. Forever at the gates of Camp Douglas, these two planes fly in silent formation, testimony to the awesome power of force and the gentle beauty of flight.

The camp is nearly deserted in October, its long, neat rows of white barracks buildings standing empty in the brilliant sunlight. Now and again, a truck can be seen driving across the parade grounds as the single, vigilant driver goes about his business of the day.

At a nearby rest area, I stop and make an entry into my journal concerning a recollection that has just come to me. I am going to Hanscom Air Force Base in Massachusetts with my father, and that day, right in front of us, a whole formation of Sabre Jets takes off with a roar. I think that both of us had always wanted to learn how to fly.

The lay and the feel of the land have begun to change. Perhaps one has to drive across the whole country a time or two to be able to catch the subtleties of these changes. Somewhere around Tomah the trees begin to decline in size. Along the side of the road, the cream-colored sandstone rock formations begin to appear, eroded by the wind into castle-like shapes and pitted with the nests of the darting cliff swallows. The land itself begins to flatten out into a broad plain which enhances the dimensions of the sky. Overhead, great galleons of clouds sail the endless depths of blue in sleepy flotillas, horizon to horizon, driven by the ancient and ever-present prairie wind. I almost feel as if I am about to shake the great monkey of the crowded East off my back and cross a threshold to a place where I can relax and breathe freely again.

Interstates 90 and 94 part company at Tomah, with the latter making its way to the twin cities of St. Paul and Minneapolis. My route for this part of the tour however, takes me west, along Interstate 90 to La Crosse, and then by state road a few miles north to Galesville and the Back Yard Patio Café, this night's concert location. The restaurant was originally called the Mill Road Café. The Mill Road Café closed for a period of time in the middle 1990s but was reopened in 1997 by Jerry Lehmann and his wife Pat as a retirement project. The cafe is an intimate place with a back porch that is perched on a cliff about 60 feet above Beaver Creek.

It is late in the afternoon when I arrive at the restaurant. Pat and Jerry are busy in the kitchen preparing for the evening dinner crowd. Beneath the glass counter just inside the entrance, the rows of pastries, cakes, and cookies fire up the appetites of all who enter. Later that night some of those pastries will play a big role in getting me to my final destination before I get to sleep.

Around 6:00 P.M the place is all but full, and the conversations are lively but politely subdued. At 7:00, it is time to start the show. Playing at the café is a lot like entertaining in your living room. The people sing and make requests. During the break two young children ask me to sing "All God's Critters." They tell me that they learned the song at camp. I guess one must believe that they have made it as a folksinger when they find out that kids are singing their songs in camp. I think that writing a song that will last and be sung for years to come is the true measure of success as a songwriter. Of course it would be wonderful to win a Grammy, but what is truly important is the music itself, and it is only the song that will ultimately carry on.

The concert at the café is over by 9:30 that evening. I spend a little time chatting with people as they leave, and everyone seems to have had a good time. One party has come down from Lake City, Minnesota, and now has more than an hour to drive before they get back home. The drive that I need to make that night, however, will be just a little bit longer.

My next performance is Tuesday evening, two nights later, in Jackson, Wyoming, so as the audience in Galesville makes their way out of the café, I begin to prepare for the rest of the evening and the drive that will take me across the state of Minnesota to Sioux Falls, South Dakota, and the Frontier Truck Stop where I'll get a few hours of sleep in my van. Physically, this is one of the toughest stretches of the trip, but in order to keep on the tour schedule, the drive must be done. It is also one of my favorite times during the tour when, on this long night of driving, I feel the most alone and yet the most in tune with myself as a far-flung traveler. I am on the dark highway, and I, along with a few determined truckers out there, belong to that late night society of road warriors that survive on truck-stop coffee, conversations on the CB, and the chatter of a radio station broadcasting out of Dallas, Texas, that caters to the truck-driving community. No matter where you happen to be driving, somehow the signal originating from WBAP, the voice of Bill Mack and his "Midnight Cowboy Trucking Network," will find its way to your antenna. The show serves the over-the-road trucker as everything from a mail-order general store for all kinds of trucking paraphernalia to an inspirational fount, supplying simple words of wisdom for those dealing with a troubled heart. It is not an easy life, this life on the road, and a troubled heart is never hard to find. There are demons between the white lines, especially late at night when Hypnos, the god of sleep, is at play and springs his tricks on those who aren't paying attention to his moves.

I, however, am armed and ready to do battle with Hypnos. My weapons include a half dozen chocolate and butterscotch brownies, a fistful of buttery sugar cookies, and two cups of dark coffee, all given to me by Jerry and Pat before I left the café. The potential energy in this cache of goodies is enough not only to get me to South Dakota, but if I am not careful may keep me flying until I get all the way to Seattle. Popping the first of the cookies into my mouth, and taking a sip of the coffee, I take the turn back onto Interstate 90 at La Crosse, and once again head west over the broad blackness that is the Mississippi River.

Once reaching the western shore of the river, the interstate climbs gradually out of the valley, past the welcoming stone marker carved in the shape of the state of Minnesota, and continues straight out in front of me for more than 300 miles to Sioux Falls.

I will keep my distractions in reserve: the CB, the radio, the brownies. I will call for those reinforcements as they are needed, but for now the miles slip by in silence. I am alert, still running on the energy and thoughts of the concert, staring out as far into the distance as I can see, trying to anticipate what I might encounter beyond the bright beams of the headlights. As I left the café, Pat's final direction to me was, "Watch out for the deer."

It is important to be especially wary of two things while driving in the fall. It is rutting season when the deer, moose, and elk sacrifice any semblance of brains for the urge to procreate. They are all over the highway at almost any time of day or night, chasing each other here and there, with no sense of anything that is happening around them. The result is obvious, and the roads are littered with the remains of love-hungry bucks and the does that are the objects of their affection.

The other thing that a driver should be leery of is falling rock. In the late fall and early winter, water seeps through the tiny fissures in the cliffs adjacent to the highways. The constant nighttime freezing and daytime thawing loosens the rock, and often this falling rock bounces down the cliff and out onto the surface of the road. I was made aware of this danger on one of my tours when a rock the size of a loaf of bread landed about 30 feet in front of me. With no time to stop or safely swerve, my vehicle took it right in the transmission. Since then, when a "falling rock" sign comes into view, I pay attention to what is going on above me, and what might be on the road ahead.

The numbers on the mile markers count down the passing of the long dark distances. I turn on the CB and listen for a while, when suddenly my attention is gained by a call on the set for "that westbound van from New Hampshire. Have you got your ears on?". With the probability being that I am the only van from New Hampshire driving across the middle of Minnesota at midnight, I return the call to the trucker who has just passed me.

"Casper the Ghost" is on a return trip to Oregon, having just delivered a trailer load of Pendleton Shirts to L.L. Bean in Freeport, Maine. We talk about things in general: the northern winters, driving at night, the locations of the best truck stops, music, nothing important, but something enough to pass the time and what is beginning to seem like the endless miles.

"Okay, Pony Express, have a safe trip." His final message comes over the air to me as the distance between us widens, and I slow for a break at Albert Lea. I know that it will be close to 3:00 A.M before I get to South Dakota, and that the next three hours driving in Minnesota will be the toughest yet.

The night has gotten very cold, the first real cold that I've felt on this trip. My breath is visible in the neon lights as I hurry across the truck-stop parking lot to the van. Giving its dashboard a pat, I utter a few words of encouragement, "Let's go my friend, let's get to South Dakota." There are times during the tours when, with the exception of a bartender, counter clerk, or waitress, I will go for days without speaking a meaningful word to anyone but my van or my guitar. Sometimes I wonder if they talk about me behind my back.

"Hey, Guitar, did you see what that idiot did today? He almost got us nailed when he scooted out of that parking space without watching where he was going. Where is this guy's mind? I don't know why I keep running for him."

"Aw, he's not so bad, he changes my strings every night and we've done a lot of shows together."

Into the night, past Blue Earth and the tiny town of Welcome, Minnesota. Now, over two thirds of the way there at Jackson, out come the heavy reinforcements, the brownies. Now open the window for just a little bit; man, oh, man it is cold out there! Buy a little more time, a few more miles. I pass Adrian, Minnesota, and begin the final stretch. It will feel good to close my eyes. Don't do it, Bill!! More cold air. Now the border! "Welcome to South Dakota." Just a ways to go now, just a little way to go. Out of the corner of my eye, I catch the image of someone or something standing at the side of the highway. Was that a hitchhiker? It must have been a roadside sign. What would a hitchhiker be doing out here?

Whatever it was, it is gone now, and in the distance the reflective light in the sky over Sioux Falls is a welcome sight. Soon I'll be able to get some sleep.

The 20-foot-high statue of Wild Bill Hickok on the north side of the highway beckons the traveler into the Frontier Village Truck Stop. I make the entrance into the village, park the van in one of the out-of-the-way spaces in the parking lot, and head in to the all-night restaurant to wash up. Returning to the van, I slide into my sleeping bag on the floor in the back, pull on a woolen cap, and finally settle in for the rest of a short but peaceful night. Soon I am asleep, as my van is gently rocked by the cold and constant wind.

Into the arms of South Dakota, this night I commend my bones
And sleep the sleep of one who has journeyed far.
Take good care of this traveler, you spirits of the road,
And when bright morning comes again, renew his heart.

CHAPTER 13

I Can Feel the Sweet Winds Blowing

Late in May of 1972 I received an invitation in the mail from Dick and Anne Albin, a couple from Kentucky, who were putting together a folk festival in conjunction with the University of Louisville. The festival was to be called the Belknap Folk Festival and would be held early that September at the Red Barn on the campus of the school. I had no idea how they had come to know my music, but it was real boost for me to think that perhaps my name was making itself known in new areas of the country.

I immediately called Dick and accepted the invitation, figuring that I could combine the festival gig with yet another trip to Texas. The Old Quarter in Houston had the weekend following the Belknap Festival open, and so it seemed as if everything would work out. In the meantime, I was as busy as I wanted to be that summer with performances all around the Northeast.

The trip south that September was to be one of the most trying experiences I had yet to have on the road. In the long run, it would also introduce me to someone who would become a dear friend, someone who would play an important role for years to come in my personal, as well as professional, life.

I never did make it to Texas that September. On the first day of the trip, just west of Buffalo, New York, the head gasket on my car decided to call it quits, and in a billowing cloud of white smoke I came to a stop just off an exit on the New York Thruway. The car was towed to a nearby garage, and I was informed that it would take four or five days before the repairs could be completed. So much for any profit that I might realize on the tour.

I knew that it would be too much to try and get to Houston this time around, so I called the Old Quarter and canceled my show. I hated to do it, but it seemed that I had no other choice. Dale said that it wouldn't be a problem, and that I should let him know when I would be in Texas again. I really had my heart set on making it to the festival in Louisville, however, and so I was willing to find a way to get there, one way or another, even if I had to walk. I told the owner of the garage that I would be back in about a week for the car, took a taxi to the bus station in Buffalo, and caught the first Greyhound for an all-night ride to Kentucky.

Louisville at 6:30 that Friday morning, the first day of the festival, was burdened with a heavy mist that bordered on continuous rain. The downtown bus station dock, with its buses idling at their respective gates, reeked of diesel fumes as I collected my pack and guitar from the driver. I had no idea where I was, other than the fact that I was in Louisville, and I had no idea in which direction I should proceed in order to get to the festival. A quick inquiry to the agent at the ticket counter provided me with the information that I needed, and a minute later, pack on my back and guitar in hand, I was headed out Third Street toward the University, two and a half miles away.

The Red Barn, the site of the festival, was appropriately named. It was a huge red barn situated on an out-of-the way lot at the edge of the campus, adjacent to the L&N railroad tracks. The building was used as a utility space for various campus gatherings, theatre performances, pep rallies, and whatever else might require a large open indoor area.

I guess that I expected to find the place teeming with performers, all playing music in every nook and cranny. What I did find on that drizzly Friday morning after a two-mile walk from town, though, was a locked barn and a deserted site with not another soul around save one.

Her name was Nancy Johnson, and she was sitting in the back seat of her VW van with the door open, playing a tune on her mountain dulcimer. I introduced myself and asked her if she knew anything about the setup for the weekend and who I might check in with to let them know that I had made it into town. Nancy assured me that the organizers would be on site before long, and that I should just make myself at home and set up my camp wherever I felt comfortable. I picked what seemed like a sheltered spot just beside a row of six—to eight-foot bushes at the edge of the lot and settled in for the duration. I had not brought a tent, but I did have a tarp and a sleeping bag, and that should be sufficient. The rain had stopped and the weather was beginning to clear. The temperature was warming, and the forecast for the weekend sounded like it would be sunny and dry.

By late morning, the Red Barn had been unlocked and the craftspeople had begun to arrive to set up their wares. I introduced myself to Dick and Anne and picked up my schedule for the weekend. The performers list included primarily local musicians from Kentucky, and I was not familiar with most of them—but there were two names I did recognize.

The first was Almeda Riddle, one of the most respected of the traditional singers from the Ozarks. "Granny Riddle," as she was called, was one of the headliners, along with a band known as the Bluegrass Alliance.

The Bluegrass Alliance was a popular attraction at one of the Louisville taverns called the Storefront Congregation and was the original manifestation of the group that became the New Grass Revival. During that time in 1972, the group included Courtney Johnson on banjo, Ebo Walker on bass, Lonnie Pierce on fiddle, Curtis Birch on guitar, and a very young Sam Bush on the mandolin.

The other name that I recognized on the list of performers was a singer by the name of Logan English. My introduction to Logan's music had come by way of Frank Reardon at The King's Rook back in Ipswich; he constantly played a recording done in 1964 entitled, *Logan English Sings the Woody Guthrie Songbag* between sets at the coffeehouse. On the recording, Logan was accompanied by the Greenbriar Boys and Judy Collins, and the album was voted by a collection of folk music reviewers as the best folk album of 1964. I had also recently read an article written about Logan in one of the folk music publications which described him as one of the "prominent performers of the traditional folk music of Kentucky."

It was at this first Belknap Folk Festival that Logan and I became friends. Now and again, if we are lucky enough in our lives, we meet someone who is an inspiration to us—a mentor, a guiding force, someone on the same wavelength as ourselves. It was that way with Logan and me. We had been scheduled to do a number of workshops together at the festival, and so I set out to find him to see if perhaps we could do a tune or two together during one of the sessions. I knew some Woody Guthrie songs and figured that there must be at least one that both of us knew. I found Logan sitting in a lawn chair at the back of his blue Ford Torino, scribbling some notes on a piece of paper. His first words to me were in the form of a question.

"You wouldn't by chance happen to know the words to 'Moonlight in Vermont,' would you? I've been working on an arrangement of the song, and I sure would like to be able to play it this weekend."

"I'm sorry." I said. "I've heard the song a couple of times, but I don't know any of the lyrics to it."

I mentioned that we were scheduled to do a few stages together and told him my name. I also mentioned that I was very familiar with his recording of Woody's tunes and liked the record a lot. Logan's face brightened and he laughed; he said that he didn't think that he would ever meet anybody who had ever heard of that recording. I reassured him that was not the case and said I thought it was a classic album.

We did our workshops and we sang together, along with so many of the other performers that weekend. On the Saturday night of the festival, after the concert, Nancy, Logan, and I made our way downtown to the Storefront Congregation to see the Bluegrass Alliance do a late set. The band had the place in an uproar. I had never seen a group with more energy onstage in my life.

We were drinking Guinness Stout, and after the band had finished their last set and the crowd had thinned a little, Logan broke into an *a cappella* rendition of "Wild Mountain Thyme," followed by a version of "The Royal Canal." Nancy and I joined in on the harmonies, and before long we had the whole tavern, including the band, singing traditional songs in four-part harmonies.

That was the way it was with Logan, the Greenwich Village singer who occasionally sang with the Clancy Brothers; the poet who agonized for weeks over the use of a single word in one of his poems; the storyteller and writer who was friends with Robert Penn Warren; the playwright who graduated from Yale Drama School and wrote plays about jazz player Charlie "The Bird" Parker and abolitionist Cassius Clay; and the man who was one of Cisco Houston's best friends, the person that Cisco came to for support when he found out that he had cancer.

This was the Logan that I came to know: the hard-drinking literary genius with a fire in his heart that would rage his entire life, and the man who kept a journal in the form of notes that he wrote as Pierrot, the tragic French clown of the theatre, to Columbine, the sweetest flower of love.

For the last day of the festival, I rented a room at a nearby hotel so that I could get some sleep before the bus trip back to Buffalo to pick up my car. The final night of the festival was a special moment. Throughout the whole weekend, there had never been a great number of people in attendance, and for the last show the house was only about half full. Yet there was a musical magic that night that I consider myself fortunate to have experienced. I remember well Logan singing, "The Ballad of Tom Joad," the Woody Guthrie song based on the Steinbeck novel *The Grapes of Wrath*, and I remember thinking how blessed I was to be listening to J.P. and Annadeane Fraley singing "Molly Darling." The closing song of the festival was an old Bahamian funeral song entitled, "I Bid You Goodnight." I don't remember who led us on that final song, but I made up my mind to learn the piece, and years later I would record it on an album called *Bridges*.

Logan showed up at my hotel bright and early the morning after the festival and offered me a ride to the bus station in Louisville. He was living at his family farm in Paris, Kentucky, and the station would be right on his way back home. I mentioned during our ride together that I would be performing at the Caffé Lena in Saratoga at the end of the month, and he asked me to say hi to Lena for him. As it turns out, Logan had performed for Lena back in 1960, just after she opened the café; they were good friends, although they hadn't seen each other in a long time.

The bus trip back to Buffalo was uneventful, and the Belknap Folk Festival would become an annual stop on my tours for six or seven years until it finally faded away in the late 1970s.

When I played my weekend at Lena's at the end of that month, I mentioned to her that I had been to Kentucky, that I had met Logan, and that he had sent along his greetings. Her face immediately lit up, and she broke into a big smile.

"You know," she said, "Logan was the second person ever to play here, just after we opened. If you talk to him again, have him get in touch with me."

I knew that Logan had moved home to Kentucky from New York to work on a play that he was writing for the Louisville Players, and that the play was his focus for the moment, but soon after I played Lena's I got in touch with him and told him that he should give her a call. Whether in the long run it worked out for the best, I guess I'll never really know, but shortly after my call to him I found that he had moved into an apartment in an old brick building right around the corner from Lena's in Saratoga.

Logan's dwelling was sparsely furnished with a sofa, two floor lamps, a table with a couple of chairs, and a writing desk complete with a typewriter and a desktop bookshelf that contained his notebooks. Accompanying the notebooks on the bookshelf was a set of the novels of James Joyce and a volume of *The Complete Works of William Shakespeare*. Over Logan's bed, a single verse from a poem/prayer was done in calligraphy and framed:

> *"From Ghoulies and Ghosties*
> *And things that go bump in the night,*
> *Dear Lord, deliver us."*

If there was any kind of extravagance in Logan's apartment, it could be found in the kitchen, for Logan loved to cook. Suspended from hooks overhead on the ceiling, or hanging from the inside of cabinet doors, there was nearly every kind of cooking utensil imaginable. Any gathering of two or more friends at Logan's was cause enough for him to whip up a gourmet meal.

The old brick building was torn down after Logan had been living there for about a year, so he moved into an apartment in a large house on Circular Avenue, a few blocks away. After a year or so on Circular, Logan settled into a second floor apartment on North Broadway. Although the interior layout in his apartments would change, Logan's furnishings always remained constant. He never seemed to need—and I dare say, never seemed to want—much more than the simple life of a writer and an artist.

Logan insisted that I always keep a key to his place, and whenever I passed through Saratoga or played at Lena's, I always had a couch available to stretch out my sleeping bag.

During the first week of October in 1972, Cynthia and I were invited by Bruce Patch and Harry Bee to attend a release party for *The Wind Harp*. The get-together was at Northern Recording Studios in Framingham, Massachusetts. It was a raw and rainy night, but everyone was of good cheer and exited about the double album project. Although the recording sounded pretty strange in content, the package had received good reviews in the media. The party lasted until about midnight, and when it came time to leave and drive back to Brookline, I decided that Cynthia and I would take Route 9 instead of the Massachusetts Turnpike, which would have been faster.

About four miles east of the studio, we were hit head on by a vehicle being driven the wrong way on the divided highway. Cynthia was severely injured and my car was demolished. The driver of the other car fled the scene, and shortly after the accident the car was suspiciously reported by the owner to have been stolen. Whether or not this was an accurate report, I will never know. I was very fortunate, but Cynthia spent a number of days in the hospital. Our relationship had once again been on shaky ground when the accident occurred, and although it was a difficult time for us both, it was especially hard on her. The recovery from her injuries took some time, and I was not there when I should have been.

I had scheduled another trip to Texas in early November, and it was on this trip that I met Karen, the person who some four years later would become my wife.

Karen was a student at Wilson College in Chambersburg, Pennsylvania, and I had been booked by the student activities committee to perform at their coffeehouse. Karen, as it turned out, was scheduled to be the coffeehouse coordinator for that particular concert. Her responsibility for the evening was to take me to dinner at the dining hall, show me where I was staying, and introduce the show. I was immediately taken with her and asked her if she might be free to spend the next day with me. The next day was a Sunday, and I thought that it might be nice to take a drive to Gettysburg and walk through the historical park. It was a foggy morning, but by noon the skies had cleared and it had become a beautiful fall day. We spent that Sunday together, and later in the evening after she had returned to her dorm I wrote her a poem. The next morning when she came to see me off on the rest of my trip, I gave her the poem.

Perhaps it was a good thing that I was on my way south and not heading straight back to New England, for my drive to Texas that November was filled with confused thoughts and feelings about my relationship with Cynthia, what I was going to do with my music, and now, of all things, what had become a yearning in my heart for this new person in my life. Although we kept in touch, I would not see Karen until the following spring when once again I was invited to Wilson to play at a folk festival sponsored by the college.

In the early months of 1973 my relationship with Cynthia came to an end, and I busied myself by getting involved with another recording project. Bruce Patch was again the producer and was willing to front the money for the recording time. The plan, as it had been for the previous album, was to shop the master tape to various labels to see if they might show it some interest. If there was no interest in the project shown by the labels, we would just release the album independently and count primarily on sales from the stage.

Although the recording went smoothly, in the months that followed the project became mired in one problem after another; it turned into what only could have been a bad dream. None of the major labels showed any interest in the tape, and so the decision was made to release it ourselves on the Catfish label. In hindsight, it was probably the perfect name for the record company, given that the project spent most of the time wallowing around in what seemed like a muddy oblivion. Soon after the album was recorded, Bruce ran out of money for the project and the whole release was put on hold. I made an offer to foot the bill for the pressings, but it seemed that everyone's interest in getting the thing released was also put on hold. Finally, after constant badgering on my part, Bruce agreed to my proposal and we began to move forward with the record. Almost immediately another problem came bounding out of the wings. The summer of 1973 was marked by the Arab oil embargo, and vinyl, being a petroleum product, was in short supply. In fact, for small pressing plants, finding good virgin vinyl was nearly impossible. Because of this shortage of good plastics, when the album *Third Time Around* was finally released, there also came with it a number of problems with the pressings. I was ready to move on to something else and forget that the whole project had ever happened. What was interesting to me, however, was that people kept coming up to me and telling me how much they liked the record. The first pressing sold out, and that was it for *Third Time Around.*

Fortunately, it was not the final note for most of the songs on the album, for almost all of them were re-recorded on later releases. It *was* though, the only recording and final fanfare of the "Staines Concerto in Eb for Mouth Trumpet and Guitar." This was much to the disappointment of some of the most deranged of my fans.

In early September of 1973, Karen joined me in Kentucky for that year's Belknap Folk Festival, and it was there that she met Logan. She was immediately impressed by his writing abilities, and soon after the festival she invited him to Wilson to do a poetry reading and seminar. I was once again on my way to Texas, and so I stopped at Chambersburg to visit with Karen and to see Logan's presentation, which was a mixture of original songs and poetry. I don't think that I will meet a more talented poet in my lifetime. With his soft Kentucky baritone voice, he was absolutely mesmerizing.

In 1973, Houston, Texas, was home to a number of folk music venues. Not only was The Old Quarter operating, but also The Green Room; Houlihan's; and a small, bohemian type of spaghetti restaurant called Anderson Fair, the appellation of the place stemming from the names of the two men who opened the doors for the first time.

Nestled away on a side street in the Montrose area, Marvin Anderson and Gray Fair had initiated an enclave of musicians and artists that had become almost a community by itself. Each morning, a collection of these locals would show up for coffee, often helping out between cups with the preparation of the noon spaghetti, salad, and garlic bread offering to the community. At 11:00 A.M. the doors would open, and through them would pass the people and politicos of the Houston business world. It was the perfect opportunity for the local musicians to do their thing, and a corner of the restaurant was set aside for lunch time "pass-the-hat" performances.

During the evening, the Fair also had scheduled music. Many of the same musicians who played during the noon hour also filled these spots, the only difference being that in the evening there was more of a concert atmosphere, and a cover charge went into effect. This also allowed the club to bring performers in from out of town.

As the years passed, of all of the clubs in Houston, Anderson Fair alone would survive. Weathering a host of owners and managers over three decades, the Fair would come to be a stop for touring musicians from all over the world and a springboard for the likes of Nanci Griffith, Lucinda Williams, and Lyle Lovett.

In 1973, I felt that I still owed my allegiance to The Old Quarter, and so I played there whenever I came to town. Almost always, however, after my own show was over, I would drop by the Fair to catch another late-night set of music. I was staying at Bill and Lucille Cade's place, and they lived only a block or two from the Fair, so it was right on my way home. There was always a party or late-night jam happening until the wee hours of the morning. The next day, bright and early, I would show up to read the paper, drink coffee, and help chop the vegetables for the day's spaghetti sauce.

I will always have a soft spot in my heart for Anderson Fair. It continues to operate today as one of the country's legendary folk venues.

* * *

Karen moved to New Hampshire after graduating from Wilson in the spring of 1974 and rented an apartment in a large old house in Dover. She would be attending the University of New Hampshire that fall as a graduate student in psychology, and I spent a good deal of time commuting from Boston to see her. Although I was happy to be spending my time with Karen during those cool, colorful months, it seemed to me that my career had reached some sort of plateau, and it was beginning to bother me. I was certainly busy playing places, but the clubs in the Northeast and my trips to Texas seemed to mark the extent of my musical world. I needed something more, and in the spring of 1975, once again adventure found its way to me. This experience would not only broaden my musical circles, but also my entire existence. It would be an adventure that would open the door through which I would pass into the next stages of my life.

The odyssey emerged from an idea that I had in the fall of 1974 when I was on one of my sojourns to Houston. I had never been to California, and it seemed to me that rather than returning to New England after one of my trips to Texas, I should just keep on heading west as far as I could go. When I told Bill Cade about the plan, he indicated that he might like to tag along. Walter Spinks, who was working at Anderson Fair at the time and had a large white panel truck, offered up the vehicle as a kind of an Argus if there were another spot that he might fill on the adventure. We all agreed that we would leave from Houston at the end of May, when I would be in Texas again, and spend all of the month of June traveling in the West. I thought that it might be nice to have Karen join me for at least a part of the journey, and everyone agreed that having her along would be fine. She had an uncle living near Houston, and it would give her a chance to stop by and visit his family before we left for the trip. She would leave with us from Houston, but because of time constraints she could only travel with us as far as Los Angeles. From there, she would have to hop on a plane for home. Walter, Bill Cade, and I would continue the trip through California and finally make our way back toward Texas by way of Nevada, Utah, Wyoming, Colorado, Kansas, and Arkansas. I would need to leave my car in Houston at the outset of the trip. Another Anderson Fair regular, Roger Ruffcorn, agreed to drive my car to Little Rock, meet up with us, and return with Walter and Bill to Houston while I started north.

The time was set. Karen would fly to Texas on that Memorial Day weekend in 1975, and after she had visited with her uncle, the four of us would head out from Houston on our grand safari. An unexpected turn of events delayed our departure for a few days.

In response to what was almost a dare from my musician friends in Houston, I had submitted a tape of my yodeling to Rod Kennedy, the producer of the Kerrville Music Festivals. The festival that year would host the first annual Kerrville National Yodeling Championships. Kerrville, Texas, had been home to Jimmie Rodgers, "the Singing Brakeman," and it seemed like the perfect place to hold the contest. The folk festival was a popular attraction in the town and deemed to be the likely host for the event. Much to my surprise, I found myself in one of the finalist slots, vying for the honor of National Yodeling Champion.

The finals took place during the festival on the Saturday of the Memorial Day weekend in 1975. It had been raining heavily all day, and the festival grounds were awash in torrents of running water and mud. There were three judges for the event: Mike Seeger, Kenneth Threadgill, and Wilf Carter (otherwise known as the great "Montana Slim"). As the contestants were eliminated one by one beneath the driving rain, I realized that I was one of the two finalists, and the judges ruled that the contest should be considered a draw. A decision was then made that there would be a "yodel off" between the last two contestants. I don't remember the name of my opponent, and mostly I was pretty amazed that I had survived as long as I had in the contest. During this last round, I expected to go down in the agony of defeat. The judges announced the winner. It was the yodeler from Houston. I was not from Houston. It must have been the other finalist. No, he was from Austin. They were congratulating me. Hot damn!

I received 100 silver dollars, a trophy, and the title of National Yodeling Champion, which I would be expected to defend the following year. What I remember most, however, was the rainbow that appeared in the brightening sky as they announced the winner. It was an incredible sight, as bright and brilliant as I had ever seen a rainbow. It lasted for only a few minutes that afternoon in Texas, but for me it would last a lifetime.

The four of us—Walter Spinks, Bill Cade, Karen, and I—headed west. We crossed the Pecos River under a spring-bright west Texas moon and stopped at Langtry the next morning. Langtry, the tiny stop along the railroad, was where the self-proclaimed "Judge" Roy Bean dispensed his own swift and final justice upon many a hapless horse thief. Judge Bean, with a Bible in one hand and a book of the statutes of the state of Texas in the other, answered to no mortal man when it came to his judgments. He was "the law west of the Pecos."

There was only one true and constant soft spot in the judge's heart, and that was for the beautiful English society woman who had become a respected actress. She was Lillie Langtry, and it was for her that he would name his town.

"The Jersey Lily," as she came to be known, did visit the town once, by train, on her way west. Standing on a platform at the back of the train, she acknowledged the cheers of the crowd, listened to the music of the assembled musicians, spoke for six minutes, and then was gone forever into the shimmering heat of the west Texas afternoon.

We camped one evening at Big Bend National Park, nestled beneath the rim of the Chisos mountain basin with towering Casa Grande peak standing sentinel above us in the fading light. Karen took some photographs that evening of the sunset and the surrounding hills. Some eight years later I would use one of these photos as the cover art for the album *Sandstone Cathedrals*.

We reached El Paso and decided that we could not continue without at least a short foray into Mexico at Juarez. Bill Cade decided to remain in the truck on the Texas side while Walter, Karen, and I hoofed it across the bridge into that border abyss of trinket shops, shoeshine boys, raunchy bars, and liquor stores that sold various distillations of the devil that were not available in the United States. Once partaken of, these elixirs tended to change one's outlook on the world, the universe, and just about anything else. The next morning I remembered a line from Shakespeare's *Othello*, a line spoken frequently by Logan after a particularly hard night. In the play, a soldier rues the consequences of the previous evening's escapades: “Oh, that a man should put an enemy into his mouth to steal away his brain!”.

We continued across the Southwest, taking some of the out-of-the way desert back roads, visiting Tombstone and the OK Corral on our way through Arizona. Finally, four days after leaving Kerrville, we entered California. With our arrival at the Santa Monica pier, I had completed my first trip across the country.

We spent a few days visiting Dick Morgan, an old acquaintance of my mother's. She had dated Dick before she married my father, and they had always kept in touch. Dick had moved to California decades before and was now selling health foods and vitamins out of his house in the suburbs of Los Angeles. I had met Dick a few times when he had traveled back East to visit his family, and I think perhaps he had never lost his affection for my mother. Once, on a visit, he had even helped me replace a blown engine in one of my old Volkswagens. He was pretty impressed with my yodeling trophy.

We explored Los Angeles, saw the Hollywood sights, and were cited for jaywalking at the corner of Hollywood and Vine by a motorcycle cop with “I-can-see-you-but-you-can't-see-me” sunglasses. I was tempted to ignore the ticket until I noticed the small print on the back of the citation that warned failure to pay the fine within the allotted period of time was a separate offense and would result in something akin to death.

Karen flew back to New England, and after a short hop down to Tijuana (which we were informed by a San Diego gas station attendant was home to *el diablo*), Walter, Bill, and I, continued up the coast of the state. We dropped in at a place called the Bluebird Café in Santa Barbara and were told that, if we were to stay around for a few days, we might be able to do a guest set on that coming Friday evening. Never ones to pass up what might be a future booking, we agreed to hang around until the end of the week.

To pass the time before the weekend arrived, we decided to take a trip up into the hills east of Santa Barbara and camp for a while. We had just about made it as far as Ojai when, on the edge of town, the fuel pump in the truck gave up the ghost. We coasted into a local service station, stuck and wondering what to do next. It was going to take three days to get another fuel pump for the truck, and we had no place to stay in town.

Out of the hot California afternoon appeared a lone figure walking down the road. With an old leather hat on his head and a guitar on a strap over his shoulder, Jerry Rau stopped at the service station for a drink. Noticing his guitar, we struck up a conversation with this character and found that he had just hitchhiked to Ojai from the Kerrville Folk Festival. Jerry had a lady friend living in town and he was there for a visit, or perhaps to stay. He wasn't at all sure himself.

Jerry's friend, Stephanie, was living at the edge of town in an old candle factory. The candle makers had moved out of the building, and a group of assorted characters from the hills had moved in with all of their earthly possessions. Jerry suggested that there might be space for us to stay at the candle factory until the truck was fixed. After he checked with Stephanie, the four of us showed up at the front door of the place: a pack of homeless, broke-down musicians, looking for the proverbial "palette on the floor."

That's exactly what it was. We spread out our sleeping bags on the floor in a corner of the place amongst the menagerie of dogs and cats, and a cage containing one huge boa constrictor. The people were nice enough, albeit a little strange, but the ice was soon broken as we stayed up most of the first night playing music and drinking beer. The snake, however, must have decided that things had gotten a little too crowded or perhaps a little too weird at the factory, so after we had all fallen asleep, it made its escape. In the morning it could not be found, but all of the cats seemed extremely nervous.

Later that week, we contacted the service station and found that Walter's truck had been repaired, so we said our farewells to the people at the candle factory and continued our journey back down to Santa Barbara and the Bluebird Café. Before we left Ojai, Jerry gave me the phone number for a coffeehouse in Minneapolis. It was called the Coffeehouse Extempore, and as it turned out, Jerry was the person who was doing the booking for the place.

Making that acquaintance with Jerry Rau in Ojai was the first of the occurrences in 1975 that would affect the future of my musical life.

It felt good to be on the move again. We stopped that Friday evening to do a guest set at the Bluebird, but the owner wasn't there, and the leader of the band that was playing that evening decided that he would rather not let anyone else onstage to play music. That was fine with us. The vibes in the place weren't all that great anyway, so we gladly left the Bluebird and Santa Barbara behind.

The next stop on our odyssey was King's Canyon and Yosemite National Park. Camping in the Yosemite Valley, surrounded by the immense monuments to the beauty of the Earth, was an awesome experience indeed. Very early one morning before Bill and Walter were up, I decided to take a hike up to the base of Bridal Veil Falls. The sun had just risen, and as I stepped into the cloud of mist at the base of the falls, I found myself totally surrounded by rainbows. Everywhere I looked color abounded, and the rainbows floated here and there in the shining brightness of the cool mist. I sat on one of the moist rocks, engulfed in this spectacle of color, when overhead a much larger rainbow appeared. I could not tell whether the moisture on my face was from the mist around me or the tears that I was sure were falling from my eyes. This was the second time on this trip that I had been the recipient of such beauty: the first at Kerrville, and now at Yosemite. I said nothing about this experience to Bill and Walter as we exited Yosemite on its eastern side, descended to Mono Lake, and began our journey back toward the East.

The Grand Tetons were the next stop on our trip. It was a last-minute decision, but Cade had heard of a place called the Mangy Moose Saloon that offered music in Jackson, and since none of us had ever seen the mountains of northern Wyoming before, it seemed like a brilliant idea to go for a visit.

We arrived in Jackson late one rainy afternoon with the Tetons totally obscured by weather. Camping just outside of town, we set off to find the Mangy Moose. Checking with one of the locals, we discovered that the place was located in Teton Village, at the foot of the mountains just west of town. As it happened, that evening's performer was Townes Van Zandt, with his band which included Mickey White and Rex Bell, two old Houston friends.

It was a Texas reunion and a wild night. Townes allowed that we should do a guest set, and we ended up closing the place down and retreating to the motor home in which Townes was traveling until we just could not stand the fun anymore. How we ever found our campsite later that night is beyond me, but the next morning we stumbled out of the truck and the tent with the sun in our eyes and the majestic Tetons in full view.

It was this first trip to Wyoming, in combination with the stories told to me by my Texas rodeo friends, that became the seeds for the song "My Sweet Wyoming Home," written in the fall of that year.

Although almost all of the trip was unplanned, there were a few stops that made sense from the outset. Bill Cade had wanted to visit an old friend, Phil Stephan, who was living up in Sunshine Canyon in the foothills above Boulder, Colorado. We could visit Phil and then head down to Denver to check out the hootenanny at The Oxford Hotel, one of the well-known folk venues in the West. Bill had known Phil when Phil was a chaplain at the University of Houston, and a call from us brought an immediate invitation to spend the night at his home. We made our way up the winding canyon road to Phil's mountainside house. It was a gorgeous day, and Phil was at his front door to meet us.

A bearded man with a strong, sincere handshake, he had retired from being a chaplain and gone to work as a counselor for a holistic health center at one of the local colleges. We spent an hour or two catching up on old times. Although he was glad to see us, he had a previous engagement out of town that evening and would need to leave shortly. Before he left, he took three steaks out of his freezer and insisted that we make ourselves at home for the night. The barbecue grill was out on the front deck. He must have known Cade's passion for a good steak, and the house was ours.

The moon rose that evening over Sunshine Canyon and three

friends gazed above to the stars, and below and before them to the pale-lit spectrum of the eastern high plains, just a little giddy about their place in the universe and the beauty of it all.

* * *

There was a line for the weekly hootenanny at The Oxford Hotel when we showed up the next evening, and the bar at the place was in full swing. Bill Cade and I signed up for early performance slots and played our songs for what was probably always an enthusiastic audience. The three of us then settled in at one of the tables in the bar to pass the night and listen to the rest of the music. The place definitely had the feel of the old West. Antlers hung high on the wall and there was a long, dark, heavy wooden bar, complete with a mirror reflecting the faces of the customers. I almost expected to turn and see the figure of Paladin out of "Have Gun Will Travel" playing cards at one of the tables.

There was quite a parade of performers onstage that night—but of all of them, only one who caught my attention and who I would remember. She was a young woman with a beautiful voice and a head of tousled chestnut hair, playing a guitar that seemed large when it was paired with her small frame. We only met in passing that night when, after her set, she came into the bar, but for some reason I never forgot her name. Our paths would cross years later in Texas when I heard that she was working with a singer by the name of Tom Russell. It was Katy Moffat who had filled the room with her music that night in Denver at The Oxford Hotel.

The next morning, we said goodbye to the Rocky Mountains and the state of Colorado and headed east for Kansas City, where we would make a brief stop to visit with one of Walter's brothers. We then headed south toward Little Rock and, hopefully, our rendezvous with Roger Ruffcorn and my car.

The target meeting point in Little Rock was at an apartment rented by Bill Haymes, another musician who toured Texas and played frequently at Anderson Fair. Bill was living in Arkansas but spent much of his life on the road traveling around the country. He had invited us to give him a call and drop by his place whenever we were in the area.

Miraculously, we all arrived in Little Rock at the same time, found Bill Haymes' place, and descended upon him, each of us in one piece, and all relatively no worse for the wear. We had stories to tell Roger and Bill of our trip, and it was the wee hours of the morning before the group of us fell asleep on Haymes' floor.

I should say I attempted to fall asleep, for after about an hour of tossing and turning on the hard wood, an undeniable urge came over me to get up, get back on the road, and start my long drive back to New England. I quietly packed my car, left a note of farewell to everyone, and made my way under a still-dark sky out of Little Rock while most of the city was just beginning to stir in anticipation of the coming day.

It had been quite a trip, I thought as I sped past the exit on Interstate 40 for the Little Rock Air Force Base. It had lasted just under a month, and I had been to a number of new places and met a lot of good people along the way. How fortunate I was to be living a life such as this, with music as a foundation and so many good friends around me.

In the next instant, I found myself missing Karen and eager to get back to my life at home. She was not someone to take for granted, and I wondered, given that we had spent so much time apart, whether our relationship would ever last.

Rain had begun to drum out a pattern on my windshield, and although the sky was brightening in the east, I could tell that the drive across Arkansas was going to be a wet one. I had had very little sleep and by this time was running entirely on adrenaline. As the day wore on, I felt as if I was racing with the storm across Arkansas and Tennessee. At times it rained so hard that I could hardly hear the radio in the car. Occasionally, a bolt of lightning would strike the ground off to the side of the highway with a startling explosion of sound that would bring me straight up in my seat. Toward evening, I emerged from under the leading edge of the system and turned north, up into the beautiful Shenandoah

Valley of Virginia. As the overcast began to dissipate and the late golden sun peeked out above the western horizon, I thought that this must surely be an evening cast for an incredible sunset. What did appear, as the sun shone at that low angle through the mist, was another beautiful rainbow, rich in color, and directly in my path.

What I can only describe as some sort of powerful revelation came over me at that point. Although I had always felt as if I were a spiritual person, I had never been very religious. I was not familiar with the biblical connotations of rainbows, and other than recognizing them as pretty phenomena in the sky or cutesy window stickers out of the 1960s, I had never thought much about them. That was about to change. In that moment, I perceived that something very important in my life had been shown, or perhaps explained, to me.

The essence of the enlightenment that day was that each of us during our lifetime is endowed with our own personal rainbow. It follows us through our life, and every once in a while when some important event happens or is about to happen to us, this rainbow makes an appearance, just to assure us that everything is okay and that things are proceeding as planned. I suppose that for some people this belief comes in the form of a guardian angel. I came to realize, as the sun set on that golden Virginia evening, that my guardian was a rainbow. We see many rainbows in our lifetime. How does one know when this special one makes an appearance? My sense is that one just knows, that a person can feel it in their heart. It is not something to look for in every sighting, but if one believes in this theory, when this special rainbow appears it will be evident by the sense of safety and peace felt by the person who beholds the sight.

I knew that it was not the greatest of spirits, that it was not a substitute for God, that it was only a rainbow. I also knew that it would follow me in my life and that I would see the rainbow again when the time was appropriate. A year would pass before I saw its colors once more.

The second occurrence in 1975 that fanned the flames of my

musical life came in the form of an invitation to the Fox Hollow Folk Festival in Petersburg, New York. Although the festival was small, it was one of the most prestigious folk festivals in the Northeast, if not the country. The real focus of the festival was on traditional folk music, but by 1975 many of the contemporary songwriters, if their writings held forth traditional roots, had been invited to perform at the event. Fox Hollow was held at a beautiful, rambling old homestead nestled in the rolling hills of eastern New York state. It was the home of the Beers family: Bob, Evelyne, and Martha. This trio of singers was one of the most respected folk music families of the time. They had performed concerts in venues ranging from local town halls to the White House, and in 1966 they had opened their home and lands to all those who loved traditional folk music.

It rained almost every year of the festival, sometimes in showers, often in torrents, and once as a flood. The first two archival recordings of what was lovingly dubbed "Fox Wallow" were celebrations to the stamina of the festival-goers and were entitled *Pitter, Poon, the Rain Come Doon* and *Clitter, Clatter, Down Come the Water.*

It was at Fox Hollow that I met many of the people who would play important roles or be inspirations in my musical life. There was Faith Petric, the "Grande Dame" of folk music in the San Francisco Bay area; Gordon Bok, one of the few performers I had ever met who could sing up to a bass note; Joe Hickerson; Andy and Bill Spence; and Alan Block, the fiddling sandal maker whose daughter, Rory, became a respected singer of the Delta blues. I met Cindy Dinsmore who, along with Dave Fry, had just started a club called Godfrey Daniels in Bethlehem, Pennsylvania. They were looking for performers to play at their new place and invited me to get in touch with them. There were so many people who brought so much heart to the festival, not the least of whom were Sandy and Caroline Paton.

The Patons, along with Lee Haggerty, owned and operated Folk Legacy Records, a small but important record label that specialized in field recordings of singers and storytellers in both the American and British traditions. By 1975, Folk Legacy had released more than 50 recordings documenting the music and oral traditions of rural America and the British Isles, from the singing of Frank Proffit of Watauga County, North Carolina, to the Scots songs of Norman Kennedy and Jeannie Robertson. I would eventually record two albums for Folk Legacy, a result of getting to know the Patons at Fox Hollow.

Tragically, Bob Beers was killed in an automobile accident in May of 1972, and although the festival carried on without Bob through the late 1970s, it eventually became another one of those casualties to time. The spirit of Fox Hollow, however, would endure and manifest itself in the Old Songs Festival held each year in Altamont, New York.

By the end of that summer of 1975, I was feeling rejuvenated, and as the fall of that year approached, I began to think about recording another album. I booked a block of studio time at Northern Recording Studios in Maynard, Massachusetts, just west of Boston, and in that October I recorded the album *Miles*.

Most of the material on the album was original, including songs like "Walk Down by the Water" and "My Sweet Wyoming Home," but I also included "Zane Grey," a song by Tom Russell, and a traditional song, "Ain't No More Cane on the Brazos," based on the lives of the inmates of the prison in Sugarland, Texas, as they cut sugarcane on the Brazos river prior to World War II. I set one of Logan's poems to music and recorded "Going Back Where the Wheatfields Wave." It was the only time that I was able to take somebody else's lyrics and successfully integrate them with one of my melodies. *Miles* was released New Year's Day of 1976 on my own independent label, Mineral River Records, and most of the initial sales were from the stage. The name for the label came from an old Lone Ranger episode, when the masked man instructed Tonto to go into a fictional town called Mineral River to observe what the local outlaws were about. For some reason the name stayed with me and not only became the moniker of my record label, but also the name of my publishing company which would publish all of my songs.

Shortly after the release of the *Miles* album, Karen and I decided to get married. By that time I had been all but living in New Hampshire anyway, so we set the wedding date as the first of May of that year. We informed Karen's parents, and although they gave us their blessing, I'm sure there was a bit of trepidation in their minds; having their daughter engaged to a folksinger must have been just a little underwhelming.

In February of 1976 I was scheduled to perform as the opening act for Doc Watson at the Main Point in Bryn Mawr, Pennsylvania. Karen's folks had been planning a trip from their home in Virginia to New Hampshire anyway, so we all decided to rendezvous in Bryn Mawr. They had never seen me perform, and after all, if their daughter was going to marry a musician, they had better make sure that he did a good show.

It was a magical evening. The place was sold out, and everybody was ready for Doc and his marvelous guitar picking. Sometimes it can be intimidating for an opener, being pretty much an unknown and knowing that the audience is there primarily for the headliner. This evening was different. Perhaps there was enough magic in the air for everybody. My set was well received, and Doc was gracious enough to listen to the whole thing. His set was amazing, and everyone left the club feeling a bit of the magic.

The next morning I went to the room at the hotel where Karen and her folks were staying, and Karen's dad handed me a copy of the morning *Philadelphia Inquirer.* There was a rave review of the concert. As it should have, the review focused on Doc Watson. At the end of the article, though, a few lines had been reserved for the opening act. It was the last line that gave us all a good chuckle. It read something to the effect that " . . . when Bill Staines left the stage, he came across as someone that you wouldn't mind having as part of your family." It seemed as if I had received a favorable review on more than one front that morning. I was always grateful for that review. In jest, it took a long time to convince anyone that I hadn't paid to have it written.

I had one more long tour to do that spring before the wedding. Frothingham Management, a Boston-area booking agency, had set up five concerts for me at the end of March in the Gold Country of California. It would be my first solo trip across the country. I booked a date in Kentucky and another in Kansas City on the way out, and I left on my first transcontinental driving adventure during a New England snowstorm.

The roads east of the Missouri River were like old friends by now since I had seen them so many times before, but traveling the distances across Kansas and Colorado by myself was a new experience. I felt very alone, vulnerable, like I was on some giant balance beam and could fall off into grand obscurity if something were to happen to my car and I was forced off of this ribbon of interstate.

It happened about 20 miles west of Limon, Colorado, on the high plains, at 8:00 at night. The alternator in my car froze up, and I came to a stop at the side of the road, in total darkness, with a frigid wind blowing outside. I could look back down the long slope of the plains and see the dim lights of Limon, miles to the east, but I may as well have been the moon.

The hours passed, with now and then a single car or semi-truck rolling by. Finally, around 11:00 that night, a Colorado state trooper decided to check out the vehicle sitting forlornly at the side of the road. I informed the trooper that I needed to be towed back into Limon. He radioed the local AAA towing service and told me that they would be by in a while with a wrecker. Then he drove off merrily on his way, leaving me once again alone at the side of the dark highway. Sure enough, some 25 minutes later, the towing service came along. Hooked up and once again in motion—although headed in the wrong direction—I was on my way.

By midnight, my car was in the parking lot of the local Ford dealership, and I was in bed at the motel directly across the street. By 9:00 the next morning, the alternator had been replaced and I was on the road again, this time westbound and in the right direction. I had made it through the encounter; more than that, a fear inside me had been erased. From that point on, with all of the driving I would do, I would never again feel all alone on the road. After that night I felt that so long as I had a credit card in my pocket, I would be able to deal with any situation on the road that threw itself in my way.

On the first of May in 1976 Karen and I were married according to the grand traditions of the South in a majestic brick church on Rivermont Avenue in Lynchburg, Virginia. My family attended, all except my father, who was now too ill to travel from New England. There was a contingent of my Boston friends including Dick LaRose; and Roger, Jesse, and Lee, the Texas odyssey participants of six years before. Logan agreed to write a poem for the ceremony, and I composed the music for the wedding march. Logan's poem was entitled "Pierrot Addresses Himself to a Marriage for Karen and Bill," and the stage was set for the affair.

On the morning of the wedding I kept thinking that, although everything and everyone seemed to be in place, there was still something missing from the day. I was wishing that somehow my rainbow would make an appearance. After all, if I did have this thing in my life that was supposed to let me know that all was going according to plan and that everything was okay in the great scheme of things, then certainly my wedding would be an important enough event to show itself.

Although it was a gray, drizzly day, the wedding went off without a hitch. Logan read his poem, and at the conclusion of the ceremony all of the participants and guests adjourned for the reception to a beautiful old country club just a few miles down the road.

By the middle of the afternoon, the sun had appeared and the towering old oak trees that surrounded the main building cast soft shadows over the stately magnolias and flowering dogwoods that dotted the grounds. With the hustle and bustle of the day's events, and with intent photographers dashing this way and that, Karen and I both had our hands full, meeting and greeting everybody who came our way. By the late afternoon many of the guests had begun to depart, so Karen and I made ready to leave for a trip to the Virginia shore.

What kind of changes would be taking place in my life now that I was married? What kind of new responsibilities would I need to face? These questions lingered in my mind as we drove off toward the shore that afternoon. These, I suppose, are questions that are pondered by most newlyweds. They always have been and probably always will be. Had I done the right thing or made the right choice of a mate?

The answers were made clear when about 50 miles down the road, a sudden rain shower in front of us and the setting sun behind us produced one of the biggest and most beautiful rainbows I had ever seen. The arc was directly in front of the car and touched down on each side of the highway. I have seen my rainbow only a few times in my life, but never has it meant more than at that moment.

CHAPTER 14

The Fall Tour, Day Six

The clatter of the diesel engine belonging to the semi parked nearby at the Frontier Truck Stop brings me out of a deep sleep. I must have been very tired not to have been aware of the truck's arrival during the early hours of the morning. I unzip my sleeping bag, slide out, and open the side door of the van. I'm immediately met with a gust of clean, cold Dakota air, driven across the plains by a wind out of the north.

I search for my boots somewhere in the tangled blur of CD boxes, suitcases, blankets, and guitar cases. I know that with the boots I will also find my eyeglasses. Oh where, oh where can they be? Ah yes, right there on the front seat. I don't remember putting them there, but there they are in any event, eyeglasses and all. Pulling on my boots and donning my down vest, I exit the van onto the great stage that is the open space of South Dakota.

During the night a passage has occurred, a passage from the eastern flatland prairies to the gently rising slopes of the western high plains. From this point, the drive will be on an ever-so-slight rise to the Black Hills, and then a steep climb into the Rocky Mountains beyond.

It is a travel day, this Monday, the sixth day of the tour. With no concert to play in the evening, my only responsibility for the next 18 hours or so is to get as far west as possible, hopefully to Buffalo, Wyoming, where it will be a fairly easy drive into Jackson for the next night's concert. It is on these days that I feel most profoundly the sense of freedom that can come to a musician on the road. Although cold and windy, it is a beautiful and bright new day, and I have nothing but miles of open highway between me and the setting of the sun behind the Big Horn Mountains of Wyoming. I feel a driven sense of elation, an inner laughter that is once again playing children's games in my heart. I want to turn down some back road off the highway, stop the van, get out, and dance drunkenly with the spirits of the wind as they fling themselves across the spaces around me. I shall close my eyes, lift my arms, and rise into the bluest of skies with the warmth of the sun upon my back and experience, again, the immense symphony of life beneath my frailest of wings.

Perhaps it is *Wakan-Taka,* the great spirit of the Lakota, that has caught me and held me aloft so that I may understand the power of the land—and yet its fragility. I have been removed from the loneliness of the miles. I begin to sing out loud so that my voice becomes one with all the others of this time and place, and I feel as if I could hold all of this to my soul until the day that I am gone forever.

One must be careful driving these long, straight distances, for once lost in a reverie it takes but a second of reality to bring about a possible disaster. I stop at Mitchell for a cup of coffee and some fuel, rejoin the interstate, and continue my journey west.

The highway crosses the Missouri River at Chamberlain, and it is there that I pull into a scenic rest area and write a few lines in my journal. It is a mighty river, the Missouri. It is a river of legend and history, of fur trappers and traders. It is a river of pioneers and explorers like Lewis and Clark, and of rough-and-tumble men with names like Andrew Henry, John Hoback, Jim Bridger, Hugh Glass, and John Colter. The Missouri is a river of the great peoples—the Lakota, Arikara, Mandan, Cheyenne, Crow, and Blackfoot—and it is a river of song.

I stand on the eastern shore of the Missouri at a modern rest area and softly sing to the river one of those songs that is very old.

> *"Oh Shenandoah, I've loved your daughter,*
> *Away, you rolling river,*
> *It's for her I've crossed your rolling water,*
> *Away, I'm bound away, across the wide Missouri."*

I wonder how much the land has changed in 200 years, and I close my eyes to try and eliminate the rest area, the highway, and the bridge. In five days I can drive coast to coast with no hardship and very little courage, and so I make the transit across the bridge to the western shore and continue on my way. In passing, I wonder what the character in that old song might have been like as he made his own way "across the wide Missouri."

A little to the west of the Missouri crossing, one comes to the town of Presho. It is near Presho that a traveler crosses the 100th meridian, also known as the "line of aridity." Generally, west of this line the annual rainfall amounts decrease significantly, and the land is much drier. The scrubby vegetation becomes little more than grass and sage, and the wind assumes the role as sculptor of the land. Bare outcroppings appear on the sides of sandy or clay hummocks and hills. At first they are small concessions to the wind, but as one travels west, these barren slopes become more noticeable. Between the Cheyenne and White Rivers of southwestern South Dakota, a huge shelf of clay, gravel, and sand was washed out of the Rocky Mountains by rivers flowing some 25 to 50 million years ago. Over the course of time the runoff from the rains, which occur infrequently but generally as cloudbursts, cut through the clay and the loose, gravelly bedrock and carved deep and meandering gullies into the earth. When this soft underbelly of the land was exposed, the wind took over, and the resulting collection of mesas, saw-tooth cliffs, and ravines supporting little or no vegetation became known by the first French trappers in the region as *les mauvais terres* or "the Badlands."

The Badlands area of South Dakota became a national monument in 1939 and in 1978 was designated a national park. Some years before, I had driven the loop road into the park and hiked some of the trails, but on this tour, time is not permitting me the luxury. I have yet to pay my respects this afternoon to Wild Bill Hickok, Calamity Jane, and Potato Creek Johnny, so I continue past the national park and the town of Wall, with its famous (or infamous) Wall Drug, and make my way further west to the town of Sturgis and the exit for the Black Hills.

They are *Paha-Sapa* to the Lakota, the Black Hills of Dakota, and from their dark, forested ridges and slopes flows the life force of the Lakota people. It is their belief that in the beginning the Creator endowed the universe with a great song, a portion of this song belonging to each separate part of this creation. It is only here in the Black Hills, however, that this song is present in its entirety. It was at Bear Butte, *Mato Pata,* just to the north, that the Lakota originated and were given their sacred instructions by the Great Spirit. At death, it is to this sacred place that the spirits of the Lakota return.

In 1874, gold was discovered in the Black Hills during a military mission commanded by Lieutenant Colonel George Custer. Although the area had been ceded by the United States government to the Lakota tribe as a perpetual sacred wilderness in 1868, and had been closed to all white men by treaty, the resulting ragtag influx of treasure seekers, traders, and miscreants led to open hostilities between the native people and the whites. For a period of time, while the government was trying to renegotiate the land back from the Lakota, the military tried to evict the gold seekers. In the end, after all negotiations had reached an impasse, the treaty was ignored and the sacred lands were overrun by the newcomers.

There have been many injustices initiated or endured by individuals, groups, or societies over the course of history. One is easily manipulated into guilt or a sense of anger over these injustices.

I do not believe, however, that I can or should hold myself responsible for events that happened before I was born. I believe that I do have a responsibility stemming from that history, and that responsibility is to learn from the results of those events. I must be a student of the hearts and minds of others, for that is the only way by which I may understand their feelings. I must be a student of the feelings of others, for we are all as one, and that may be the only way by which I may come to know and understand my own self. In order to be true to my music, in order to be able to impart anything of value to others through my craft, I must strive always to be a student of life, to be observant of the smallest of things that make up the larger body, and to never give up the quest to understand what is just beyond the farthest horizon. I feel renewed in that responsibility as my van travels up the road to *Paha-Sapa*.

The long-haired figure, cast in bronze, sits leaning back on two legs of a chair, the piercing eyes staring up the main road at the strangers that pour into town. It *is* his town, you know, Deadwood. It has been his town ever since he arrived here in July of 1876. His name is James Butler Hickok, a Civil War spy and sharpshooter for the Union Army, a town marshal in Kansas, a scout for Custer's Seventh Cavalry, and one of those colorful characters of the West that was feared by men and admired by women. He was a big man, standing six foot three, and he hated lawlessness. Recently married in Cheyenne to Agnes Lake, an old friend, he planned on settling down and living a simple, quiet life. Hickok traveled to Deadwood that July in hopes of earning enough money, either as a lawman or prospector, to make retirement possible. Unfortunately, his reputation preceded him, and as it had happened so many other times in the West, there was always someone waiting in the wings who either held a grudge or wanted a greater reputation of their own. On August 2,1876, just a short time after his arrival in town, Hickok was murdered by Jack McCall, shot in the back of the head while playing poker in Saloon #10. He was buried near town in Ingleside Cemetery. As the population pressure in the area grew, his body was exhumed and reburied in Mt. Moriah Cemetery on the side of a nearby hill.

There was a trial for Jack McCall, although no conviction resulted. He fled the territory, but some years later he was overheard boasting about committing the deed, and he was arrested by local lawmen. Upon his return to Deadwood there was a second trial; he was found guilty, and off he went to the gallows.

One of Wild Bill's steadfast admirers (although their intimacy has always been nothing more than conjecture) was Martha Jane Canary, otherwise known as "Calamity Jane." She was a strong, independent woman who at one time in her life had been attached to an Army supply train as a bullwhacker. In one battle, she managed to save the life of a captain. After the fight, the officer complimented her by saying, "Jane, you're a hell of a gal to have around in a calamity." The story, and the name Calamity Jane, followed her for the rest of her life. Her admiration for Hickok was well known, and it devastated her when he was gunned down in front of her eyes. She visited his grave often, and 27 years later, at her death in 1903, she was buried beside him on that hillside in Mt. Moriah Cemetery.

Johnny Perrett left Wales for the United States when he was 17 years old to seek his fortune in the West. He was small in stature, being just under five feet, but the folks around Deadwood always claimed that he had a big heart. Before making his way to town, he had held a number of jobs, from farmer to cowpuncher, but his small size had always been a problem when he was looking for work. At last he decided to try his hand at prospecting. He filed a claim on Potato Creek, outside of Deadwood, and commenced a life which alternated between solitude in the summer when he worked his claim, and notoriety each winter when he came to town and entertained the citizens with his guitar playing and fiddling. "Potato Creek Johnny" was a favorite with children, perhaps because he was so small, and they would follow him up and down the streets as if he were a pied piper. In 1929, Potato thought that he had hit the jackpot when he came upon a gold nugget that was the size of a small pistol. It was the largest nugget ever found in the Black Hills, but when it sold the nugget only brought him $250. When the town of Deadwood initiated their Days of '76 celebrations, Johnny was invited to participate and soon became a popular figure in the parades. Decked out in his buckskins and pushing his prospector's wheelbarrow complete with picks and shovels, he was always cheered by people in the crowd when he passed them. Potato Creek Johnny died after participating in only a few of the celebrations; out of love and respect, the townspeople laid him to rest next to their other legends, Wild Bill and Calamity Jane.

I have visited the graves a number of times over the years—not so much because those who lie there are legends, but because they were real people. They are of those smallest of individuals who make up the great body of history. It is that contact, that connection with the timeless stories, that I seek. They are here in these hills. They are being told each day by the wind that blows through the gulches and along the sacred ridges. They will always be here until forever passes away.

It is late afternoon by now. I stop for a shot of whiskey and a quick meal in one of the saloons on the way out of town, gamble away a few dollars on the slot machines, and figure that just by breaking even my luck was a whole lot better than Wild Bill's.

I head north, back up over the hills to Spearfish, take the interstate west past the National Military Cemetery, and enter Wyoming at Beulah. It is a little over 150 miles to Buffalo, and with the change to Mountain Time earlier in the day, I figure to be at my hotel by 8:30. It is dark now, and once again those broken white lines come at me in what seems like a never-ending supply. I pass the exit for Devil's Tower and Sundance, Pine Haven, and then Gillette. I wrote a song once on commission for Burlington Northern Railroad that mentioned Gillette, Wyoming. I try to piece together some of the melody as the lights of the town's coal plants and oil refinery illuminate the scene in front of me; alas, it is to no avail, and the town, as well as the song, slips away into the darkness.

It is coming on to 9:00 when I take the Wyoming Route 16 exit and head into Buffalo. It is one of the oldest towns in northern Wyoming, and it was in and around this area that many of the skirmishes between the whites and the Sioux, Arapahoe, and Cheyenne occurred. Fort Phil Kearney, built to protect travelers along the Bozeman trail, was located some 17 miles to the north, and between 1866 and 1868 it was frequently besieged by Chief Red Cloud of the Sioux in what was known as Red Cloud's War. In 1868, when the land around the Black Hills was ceded by treaty back to the native tribes, the fort was abandoned by the military and immediately burned to the ground by the Indians.

My first and only stop for the night in Buffalo is at the Crossroads Hotel. It is one of those places along the road—whether they be restaurants, hotels, saloons, or truck stops—that have become regular haunts for me. Anyone who spends a good deal of time traveling by themselves knows the importance of these habitual stopovers and personal landmarks. Sometimes these places provide the traveler, so far from home, with the only sense of consistency and bearing. I know, for instance, as I enter the lounge at the hotel, that the clientele for the evening will be a mixture of hunters and businessmen, all on the road and all watching the Monday night football game. It doesn't matter which teams are playing; the fact is that the television is a comfortable, common focus for all of us that somehow keeps the loneliness on the road at bay. Ordering up a dry vodka martini, I scan the napkin-size bar menu for something that looks appetizing. A loud cheer erupts from a group of hunters sitting in the corner near the popcorn machine as the quarterback is brought down for a five-yard loss. The bartender arrives with my drink. The olives have been skewered with a plastic pick sporting a bucking bronco at one end. The bitter, slightly salty liquid warms my being. Tomorrow morning I'll cross over the Bighorns, but tonight in Buffalo, Wyoming, it is second down and a long 15 yards to go.

CHAPTER 15

River, Take Me Along . . .

My father died in June of 1976. He was only 66 years old, but he had been ill for some time. I can't say that I was totally surprised when I finally heard the news, but it came as a hard blow.

Soon after our wedding, Karen and I went on an extended camping trip all over the West, visiting the national parks and getting to know the country together. A portion of the trip took us to southwestern Montana, where we spent about ten days hiking and camping on the Branham Lakes in the Tobacco Root Mountains. We had been out of touch with the rest of the world for some time, and when we arrived in Sheridan at the end of our wilderness stint, I called my mother. She broke the news to me. The funeral had been delayed once already and was now scheduled for the next day. There was no way for us to get back home in time. The nearest airport with possible connections was in Idaho Falls, and that airport was closed temporarily because of the flooding caused by the collapse of the Teton Dam on the Snake River. I was simply not going to be able to make it to the funeral. My mother suggested that family matters could wait until we returned at the end of the month, and that there was nothing to be gained by cutting our trip short, so we continued, making the best of a sad time.

Jumbled thoughts and long-faded memories of my father were lying uneasily on my mind until one night in Wyoming. While Karen and I were camped at a state park, I told her that I needed to spend a few moments alone and wandered away from the campfire. There was a small creek nearby, and it shimmered in the crisp light of the full moon. I sat down and listened to the soft sounds of the water as it passed by, and I felt a sense of real peace come over me. I realized that if one dies, and that is the end of it, it is simply a meaningless exercise to try to communicate to them what is in your heart. If out of that person a spirit remains, however, and within us and around us we sense that spirit, then our thoughts and our feelings will surely find their way home.

I could hear my father's violin now in the trees above the water. It is a sad thing for me not to have known him better as a person while he was alive, but it is also a wonderful thing to still be able to hear his music.

Upon our return from the West, I decided to give Jerry Rau a call. Jerry's time in Ojai had not lasted very long, and in July of 1976 he was back living in Minneapolis and once again doing the booking for the Coffeehouse Extempore. I was planning a road trip in the fall and figured it would be a good opportunity to visit Minnesota, renew my acquaintance with Jerry, and expand my listening audience. I called him and he agreed to book me into the Extemp that coming October. In fact, he said, there was a live radio show broadcast out of St. Paul, and the host of the show just might be interested in having me do a tune or two on the air. I made a note of the booking in my datebook and then proceeded to make the other phone calls that would piece together the rest of the tour.

It was a time of change in the Boston folk music scene. Many of the clubs that had been around since the 1960s were either closed or were about to close down. The King's Rook in Ipswich was gone; The Unicorn, The Turk's Head, and The Loft had all closed their doors. It seemed that the coffeehouse era had become a thing of the past. Rock-and-roll dominated the live music scene around town, and disco was the new thing.

Folk music, however, showed its true strength and ability to endure, to push its way from beneath the pavement back into the shining light of a new day. It would not be swept away, and much like jazz it managed to establish a permanent niche for itself in the great world of music. Folk song societies appeared and presented concerts in church community centers, and opened coffeehouses in church basements. In the New England area alone, the list went on and on: the Hartford Folk Song Society, the Woodshole Folk Song Society, the Branford Folk Song Society, the Worcester Folk Song Society, the South Shore Folk Music Society, and the New York Pinewoods Folk Song Club. Around the country, there were the Philadelphia Folk Song Society, the Houston Folk Song Society, the Seattle Folklore Society. The outlets for the music were still there. Sometimes one had to look hard to find the venues, but they were there, and the music would not die.

One of the most important reasons that the music held its ground was its availability over the radio airwaves and the consistency of the programming. Folk music still had a voice on public and community radio, and there were some dedicated announcers who stayed true to the tradition: Dick Pleasants in Boston; Oscar Brand and Dave Sear in New York; Gene Shay in Philadelphia; Dick Cerri in Washington, D.C.; Phil Shapiro in Ithaca, New York; and Jackie Alpert in Albany, New York; they all carried that voice to the people, and folk music stayed alive.

For the few commercial coffeehouses that remained, it was a struggle to stay alive. Some did though. Whether it was out of sheer determination or some sort of grand destiny, their doors stayed open.

The Club 47 was closed in 1968, but in 1969, at the same address and in the same space, Bob and Rae Anne Donlin opened what would become one of the all-time legendary and lasting coffeehouse venues, Passim.

It was at Passim in July of 1976 that I met Guy Van Duser and Billy Novick. I was appearing at the club for a weekend gig, and Guy and Billy were booked as the opening act. Needless to say, I was blown away by Guy's guitar playing and Billy's clarinet wizardry, and by the end of the weekend the three of us were onstage doing what amounted to a swing-folk-Dixieland version of "My Grandfather's Clock." It was the start of a musical and personal pair of friendships that continue to this day. I discovered that Guy played bass, and I invited him out to the Fox Hollow Festival that year to accompany me on guitar and bass during my sets. Guy would provide the lead guitar accompaniment for my next ten albums.

It was a summer of new friendships. It was the summer that I was introduced to the music of Jeanie Stahl and Mason Daring. I had actually met Jeanie some years before when she booked me into her school coffeehouse at Wellesley College.

Jeanie had a beautiful voice and was also performing around town, doing mostly traditional music along with some of her own songs. One evening, booked to do a guest set at a club near MIT in Cambridge, she met Mason Daring, who was appearing as the scheduled performer for the night. The two struck up a friendship and soon began singing together. Their voices blended delightfully, and the combination of Mason's pop-oriented arrangements and Jeanie's traditional approach led to a musical style that was unique, compelling, and all their own.

How it was that I first came to hear Jeanie and Mason sing together as a couple I don't recall, though I believe it was at one of the Sunday afternoon radio shows broadcast live during those years from Passim. I do know, however, that I fell in love with their music; even better, I got to know them as friends.

I had written enough new material by the fall of 1976 to do another recording. At Fox Hollow that summer, I had been invited by Sandy and Caroline Paton, who owned Folk Legacy, to do an album for them. Although that would have been great, I wanted to do one more recording at Northern Studios before I moved on. I booked time at Northern in November, called Guy to play guitar on the project, and began putting together material for the album. Sandy and Caroline were gracious enough to leave the door open for me at Folk Legacy, and knowing that I loved traditional music, they suggested that I take whatever of my own material was left after the fall project at Northern, mix in some traditional pieces, and do an album for them in Connecticut over the winter. I thought that the idea was perfect, so by September of 1976, I had two prospective albums on my mind. I called Guy to play on this second project as well, and he agreed—although by this time he must have been thinking that perhaps I was just a little crazy.

The fall tour that year was a huge triangle—New Hampshire to Texas, Texas to Minnesota to play at the Coffeehouse Extempore, and from Minnesota back home to New England, with a few stops along the way in Johnson City, Tennessee; and Kansas City, Missouri. I had been playing music full time now for 7 years, and after putting 11 cars to rest, it was beginning to feel like I was racking up the miles. Driving around the country was no big deal anymore. I'd leave home in New Hampshire, close my eyes (figuratively, of course), and two days later I would be in Texas. Easy as pie, nothing to it. Leave Texas, close my eyes, and lo and behold I was being welcomed to Minnesota. I loved it. I could drive all night on just a few hours of rest and show up in the next town ready to do a show. After all, wasn't this what it took to be a real road warrior? Wasn't this what the life of a road musician was all about?

I arrived in Minneapolis a day before my gig at the Extempore and called Jerry Rau from the outskirts of the city to get directions to his place. His apartment was in a big old house near the corner of Chicago and Franklin, and he and his lady friend, Barb Trow, invited me to stay with them while I was in town. It was good to see Jerry again. In just the short time we had spent together at the candle factory in Ojai the previous year, I felt as if I had come to know him as a kindred spirit. He was passionate about life and the things around him, and he lived that life simply, one day at a time. Jerry had been a sergeant in the Marine Corps in the early days of our involvement with Vietnam. The Marine Corps had been his life until disillusionment with the U.S. government's policies prompted him to rethink his direction. He returned to Minnesota after his discharge and, having learned to play the guitar overseas, became a street singer. He was the gentlest of people, with a wisdom about him that I had known in only a very few others. Perhaps it was because Jerry had seen life in its extremes that he was so able to put everyday ups and downs in a proper prospective. To Jerry, small daily calamities were never as bad as they seemed to others; similarly, he felt that the good things that came to him in his life should be appreciated and never taken for granted, for any life could change in an instant.

Barbara recognized this free spirit in Jerry, and when he called from California after his Ojai experience to say that he was on his way back to Minneapolis, she was willing to take him back into her life. She offered to leave the door of the house open for him when he arrived in town. Barbara made her living as a computer programmer and was working for the city of Minneapolis at the time, so a good deal of her life was spent in the techno-world of computers at the Hennepin County Government Center. Jerry seemed to offer what she felt was a balance in her life, a balance between the cut-and-dried mathematical world of her daily routine and the free and almost folly-like world of the artist. They had been together for about three years, meeting one night through a mutual friend at a musical get-together in town. Although opposites in many ways, Jerry and Barbara managed to keep their relationship going for some seven years, until the early 1980s when they finally broke up. Over those years, whenever I came to Minneapolis, they were always there as friends, and often as an oasis in a vast, dry emptiness of what was sometimes a crazy world.

The Coffeehouse Extempore was located at 325 Cedar Avenue, in an area of Minneapolis known as the West Bank. It was a working-class Swedish neighborhood until developers moved in, buying up the houses and driving out the Swedes in hopes of ultimately putting up a host of high-rise apartment buildings. Until the developers were in control of the area and could move on the construction of the high rises, they rented many of the houses to students who were attending the nearby University of Minnesota. Figuring that the student population was a transient one and could easily be displaced, the new developer-owners offered low rents and encouraged, at least for the time being, the student influx. What they hadn't foreseen, however, was the fact that along with the students, there came a bohemian culture of artists, musicians, and theatre people. The West Bank of Minneapolis, its name derived from the fact that it was located on the western bank of the Mississippi River, was now becoming more like a Parisian *West Banke*, a bastion of alternative culture and the arts. Neighborhood theatre spaces opened along with restaurants, bars, co-op markets, and cafes. Many of the students decided that the West Bank just might be a good place to live after graduation. Rents were low, and the atmosphere generated in the neighborhood suited their fancy. Some years later, attorneys who had been law students and lived on the West Bank during these times actually became leaders in the fight to preserve the district as an enclave for the arts.

It was here, conveniently situated in the center of West Bank activities, that the Coffeehouse Extempore opened its doors in the mid-1960s, first on Riverside Avenue, and then a block away on Cedar. Originally chartered as a drop-in center for teenagers, it soon became a gathering place for not only teens, but a host of other colorful neighborhood characters. The Extemp, as it was fondly called, was in actuality two environments: the Tea Room and the Music Room.

The Tea Room was the domain of the local philosophers, intellectuals, self-appointed psychologists, card players, and anyone else who wanted a warm place to read the daily newspaper. There was always an animated conversation going on somewhere in the room, usually over dark coffee and doughnuts that had the reputation of really being "holes surrounded by cement." Now and then some lost soul, burnt out on drugs or suffering from an overdose of life, would find his way into the place and settle down into one of the seats by the front window, staring out of dark, hollow eyes at the incomprehensible earthlings as they passed by along the sidewalk, thinking to himself, "How far removed are they from this higher plain upon which I travel," and then silently and softly drifting off into a deep afternoon slumber, only to be awakened again by a cry from within his body that demanded another hit.

The Music Room, the performance space of the Coffeehouse Extempore, attracted a different yet equally diverse set of characters. These were the musicians—many local, and many from the other music scenes of the Midwest: Milwaukee, Chicago, Madison, and Iowa City. In the early years of the coffeehouse, the four black walls of this room would absorb the music of Leo Kottke, Michael Johnson, Barbara With, Lonnie Knight, Sean Blackburn, Becky Riemer, Dakota Dave Hull, Greg Brown, Spider John Koerner, and a host of others. Late in 1979, the coffeehouse expanded to the upper floor of the building at 325 Cedar and subsequently became a favorite stop for musicians from all over the country and the world: Bok, Tricket,and Muir; Claudia Schmidt; Silly Wizard; The Tannehill Weavers; Jim Ringer and Mary McCaslin; Suzy Bogguss; Nanci Griffith; Stan Rogers; Sally Rogers; Aileen and Elkin Thomas; Bob Bovee; Bob Zentz; they all came to play. Paul Geremia, Steve Gillette, Priscilla Herdman, Anne Hills, Jeff Cahill, Van Mertz—they too, knew the Extemp; Peter Ostroushko, Dave Moore, Robin and Linda Williams, Garrison Keillor—they were all part of the spirit of the Extemp. But the Coffeehouse Extempore was more than just a music venue, it was a tapestry woven of people's lives and dreams, it was a single heart formed of many hearts, and it was to the Coffeehouse Extempore that I came one October weekend in the fall of 1976. I was just another musician with a song to sing and a friend that did the booking for a coffeehouse.

There were probably enough regulars who showed up at the Extemp each weekend, no matter who was performing there, to guarantee at least a small audience for a new face in town. I was booked into the club for a Friday and Saturday that fall, and on the first night the audience turnout was about what Jerry had expected for a first-time performer in Minneapolis. Attendance of 50 or so regulars was about average, and he figured that the audience would build over time, especially if he could manage to get me on this radio show he had been talking about the following day.

On Saturday morning, Jerry called Garrison Keillor, who hosted a radio show each weekday called "The Morning Prairie Home Show." A live version of the morning show was broadcast late each Saturday afternoon from the auditorium of the St. Paul Ramsey Arts and Science Center. Since the live show carried on the same personality as the morning "Prairie Home" format, the Saturday broadcast was dubbed "A Prairie Home Companion Show." Jerry informed Garrison that there was a performer in town playing at the Extempore who could yodel, and Garrison told Jerry to send me on over to be on that afternoon's broadcast. My appearance that afternoon on "A Prairie Home Companion" would be the first of what amounted to 20 or so spots I would do on the show over the next 6 years. The broadcast that afternoon also had a profound affect on my musical life, for when I showed up at the Extempore that evening, there were close to 300 people lined up along the sidewalk, waiting to get into the place. My first thought was that there had been some sort of a mistake or perhaps an accidental double booking. Certainly there was no reason for all of these people to be waiting in line to hear me. Jerry was not a bit surprised. He knew the scope of influence that Garrison Keillor wielded in the Twin Cities. A good word about a performer from Garrison went a long way toward bringing out an audience for that artist. That was the way of it, and because of Garrison Keillor, that weekend my musical life was changed forever.

Some years later, I was having breakfast with Garrison after playing on his morning show, and I thanked him for what he had done for me. Although I can't remember his exact response, I'll not forget the gist of what he had to say. It was simply that he could get the people to come once to see a performer, but after that it was up to the performer to bring them back. All he did was play the music. All he did was open the door. Garrison made me feel good about my myself that day, but more importantly he instilled within me a confidence in my own music, in my own performing ability, that I had not known before. This was his true gift to me, a gift that I shall always hold dear.

Before I left Minneapolis, Jerry booked me for a return to the Extempore that coming February. I started home from that fall tour excited and ready to go to work on the first of the two albums slated for the fall and winter. A month later Guy Van Duser and I went into the studio to record *Old Wood and Winter Wine.*

I was going to call the album *Old Wood and Chestnuts*, but when I told Guy of my plan, and his face took on a look of absolute horror, I immediately changed my mind.

Why use the word "chestnuts," Guy asked, when most of the songs were new and original? I had no idea that chestnut was a term describing an old, worn-out, over-done standard, so the title *Old Wood and Winter Wine* carried the day.

The deal with Northern Studios was that they would front me the studio time for the recording, and I would pay for the pressings. The album would be released on my Mineral River label, and they would hold onto the master tapes until I had paid them back for the studio time out of album sales.

Even though *Old Wood and Winter Wine* was technically a Bill Staines' solo album, all through the recording process I had felt that Guy's contribution to the effort was so important that he deserved more recognition than a simple liner credit. The title for the album therefore became *Old Wood and Winter Wine: Bill Staines with Guy Van Duser*. Guy was an accomplished artist as well as an incredible guitar player, and he agreed to do a pen and ink drawing from a photograph that Karen had taken of the two of us for the cover.

Once again, most of the songs were my own, but I also included a piece entitled "Osceola's Last Words" by a Florida songwriter by the name of Will McLean, and another piece entitled "The Years that Come to Pass" by my friends Mason Daring and Jeanie Stahl. Rounding out the list of songs on the album was the true old chestnut, a song that Guy and I always had fun playing, "My Grandfather's Clock."

It was the last album that I would record for Northern, for some months after the release of *Old Wood and Winter Wine*, the studio closed. All of the tapes and production materials had been sent to a pressing plant on Long Island, and before I could recover the tapes, the pressing plant also disappeared. The long and short of it was that the master tapes were lost, and when the stock of *Old Wood and Winter Wine* albums that I had sitting in the basement was depleted, that was going to be the end of the project. My basement shelves, however, were about to collapse under the weight of the nearly 4,000 copies of the album, so I knew that it was going to be available for quite some time. I was still also storing copies of the *Miles* album, so by the spring of 1977 it was beginning to seem as if my record label and business were about to take over the basement of our house.

Inasmuch as we are all constantly learning from trials and tribulations, successes and failures, during our time on this earth, this was a period in my life where I felt I learned four important lessons. Two of these came to me as a result of the recording of the album *Old Wood and Winter Wine*.

The first lesson was garnered from one of the recording sessions, when each of the musicians involved had a different sense of how a particular song should sound. They eventually turned to me, as the artist, for the direction they needed. I, as the producer—and even as the artist—had no idea what I wanted for the song. We waded through the session and recorded the tune, but I made up my mind at that moment that I would never to go into a recording session again not knowing exactly what I wanted to achieve in the end. I might not know *how* to get the result that I wanted—experimentation was fine there—but I would definitely have a clear idea of what that final result should be. It is not enough to recognize what you don't want out of a session; a good producer must know the mind of the artist, see clearly where the road to the end result lies, and be able to lead the musicians along that road without hesitation. The road should be wide enough for musical experimentation and coloring, but always constant in its direction.

The lesson was simply be prepared and know what you want before going into a studio.

The second lesson was to stay in control of all of the pieces of a recording project: know where the tapes are, hold onto the original artwork, and be aware of the details so that nothing might inadvertently get lost along the way—basically, a lesson in management.

The other two lessons I learned from Mason Daring. Mason, along with being a musician, was also a music lawyer. The first of these two lessons has probably been taught in business courses since the beginning of time, but when Mason gave me this advice, it made a lot of sense to me. The lesson is that "*no* deal is better than a *bad* deal." When you have no deal, you have nothing, but when you are saddled with a bad deal, you have nothing but grief.

The second lesson I learned that fall from Mason was that if a song is a good song, with universal appeal, then that song does not have a life span. One should not be afraid that a song will lose its potency or potential just because it has been around for a while. There have been many songs that have become well known dozens of years after they were written. A good song, no matter how long it has been around, will still carry itself when heard for the first time. I learned from Mason that as a writer I shouldn't get discouraged if one of my songs isn't picked up and recorded right away; I shouldn't be foolish by signing away the rights to a piece just to see it recorded; and I should not have to look back on some bad deal that I fell into just because I thought that I needed to move quickly or a song would get lost. If I believed my music was strong enough to last, then I should also believe that it would have its time in the light. This was the lesson of patience, and over the years this lesson has served me well in what has sometimes been a frustrating and confusing road through the music business.

In January of 1977, Guy and I traveled up into the snowy hills of western Connecticut to the mountainside home of Sandy and Caroline Paton and Folk Legacy Records. Over a course of three days and nights we recorded the album *Just Play One Tune*

More. The recording was not very complicated, considering the fact that there were only two musicians playing on the record, and most of the tracks were done by the end of the second night. The third night, we hosted a party at the Paton's and invited members of the Hartford Folk Song Society to come and lend their voices to the project. The result was an album that captured the feeling that friends had gathered in a down-home living room to sing some great old traditional tunes and listen to a few contemporary ones. It was the type of recording project that had worked well for Folk Legacy, and the type that had been their forte for years. The front cover was standard Folk Legacy issue, a black and white photograph of the artist. The back cover was solid black over the left two-thirds of the jacket, with a white area on the right third that listed the album credits. For *Just Play One Tune More*, I also wrote a poem describing a recent night's after-hour festivities at Anderson Fair in Houston and included it along with the credits. The scheduled release date for the project was late spring of 1977—or, hopefully, at least in time for the Fox Hollow Festival that summer.

It had been a productive fall and winter, and it felt good to return home from Connecticut with another album under my belt. I felt fortunate to have a wife who was willing to give me the space to travel and play my music, and fortunate above all that I was able to reach people and get my inner feelings across to them through my songs. I was busy all the time (although still continually amazed that anyone would pay good money to hear me sing) and I was learning about life from the people that I had met and from the great open road that had carried me to so many places.

At the same time, I felt as if this existence, this life of mine, was also very fragile—that it might fly away from me at any moment, that I might change and become someone else or lose the fire in my heart. I had a sense that I wanted to tell everyone who I was at that very moment; I wanted to preserve my thoughts and feelings so that I would never forget who I was at the time. One afternoon at the end of January, just before my 30th birthday, I sat at home and wrote the song "River." It did not take very long; the words came as easily as the arrival of a new day. The song was simply the story of my life and an attempt to hold onto the feelings that I held so dear. Little did I know at the time that the song was also the story of so many other lives, and that instead of being a song about the past, it was really a song about an enduring passage through this world—a passage continually renewed, steadfast and timeless in its duration. I will always sing "River." I did not change, and there is still a fire within that same inner hearth.

Returning to Minneapolis in February of 1977, I wondered what the weekend would be like at the Extemp. I told myself that I was not going to be surprised or disappointed if the place was not full; more than likely the crowd would be respectable but small. I was scheduled to do Garrison's show again, and the tour was basically the same as the one the previous fall, only in reverse—Minneapolis, then Texas, and a couple of stops here and there. When I arrived at the Extempore that Friday afternoon, Jerry told me that the club was sold out for the weekend. Of course I welcomed the news, but it still made no sense to me. Why was I playing to 300 people a night for 3 nights in a row in Minneapolis, and then for 14 people at another place in Chicago? I knew, obviously, that it was because of the "Prairie Home Companion" show. Still, over the years, whenever I returned to the Extempore to perform, the first question I asked upon my arrival was, "What does it look like for the weekend?" The answer was always, "Sold out, what did you expect?" The truth was that I expected nothing, but I had fallen in love with the Extempore and the people of Minnesota who were making that place a shining part of my life.

I wanted to know more about these people of the Midwest, who they were, how they felt about themselves, and what of their heritage. I began during the spring months of 1977 by reading the books of O.E. Rolvaag: *Giants in the Earth*, *Peder Victorius*, *Their Father's God*, and *Boat of Longing*. I read the stories of Willa Cather, stories of the prairie people: *My Antonia* and *O Pioneers!*. I was beginning to develop a recognition of the differences in the ways and the personalities of the people that make up this land. At the same time, I saw that we are all part of the same story, that we are all on a marvelous journey together toward some common destiny. What might it be, this common destiny? The only answer I know for sure lies beyond our farthest horizons, beyond the scope of each of us as individuals. It is, however, our story, each and all of us, and it will be told in its entirety only over the long passing of time. I came to believe that I was put here on this earth to create music, and that it would be through this music that my own contribution to this great story would be realized.

With the summer months came the folk festivals and outdoor parks concerts. I was invited to the Kerrville Country and Western Jamboree and flew to Texas as a former Kerrville Yodeling Champion. I still only knew four yodeling songs, but that was enough to get me on the bill with Crystal Gayle; Merle Kilgore, who wrote "Ring of Fire"; and a very young fiddler by the name of Mark O'Connor, among others.

I had also been invited to Fox Hollow in early August. As always, it rained heavily, turning the festival grounds into a quagmire and the participants into beings that looked like characters out of the film *The Creature from the Black Lagoon.* On one of the evenings during the festival, I sat by a small fire beneath a campsite awning with my friends Debby McClatchy and Faith Petric, playing some music, drinking wine, and basically trying to stay warm and dry. As I recall, Faith was singing a version of "Waltz Across Texas" when a couple of fiddlers ducked in out of the rain, pulled out their fiddles, and softly began a Texas-style duet behind Faith's vocals and guitar playing. I don't know what it was about the sound of the two fiddles lofting across the campground, but the effect was the same as an alluring light to a host of moths. Not more than a few moments had passed when another fiddle player arrived, and then another, and another, until the three of us found ourselves surrounded by a dozen or so musicians, and the area under the canopy could shelter no more people. We played "Devil's Dream" and "Cotton-Eyed Joe," and Debby sang a song out of the California gold rush. Surrounded by this ensemble, I found myself transported back to the days when, as a clarinet player, I was immersed in the music of my high school orchestra. It had been the only other time in my life when I had been at the center of such a sound. We played on through that cold, damp evening at Fox Hollow, one tune after another, until it was late and the fire began to ebb. At one point, I noticed a young couple in the next campsite dancing to our music. I did not know them, and I had no idea that some three months later in October, during a return trip to Minneapolis, this young couple and the memory of that night at Fox Hollow would return to me as the essence for the song "The Roseville Fair."

It was a busy fall, that fall of 1977. I was on the road quite a bit, playing in Montreal, in New York state, and all over the Northeast. For the third time that year I returned to Minneapolis, and Jerry and I traveled together down to Kansas City, where we performed at a place called The Fool Killer.

I had just written "The Roseville Fair" at Jerry's apartment and began to perform it on that trip. People seemed to like the song, and I felt sure that it would be a "keeper." When I returned home after the tour, I played the song for Karen. We both sat on the sofa in our apartment, and when I had finished singing it to her I noticed that she had tears in her eyes. I will never forget how good it felt to please her with that song. I was spending a good deal of time on the road, time away from her, but I think that what came through in the writing of the piece was the strong desire that I had for a lasting love. It is a desire that we all have, and yet one that is so often not realized. Perhaps in "The Roseville Fair" we all get to see that dream come true, if for just one moment.

Originally the song had three verses, but soon after I wrote it I played it for Logan English in Saratoga, and Logan felt that perhaps the third verse was a little too saccharine. He suggested that I cut out the beginning of the verse and replace it with an instrumental part, which I did. As far as I know, there have been only two recordings of the song as it was originally written. Those recordings were done by Jim Ringer on his album *Endangered Species*, and by Jerry Rau on his recording *Just Happy to Be Here*.

"Now the years have gone, and the time has left us,
Oh, your face is kind, and your hair is gray,
But I'll tell you again how much I love you,
With simple words, in a simple way."

"The Roseville Fair" was the second song in a trio of songs that I wrote back-to-back during that time. The third song, after "River" and "The Roseville Fair," was "All God's Critters Got a Place in the Choir," composed in the winter of 1977. For some reason, it would be these three songs by which most people would come to know my writing. "All God's Critters'" was first performed at the Unicorn Coffeehouse Series at SUNY in Fredonia, New York, at the end of 1977. At the time, I wasn't even sure that I liked the song; after all, it was really just a doodle, and a little out of my ballad songwriting style. To be honest, I was pretty amazed at the enthusiastic response given to the song at the Unicorn that night. It was not long before I had developed quite a fondness for the piece. What had been conceived as only a cartoon of a song—but with the simple concept that we all belong in some way to a great choir—would come to have a life of its own. "A Place in the Choir" may turn out to be the one composition of mine that will endure beyond any dim recognition of my name; as a songwriter, that would be the ultimate reward.

Sometime during the last few weeks of 1977, I received a phone call from a fellow who introduced himself as Steve Nerney. Steve, an astrophysicist, had made his way to New Hampshire and was currently teaching a course on "man and his environment" at New Hampshire College in Manchester. He was a friend of Phil Stephan's in Colorado, and when Steve mentioned to Phil that he was off to New Hampshire, Phil remembered me from the 1975 trip through Colorado with Walter Spinks and Bill Cade. Phil suggested that Steve look me up and that perhaps we might get together to play some music. Steve had come across a copy of the Evolution album, liked it, and was calling to see if I might have any spare time. I think that he was feeling a little out of place, a California boy on the East Coast, and so during the winter and spring months of

1978 we met every Tuesday evening to play music together, alternating between his place in Concord and my home in Dover.

It was fun playing music with Steve, but beyond the music, I found him to be one of the most interesting people I had ever met. One immense regret that I have had over the years is that I did not record on tape some of our late-night get-togethers when, over a bottle of rum, we would philosophize about everything from the dynamics of time to the future of the universe. How difficult it was to corner him with some philosophical question about the galaxy or some other subject! He would just sit back in his chair and refuse to answer on the grounds that he was a scientist and did not have to answer the question. His excitement as he told me stories of legendary mathematicians was contagious, and once he even explained to me what was so funny as I stared blankly at the pages of equations in a mathematics joke book.

In May of 1978, after one year at New Hampshire College, Steve received a 2 1/2-year research grant from the government and returned to California to work at Ames Research Labs in Palo Alto. That summer, as Steve was on his way back to the West Coast, Karen and I, along with a group of musicians from Boston, showed up on the front steps of Folk Legacy to do yet another album. The recording (as usual) contained mostly my own material, but I also included (as usual) some traditional pieces, including "The Rivers of Texas," which had always been one of my favorite tunes. I had a good feeling about the recording sessions, and by the time the project was done, I knew that the album would be one of my favorites.

Karen and I had just moved a few miles out of downtown Dover into an old colonial house surrounded by farm fields of winter rye, horses, bobolinks, whippoorwills, and gangs of noisy blue jays. It was from these sounds of the country that I came up with the title for this latest album: *The Whistle of the Jay.*

Because of Folk Legacy's production schedule, the album was not scheduled for release until the winter of 1978-79, so I spent time that fall working on the liner notes and the artwork for the cover. Karen took some photographs of me standing by the river that flowed near our home, and Folk Legacy, in a departure from their traditional cover format, placed a photo on both the front and the back of the album. In a major artistic leap, the front photo was reproduced as a high-density print with no shadows—although, as if not to bow too much to all of this high-tech froofraw, the cover was still printed in black and white. After all, it was Folk Legacy, and we all agreed that a certain amount of tradition must be maintained.

The summer of 1978 saw the passing of the Fox Hollow Festival, as well as the Belknap Folk Festival in Kentucky. There were other festivals, though, that remained strong. Winnipeg, Philadelphia, Vancouver, Kerrville, and the National Folk Festival in Washington, D.C., all continued to prevail. At a time when inflation was rampant, gas prices were soaring, and the economy was barely putting along, the music continued to live on. It was all that I knew now, this music, and with each passing year it became for me more and more of a lifelong commitment.

CHAPTER 16

The Fall Tour, Day Seven

There is a low cloud cover that hangs over Buffalo, Wyoming, as I start the seventh day of the tour. With the temperature hovering around the freezing mark, the road feels slippery. Just west of town, where it ascends into the Bighorns and disappears into the mist, I can see where there is a light snow falling, leaving a fresh white cover on the slopes of spruces, tamaracks, and firs. Today I traverse an area of the country that is one of the most mystical places I know.

The road follows an old travel route used by the tribes of the area as a passage between the winter camps on the Platte River to the south and the summer camps near Bridger, Montana. As I begin the western ascent into the mountains, I pop a cassette into the van's tape deck. It is the soundtrack from an Omnimax film entitled *The Blue Planet*. The film itself is a magazine-style documentary that explores many of the facets of a vibrant and changing planet Earth. The soundtrack, I found some ten years earlier, if taken as a separate musical composition, provides the perfect mood complement for a journey through and over the

Bighorns. Keeping my speed at a constant 45 to 50 miles per hour up the long climb, the varying musical colors and ghostly motifs of the piece guide me into a dream-like world of ancient travelers and mountain spirits. I ascend into the falling snow and dark evergreens somehow comforted and carried along by the haunting melodies. The van is my pony once again, willing, heart-strong, and deliberate, hugging the high mountain walls and negotiating the curves of the trail with practiced steps and intention. Higher and higher into the snow and mist, until the blanket of gray begins to lighten and I can make out the opalescent image of the morning sun. The incline, although never steep to the extreme, begins to subside, the gray turns to gray-blue, and in the next few moments I emerge into a sun-bright world of high mountain meadows, drenched in the colors of the West—bright blue sky, gray rock, white snow patches, dark green spruces, and golden tamaracks aflame in their fall finery. I am at the crest of the Bighorns, where the cold, immaculate air carries the slightest fragrance of juniper and sage. In front of me, unfolded in a majestic panorama, is the western side of the range.

The descent begins on the high walls of Ten Sleep Canyon. I stop at this spot every time I travel over this trail. It is here that the magic is greatest for me. I pull to the side of the passage and take a walk along a short loop path that descends a few feet from the road. I pinch a sprig of juniper from a nearby shrub and a sprig of sage from an adjacent low-lying bush, mix them together, and place them in a small glass vial. It is for a purpose.

There have been times, when struggling with a low moment in my life, that I have opened the vial and placed a pinch of this mixture between my fingers. With the slightest pressure on the blend, it offers up the fragrant essence of this place of peace and clarity, and I am here once again, able to survive the dreariness of reality.

I return to my van, start it up, shift into gear, and begin my descent along the switchbacks and curves of the canyon. High on the south wall, I look to the monument erected in memory of an English nobleman who fell to his death at that spot while big-game hunting in the late 1880s. As rich as he was, the monument is just barely visible and is nothing compared to the beautiful canyon before me that drops away to the west and opens up at the town of Ten Sleep.

It took 20 days for the sojourners of yesteryear to make the trek across these mountains. It was here, where the town of Ten Sleep is now, that they stopped to camp, knowing that half of their journey was behind them. It was at this spot, four years before, that I rolled to a stop, helpless, having destroyed my transmission by running over a large rock at one of the switchbacks high up in the canyon. I was taken in for the afternoon by the lady of a house that was located at the foot of the canyon, a woman whose husband, as it turns out, was the superintendent of schools for the town of Ten Sleep. She allowed me to use her phone and gave me coffee and cookies while I waited for the towing service to arrive from Worland. I rented a car in Worland, continued my tour to California for a week with the rental, and then returned to Worland to pick up the van. Two nights later, I was on stage in Oregon, having driven hard to make up for lost time. I could only ask myself, "What's another 1,800 extra miles anyway? It is just the way that one manages a bit of misfortune and copes with rocks in the road."

On through Worland, past the dealership that repaired my van, and then through Thermopolis, Riverton, and Dubois to Jackson, where I have a show to do tonight at Doornan's. Actually, Doornan's is located at Moose Junction, just north of the town.

Bob Doornan and his wife, Pat, operate the place which has been in his family since the 1940s. It was at Doornan's that I first performed in the Jackson area in 1982 at the invitation of a fellow by the name of Jim Day who had moved to Wyoming from the East Coast. Over the years, Jim became one of the instrumental forces responsible for bringing a lot of good music into the mountains, as well as operating a bakery called Teton Breads and Bagels.

After running through a gamut of venues in the town, including the Red Garter Theatre, the Wort Hotel, and the Snow King Ski Resort, I returned to performing at Doornan's in the early 1990s, and it has become my "Sweet Wyoming Home" at the base of the beautiful Tetons.

It is the middle of the afternoon when I make the descent out of Togwatee Pass and Teton-Bridger National Forest, onto the flat plains of Jackson Hole. People unfamiliar with the area are often confused about the difference between the town of Jackson and the geographical area that is known as Jackson Hole. They call the town itself Jackson Hole, and if one mentions the name "Jackson" alone, they have no idea where the place is located. It is the town of Jackson that is situated within the confines of Jackson Hole.

The Jackson Hole area is actually a wide valley bordered on the east by the Gros Ventre Mountains, and on the west by the Teton Range. The French trappers and the mountain men of the West fondly dubbed the peaks of the area Tetons because of their perceived resemblance to women's breasts. It was in this area of northwestern Wyoming and eastern Idaho that, between 1825 and 1840, some of the great gatherings—called "rendezvous"—of mountain men took place.

The rendezvous was scheduled each year at the close of the trapping season, and it was here that the trappers would deliver their winter's harvest of pelts into the hands of the fur-trading companies in exchange for money and another season's supply of lead, powder, traps, and provisions. Mostly, the rendezvous was a great excuse for a giant party, and it was here that the loneliness and isolation of the trappers exploded into wild frivolity and passionate discourse on the joys of love, liquor, and life.

It seems that in some ways the modern-day Jackson is just a continuation of those long-ago parties. It is a town which thrives on the rewards that some people shower upon themselves for having lived what they perceive as productive and important lives. I do not condemn this, for I suppose that it is a natural thing to want to enjoy life to the utmost of one's resources. What I question, though, is the perception of importance, for it is not money or power that makes one human being more important than another, it is what the final and sum total of their existence will mean to the positive outcome of the great God-granted living experience that we all share.

It is late afternoon, and I am making my way south along the road that leads to Moose Junction and beyond to the larger town. The eastern slopes of the Tetons turn a purple gray as the sun continues its decline into Pierre's Hole, Jackson Hole's companion valley on the western side of the mountains. I pass the turn for Jenny Lake, and pass another turn for the Chapel of Transfiguration. I slip by the road to Doornan's, having made a reservation at one of the hotels in town, and drive by the cutoff to Kelly, where some years before I stayed in a yurt. I skirt the border of the National Elk Refuge and enter Jackson on the north side. I pass the town square with its antlered archways, take a right at the stop light by the Million Dollar Cowboy Bar, and head for my hotel.

It is another old and familiar routine: late afternoon arrival, dinner in town at one of my favorite restaurants, and then a short run back up the road to Moose for the show later that evening. I have come to rely on these old routines when I am on the road. I know that I must also gird myself for changes. Nothing ever remains the same for long periods of time, and when I am told at the entrance to the Cowboy Bar that La Chispa, one of my favorite Mexican restaurants in the country, has now become an upscale French eatery, I reel at the information and seek recovery at the local Kentucky Fried Chicken.

I was once told by a young lady in San Francisco that my return trips to that city in the fall of each year had an important stabilizing effect on her life. She had come to rely on my appearances as a sort of touchstone and knew that, as chaotic as her own life might be, there was always a constancy in my touring. Inasmuch as I was flattered by her observation, I could not help but chuckle at the idea that someone could find stability and constancy in a life as transient as my own.

I think, however, that over the years I have come to understand and feel her reasoning, for my fall tour has come to mean the same to me. I am constantly fascinated at how I can pick up a conversation, almost in mid-thought, with a friend that I have not seen in more than a year. It is as if time has stood still. I frequently have to remind myself that when I return to a town, a significant measure of time has really slipped away, and that since my last tour the lives of the people that I know may have been immensely changed forever.

And so it is with these thoughts on my mind that I arrive at Doornan's, unload, and set up for the show. The concert is sold out, and as the audience arrives, I stop to chat with Bob and Pat, who have taken their traditional places at a table to the right of the stage.

There is a special spirit about this place. It reaches out and says to me that I belong here. It is not only at Doornan's, but at so many other places like it along the road. The spirit tells me that I am not just a visitor, that I am not just a skater gliding above some deep waters, but that I have a place amongst all of the people of this land. The spirit directs that I must tell a great story in the way of small chapters. I look into the eyes of the people who have come to hear me this night in Wyoming, and I feel that what is in their hearts is not only their story, but also that of my own.

CHAPTER 17

Going to the West

By the time *The Whistle of the Jay* was released late in 1978, I had written more than 50 songs, and Mason Daring suggested that I form my own publishing company. Although I had secured ownership copyrights for each of the songs, until that time most had remained unpublished. The exceptions were the tunes of my own that I had recorded on *Just Play One Tune More*, and those had been published by Folk Legacy.

Mason could not have given me any better advice. It would be the same advice that I would give to many of my songwriter friends in the years to come. I filed the appropriate papers with the state of New Hampshire and affiliated with BMI as both a writer and a publisher. Mineral River was now not only in the business of releasing records, it was also a publishing company. Sandy and Caroline Paton were kind enough to release the publishing for the songs that I had recorded for them, and from then on Mineral River secured all of the copyrights for my songs. I think perhaps it was a bit confusing when I told people that I didn't own the rights to my music. It was simply that Mineral River owned the rights, and I owned Mineral River.

I found that understanding the publishing business went a long way toward understanding the music business as a whole. I came to realize that a good part of what goes on in the music business is just the simple application of a few basic formulae. If a person learns to add one and one together, then it holds true that they can add one million and one million together. Likewise, recognizing a good deal from a bad deal in the "biz" is often just the same application of formulae.

If a songwriter retains the publishing rights to a song through their own publishing company then, as an incentive given to an artist to record the song, that writer's publishing company might opt to deal away a portion of the publishing rights or royalties to the artist. Going the other way, if a writer signs the rights to a song over to another publisher as soon as the song is written, then the writer has given up control over the material, and likewise the ability to shop the song on their own terms.

Mason's axioms that "no deal is better than a bad deal" and "a good song does not have a life span" were beginning to find practical applications in my own musical career. Many years later, I would receive a phone call from a representative of a well-known country music star telling me that the artist had heard my song "A Place in the Choir" and was interested in recording it. According to this person, they would need to have me sign over the publishing rights to the song, and then they would be willing to spend $100,000 for the promotion of the recording. Something inside of me counseled caution, so I made a counter offer. I would be willing to evenly split 80 percent of the publishing with the artist, and we would pay a third party the remaining 20 percent to administer the payment of the royalties. I thought that it was a fair deal. We both knew that we would be paid by the third party, the artist would profit, and I would still have the rights to the song. They cooled on my offer, so I walked away from the prospect. A few weeks later, I received a phone call from a senior editor at E.P. Dutton book publishers, wondering what they would have to do to get the song out as an illustrated children's book. I still had the publishing rights to the song and knew that Mason's lessons had served me well.

In January of 1979, I approached Bob Donlin, who ran Passim, with an idea. It was simply that nothing much was happening at the club during the week in the middle of January, and it might be fun to get together with Mason and Jeanie, Guy Van Duser and Billy Novick, and a fiddle player by the name of Stuart Schulman, to present some sort of a mini-folk festival at the club on a Tuesday and Wednesday night. Bob had some dates open that month, so we all got together and put on a show that Bob billed as "The Passim All Stars." We weren't exactly sure how the thing would fly with such a short time available to promote the show, but Bob had to turn people away at the door for both nights. It was the start of a ten-year tradition at the club. Every January, the All Stars would come together for two nights at Passim and just have fun playing music. Bob even had T-shirts printed up for the shows—but he ended up giving most of them away, seeing how there wasn't a great market for T-shirts in the middle of the winter. I always kidded him about the shirts, suggesting that perhaps we should try baseball caps, too. Needless to say, his enthusiasm at the suggestion was a bit more than underwhelming. The musicians that made up the All Stars became the team that would be the core group that I would use in the studio for my recordings for Rounder Records for the next ten years. We were good friends then and remain so today.

In April of that year, I received a phone call from Ralph Silva who ran the Me and Thee Coffeehouse in Marblehead. Ralph had come up with the idea of booking one of the windjammers that sailed out of Rockland, Maine (the Lewis R. French) for a week and selling tickets for the cruise to the folk music community on the north shore. Regulars who frequented the Me and Thee would be given an advance opportunity to reserve space on the ship. I was invited to be the musician on board for the week, and it would be a free vacation for Karen and me. It was the highlight of the summer that year, cruising the waters off the coast of Maine and listening in the warm evening as the folks sang along with me beneath a fading sky.

Steve Nerney called that summer from California. Through his church, he had become acquainted with a woman by the name of Jean Finke, and he suggested that the two of them might be interested in booking a tour for me on the West Coast. The San Francisco Folk Song Society had expressed an interest in having me play for them, and Jean figured that she could arrange some more performances up and down the peninsula. I jumped at the idea, and in the fall of 1979 I began the tradition of leaving home in October and playing my way across the country to the West Coast and back again.

My first tour included stops in Kansas City; Lincoln, where Jerry Rau had introduced me to Paul and Dixie Moss, who opened their home to traveling musicians for house concerts; and the Swallow Hill Music Association in Denver.

Swallow Hill was the brainchild of Harry Tufts, who operated the Denver Folklore Center at 608 East 17th Avenue in Denver from 1962 until 1979. In 1979, with the Folklore Center about to close its doors, Harry envisioned a nonprofit folk music society that would sponsor concerts and fill the void that would be left by the closing of the Folklore Center. He contacted some interested and dedicated people in the Denver folk music scene, and within months Swallow Hill came into existence. During that first year, the Swallow Hill concerts were still actually held at the Folklore Center, but before long an alternative space was found for the shows, and the center finally closed down. Because Harry was also a musician in his own right and had recorded for Folk Legacy, he was acquainted with my music and had offered me a gig that fall on my way to California.

It was a small group of people that showed up to hear me that night, but it was the start of a relationship with Swallow Hill that would continue some 20 years later.

I arrived at the California state line on Monday, the first of October in 1979, and stopped at Donner Lake to celebrate my successful traverse of the country with a bottle of wine and a picnic lunch. It was a warm, sunny day, and the soft pine needles felt good beneath my body as I lay back and gazed at the sky through the canopy of trees. A group of Steller's Jays, emboldened by the sight of my food, advanced in slow but determined steps, hoping to pull off a robbery and quick retreat with the spoils. I began playing a game with them, lying still until they were almost upon me, and then sitting up, causing a minor panic amongst their ranks. After a few minutes of this advance and retreat, I broke up what was left of the crackers and shared my celebratory repast with these winged denizens of the Sierra.

I called Steve Nerney from a nearby phone booth to let him know that I would be arriving late that afternoon, and he gave me directions to his apartment in South San Francisco. It was my first time in the Bay Area, and I felt the excitement of adventure building within me as I crossed the Carquinez Strait, passed the industrial city of Richmond, and caught my first sight of the Golden Gate Bridge across the silver expanse of San Francisco Bay.

So here it was, the jewel of the West, the city of fog and lights, of earthquakes and bridges, of mansions and golden dreams, of hills and cable cars, and of the ever-present passing of lives. It was the place that I had read about in the books of Jack London and the colorful hip prose of Jack Kerouac. I stared at the city before me, and it was a feast unto my wanderer's soul.

I crossed the Bay Bridge and wondered at the names of the places I passed: Treasure Island, the Embarcadero, and Mount Sutro. It was a late Monday afternoon, and the rush-hour traffic was building along the main artery, Route 101, that cuts through the center of the city. I made my way south, darting and dodging back and forth through the shiny cars and trucks until at last I found the exit for South San Francisco and followed the directions to Steve's apartment.

My first concert of the week was on Wednesday in San Carlos for the Peninsula Folk Club, where I met Jean, who had done most of the footwork for the week's tour. Then on Thursday it was off to Davis, where I was to perform at the Palms Playhouse.

The Palms was little more than a sheet-metal barn with a seating capacity of around 150 people. Located just off of Interstate 80 on the south side of town, the entrance to the dirt parking lot was guarded by two majestic palm trees that towered over the surrounding hedges. The Palms was operated by Linda McDonagh, and served as the home for local theatrical productions, as well as a musical performance space for acts that were touring the country. In my case, it was the Davis Folklore Society that was sponsoring the concert. Steve had some friends who were living in the area and the Palms was all but full for the show.

The next day, Friday, I was scheduled to do a house concert in Marin County, north of the Golden Gate Bridge; on Saturday, Jean had set up a concert in Redwood City that I would be sharing with Carol McComb, one of the Bay Area's singing and songwriting legends. I was particularly looking forward to this concert, for I had only heard Carol sing once before in a live performance. That was 14 years earlier at the Newport Folk Festival when, on a very special Sunday afternoon, she and her partner Kathy Larisch had graced the stage with their music as Kathy and Carol. It was on this Saturday night that I first heard her sing her song "Secret Garden" and fell in love with it. Some four years later I would record it on my album *Bridges*, and it would become one of the most requested songs in my repertoire.

On that Sunday, I performed for the San Francisco Folk Song Society at their coffeehouse called Plowshares. After the performance, everybody at the show adjourned to Faith Petric's place on Clayton Street, where a party had been in progress for most of the day. It was Faith's 60th birthday, and it was good to see her again. It had been more than two years since we had played music together into the rainy, early hours of the morning at Fox Hollow, and it was a grand reunion.

While I was in California that year, I also called my old friends Marty Pike and Dabris Ievins, who had moved from Boston to San Francisco in 1977. Dabris had given up the Charles Street music scene in 1976 went on an extended visit to see friends in the Bay Area. Plagued with health problems, he found the climate more suitable to his tastes, and he returned to Boston and convinced

Marty that they should take up residence "by the Bay." Dabris was not fond of New England winters. Marty and "Dabs" immediately invited me to stay at their place on Whitney Street while I was in town. Although I had already made plans to stay at Steve's on that first trip, on subsequent trips to San Francisco I always had a home at Marty and Dab's.

Marty and Dabris, who had also been showing up at my shows that first tour, were also at the party in Faith's home that Sunday. I was pleased that all of my San Francisco friends, old and new, had taken so well to each other. These were the friendships that would become the foundation for my life on the West Coast throughout the 1980s. Even when Steve Nerney took other jobs around the country, he would always fly back to California for the week that I was in town. It wasn't until Dabris' death of a heart attack in 1987 that this core group of friends would drift away from the Bay Area for good. Marty continued to live on Whitney Street for a few years but then eventually moved back to New England. Steve, with his new wife Myra, had already moved to New Mexico to teach at San Juan College. Occasionally he would bring me in to the school to play a concert, but San Francisco would never be the same for me, and the bright mornings that I spent sitting in the sun on the front landing of Whitney Street would become only the warmest and dearest of memories.

On my way back from the West Coast that fall, I once again performed at the Extempore in Minneapolis. When a few days later I pulled into my driveway at home in New Hampshire, the very first of my fall cross-country tours had come to a successful completion.

CHAPTER 18

The Fall Tour, Day Eight

It is the bright moon and the morning star in the sky above that command the attention of this traveler as I drive by the dark butte that stands at the southwest side of Jackson. The high slopes of the surrounding hills begin to take shape as imminent dawn makes itself known to this cold mountain country. The road that I am taking out of town forks about ten miles south of Jackson. I take the left fork, Wyoming 189, which begins to climb out of the Jackson Hole area onto the high tableland of western Wyoming. It is a Wednesday, and once again a travel day, for my next concert the following night is in Arcata on the northern California coast.

My route this day takes me south, down the western side of Wyoming, past Bridger National Forest to Evanston, and a westbound reunion with great Interstate 80. It is middle morning when I enter Utah, and after 30 miles I make the long sweeping turn to the left at Echo and enter the Wasatch Mountain Range from the east. I pass the exit for Park City, home of Robert Redford's Sundance Film Festival, and in half an hour make my descent out of the Wasatch, down the winding canyon to Salt Lake City, the

Great Salt Lake, and the giant basin which defines this area of the American West.

Every couple of years, I stop in Salt Lake to do a concert for the Intermountain Acoustic Music Association, but this is an off year. Instead, I head straight through the city and out onto the salt floor plain and due west to Wendover, Utah, 101 miles away.

It is 100 miles of stark and barren country, dry and blinding white in the noontime sun. Every few hundred yards along the highway, a collection of stones, manipulated by some passerby, spells out a message to travelers that "BOB WAS HERE" or that we all should "HAVE A NICE DAY." Now and then one of these collections of rocks is laid out in the shape of an arrow, pointing to nothing in particular. All of these designs are accompanied by the mandatory set of footprints in the salt bed leading to and from whatever the message on the ground might be.

A few miles east of Wendover, a lone 25-foot sculpture of some kind of nut tree emerges from the soil, surrounded on the ground by the broken shells of what are nuts that have supposedly fallen from the tree. I love these preposterous ornamentations. One finds them all over the country. Along the Garden State Parkway in New Jersey, there are tall metal communications towers that are disguised as giant pine trees. In the middle of a field in Wisconsin, a half dozen telephone poles protrude from the landscape, all at the same angle, brightly painted, and all equipped with wooden feathers that make them appear as if some immense archer has loosed the contents of his quiver from miles away. It is a tribute to our makeup as human beings that our art somehow manages to find an inroad into the most unlikely of places and be born out of the most unusual materials.

I complete the crossing of the salt flats and climb the long hill that overlooks Wendover with its hotels and state-line casinos. I have occasionally driven the salt flats at night, after my concerts in Salt Lake City, with the lights of Wendover visible across the desert miles, and slept under the beckoning arms of the animated cowboy that towers over the parking lot at one of these meccas. At one time the pulsing glow in the night sky emanating from the lights of casinos in this country was something unique to Nevada or the New Jersey shore, but nowadays that nocturnal glow seems to be visible almost everywhere, from the northern woods of Wisconsin to the southern gulf coast of Alabama. It is an insidious business. A friend once remarked to me that "when it becomes more fun to play the game than it is to win, then it is time to back away." I am glad that my traveling schedule is tight, for recently it has become time for me to admit that I should keep a wide berth between myself and those rolling oranges and cherries.

It is 415 miles across Nevada to the entrance to Donner Pass on the eastern slopes of the California Sierra. Out of the high mountain country now, the day is sunny and warm. I drive through the afternoon, stopping frequently for coffee. It is a long, straight, and hot band of highway out before me—for a weary traveler, an invitation to drowsiness. Occasionally there is a long climb up to 6,000 feet or so, and then an equally lengthy descent. It is on these descents that the semis come flying by you like you've just blown an engine on the third lap at Indianapolis. Some of these trucks are more like trains, with two or sometimes three trailers tagging along behind them, floating and swaying as if at anytime they might break for the hills with complete minds of their own.

By the middle of the afternoon, I have made the descent out of Emigrant Pass and passed the town of Battle Mountain. By early evening, I am on the outskirts of Reno, having passed Winnemucca, the Humboldt Mountains, and the Humboldt Sink. I roll on by the exit ramp for Mustang, famous for its brothel, the Mustang Ranch. When the place closed down in August of 1999, the owner, one Joe Conforte, was forced to surrender the assets, sans ladies, to the U.S. government for back taxes. I often wondered how the government must have dealt with that baby of a situation and the resale of the property. I could picture an ad in the local real estate listings:

For Sale at Auction by U.S. Government.
Multiple-Bedroom Fixer Upper,
Well-Known Historical Landmark. Real Cheap!

I leave Reno behind, with its flashing colored lights and hotel casinos outlined in neon. There is nothing in this place for me, no one that I want to see, nothing that I want to know, and as early evening approaches I begin the long gradual ascent out of Nevada and chase the declining sun up into the grand Sierra.

My hotel for the night is a rustic collection of buildings on the shores of Donner Lake, not far from the spot where, on my first tour to California some 20 years before, I shared my celebratory picnic with the local winged denizens. I know that I have a formidable distance to cover the next day before my concert in Arcata, and I plan on making it an early night.

After settling into my room, I take a walk to the shore of the lake, stretch out on one of the benches provided for the guests of the hotel, and stare up through the tall trees at the profound panorama of the starry cosmos. It seems as if God has left all of the lights in heaven burning this evening, and while the ripples of the lake slap out a gentle rhythm against the shore, I ponder what it must be like to be a star and burn that brightly in the sky.

It is an unlikely moniker that we have bestowed upon our celebrities, that of being a star. First of all, a star gives off its own light. If one were to place two people in a darkened room, one a "star" of sports, screen, or television, and the other a representative of "the regular folk," I would be willing to bet that a light meter would show little difference between the two people.

True heavenly stars are constant, although their positions in the sky may change because of the daily rotation of the earth or because of the planet's seasonal position around the sun. The true star returns year after year to its same place in the sky. How many of our "star" athletes exhibit this same constancy? It seems increasingly that, nowadays, their actions and attitudes are more in tune with the shifting, unpredictable dunes of a desert. Stars rise far above our heads and are untouchable, at least at this writing, while the "stars" of stage and screen, the last time I checked, still walk upon this good Earth. Yes, I believe it is a strange moniker we have given our celebrities.

A meteorite leaves a brilliant, cold, fiery trail across the northern sky, and a warm breath of wind spurs the arms of the trees to release a shower of pine needles. They softly fall in a rustle near my bench and bring me to an awareness once more.

It seems to me that if one makes a living as an artist for 25 years, then that person, whether they be a musician, painter, actor, or dancer, must certainly have been endowed with some sort of talent. One does not survive for that long in the world of performing or visual arts with no talent. Given that this is true, then it holds that any artist having made their living for that long must become at least one of two things: either they become a celebrity, or they become a legend. Everybody, it seems, knows the celebrities, but it is those celebrities who know the legends.

Ask a well-known jazz trumpeter to list those musicians who have been influential in his life, and my bet is that he will recall a lot of people whose names are mostly unknown to the general populace. Ask a well-known dancer to list those who have guided her steps, and you will probably not recognize many of the names. It is these people, however—these old jazz cats that have played the back street honky-tonks of New Orleans for most of their lives; the high school drama or dance instructor who, through the years of teaching has learned how to nourish the heart and soul, and open the eyes of a young actress—who are the true legends. They are not well known, but they are well loved.

I know a few celebrities and can even count some of them among my good friends, but I know many, many more artists who are legends. They work hard and they live hard. They create, and it is within their creativity that they find the reason and strength to continue with their endeavors. Their names are not household words, and yet their contributions to the rich and vibrant world of the arts will always be profound.

I can only hope that my music will in some way make a difference in the lives of others. Will I ever be a star? I rather doubt it, and so I guess that I will have to settle for simply gazing at them as they twinkle just above my head on this warm and peaceful night in California.

CHAPTER 19

Rodeo Rose

How long is a mile? Technically it is 5,280 feet; alas, it can also be an infinitesimal space when it comes between people. Karen was growing restless and was ready to move back to Virginia by the end of 1979. It seemed as if I was on the road most of the time, and she was spending long days and weeks by herself. We had reached some sort of plateau in our marriage, and our relationship seemed stuck, without any sense of growth. Was my marriage to go the same way as the marriages of so many other musicians?

We seemed to weather the storm, at least for the time being, but now I was haunted by the uneasy, uncertain feelings of a foggy future. It had been a cold month, that January of 1980, and on the 23rd of the month, the winter's first heavy snowfall blanketed the fields around us. I was glad that I had found the time to gather enough fuel from the nearby woods to feed our wood stove and fireplace.

By February I was back on the road, doing shows in Oneonta and Potsdam, New York, with a weekend performance at the Caffé

Lena in Saratoga. I was staying at Logan's place across the park from the Caffé. He was not looking well and had been drinking heavily for some time. I'm afraid that I was not the greatest of influences on him when, at two o'clock in the morning, the two of us would frequently be found singing old Irish ballads at one or another of the local saloons.

I asked him what he thought of two songs that I had recently written: "Prairie Song" and "The Sampler Song." His response, through somewhat glassy eyes, was that he thought that I was really not capable of writing a bad song, but that he wished that I would. This would give him an inkling that I was finally reaching beyond my "limits for something new" and that I was not "stuck in an easy rut." That statement from Logan would enable me, years later, to complete two projects that I probably would never have attempted out of fear of either my literary or musical ignorance. *The Alaska Suite* and this book may well have remained just grand ideas, locked inside of me for want of the key that would allow me to fail. Logan English provided me with that key.

On the weekend before Valentine's Day that month, Guy Van Duser and I flew to Minneapolis to do a concert sponsored by "A Prairie Home Companion" at the World Theatre. The first show was a sellout; a second performance was added and also sold out. At 650 people per show, this was big-time for me. I was ecstatic about the weekend. The performances had gone well, but because of the way that things were at home, I was feeling troubled and very lonely on the return plane flight with Guy.

That concert was rebroadcast nationally three or four times over the next six months, and a photograph of the theatre marquis for that show found its way onto the cover of the *A Prairie Home Companion, the First Five Years* anniversary album.

Upon my return home, Karen and I decided to spend a few days at an old inn on the coast of Maine, just to get away, and for a change of scenery.

By March of 1980, I was putting together a collection of my songs to be published by Folk Legacy in a book entitled *If I Were a*

Word, Then I'd Be a Song, and by that April I was already thinking about recording another album.

I was approached by Mason Daring, who was interested in being the producer on one of my album projects. Mason's plan was to round up some investors and do a "no-holds-barred" album of my songs, and then shop the master to a major label. A new facility known as Blue Jay Recording Studios had opened in Carlisle, Massachusetts, and during the month of May we began recording the basic tracks for the album *Rodeo Rose*.

I was in hog heaven. We hired string players from the Boston Symphony, we got Jonathan Edwards to sing some of the harmonies, and we even rounded up a percussionist who could play the steel drums on one of the songs. It was going to be my "hit" album. I loved the experience, the music, the people, and the studio education. Was it a hit? Well, not really, but the album was released by Philo, a small folk music label out of Vermont. Philo eventually went out of business and was bought by Rounder Records. In the years to come, the defunct label Philo would become Rounder's outlet for their stable of contemporary singer-songwriters.

By the middle of July, *Rodeo Rose* had been recorded, so Karen and I planned a return trip to the West. I was performing at the 1980 Winnipeg Folk Festival, and that event seemed like a good opportunity to see western Canada, revisit Glacier National Park, and spend a few days with one of Karen's college friends who was living with her husband in Boulder, Montana.

We camped across the north shore of Lake Superior and arrived at Winnipeg on Thursday, the day before the festival was to begin. I was to do two workshops, as well as a concert set on the Saturday afternoon. A number of my Minnesota friends had shown up for the weekend, but it was the re-acquaintance with one old friend, and the discovery of the musical life of a new friend, that I would remember most from that festival.

The old friend was Brian Bowers, autoharp player extraordinaire. I had known Brian since the early 1970s, and although we rarely saw each other—perhaps only once every three years—I still thought of him as a good friend and one of those genuine kindred spirits of the road.

Brian's main performance at the festival was to be on the Saturday night concert. He was slated to follow a group called the Original Sloth Band, headed up by Ken Whiteley, who later produced many of Raffi's recordings. The band was a Toronto legend, and on that Saturday night it consisted of at least a half-dozen players who tore the place apart with a set that bordered on a folk-rock-gospel style of music. There must have been 15,000-20,000 people in the audience, and the Original Sloth Band had them all up on their feet, dancing and grooving with the music. The band could have rocked all night, but, of course, there were other performers yet to come on the show. I was not envious of the position that Brian was in, having to follow such a high-energy set. What followed, though, was one of those moments in performance that I have seen but only a few times in my life, and a demonstration of what music is really all about.

After a brief introduction, during which a considerable number of the audience members were still cheering for more music from the previous players, Brian walked onstage, carrying his autoharp. He stood at the microphone and softly spoke ten words. "I'd like to play for you "The Old Wildwood Flower."

There was something in his demeanor, something in the way the words were spoken, that quietly demanded my attention. At that moment, I felt that Brian was providing me with the opportunity to receive a beautiful and special gift. It wasn't just another Carter Family song, it was "The Old Wildwood Flower." It wasn't just a beautiful melody, it was a melody that contained within a sense of all of the beauty that is around us. It wasn't just Brian Bowers on stage, it was a quiet man who respected this old song, and by performing it was carrying on an ancient musical tradition.

I had to listen. I had no choice, and neither did the audience. As Brian's autoharp began to sing, a change occurred. The sound of the instrument was no longer subordinate to the cheers of the masses. It had become a simple, overpowering voice that was reaching out to everyone. The music leapt from the stage, the clear high notes of the instrument carried on the backs of the rhythmical low-string chords. As to whether Brian himself ever had an inkling as to what was happening I could not tell, for he seemed lost in the love of the music, and once again it was that music of the true heart that had prevailed. That night I learned how important it is to respect the music that you, as a musician, are privileged to play. It is this respect that ultimately brings the music to life.

Brian's solo set that evening was as compelling as any that could have been rendered by a 70-piece orchestra, and I considered myself lucky to have been there to experience the moment.

That year at Winnipeg I was also introduced to the musical heart and soul of David Amram. David had been a regular performer at Caffé Lena for years, a seemingly somewhat crazy character of musical legend who wandered through life with a dumbek drum under one arm and the original score to a concerto for violin and orchestra under the other. Logan considered David a genius, and when Amram appeared at her café, Lena would always bill him as a true renaissance human being. I knew David Amram only by reputation, but a serendipitous encounter with one of his fans would come to open a window into the life of a man dedicated to the true sense of all music.

David's philosophy and approach to musical creativity and performance would be set out for me in one single concept, exacted from his autobiography, *Vibrations*. It is the principle that "one should never think more of themselves than they do of their music."

But I did not know this at the 1980 Winnipeg Folk Festival. I was just standing by the trailer that served as the instrument check for the performers. In front of me, checking his violin, was the great jazz virtuoso Stephan Grappelli. As the maestro turned to leave, Amram approached him with a wide smile. The two shook hands and wandered away together, conversing in fluent French.

A sense of curiosity welled up inside of me and I began to wonder who this renaissance man really was and what he might be like as a person. At this moment, he was wearing an old beat-up straw hat covered with souvenir pins from the places that he had visited, but I knew that 24 hours later he might be at the podium dressed in white tie and tails, conducting the Houston Symphony.

A long-haired young man of about 20 hurried up to me. He was adorned in typical festival clothing—T-shirt, shorts, and sandals—and in one hand he carried Amram's book. He asked me if I had seen David around recently, and when I told him that the subject of his quest had left just moments earlier, he thanked me, turned, and mumbled something to the sky about getting David to autograph the book that had seen him through so many tough times the previous summer. I wondered what it was about this particular book that could have put a person into such a frenzy, and decided that *Vibrations* would be my next reading project.

After Karen and I returned from our trip that summer, I discovered a copy of *Vibrations* in a used book store in Saratoga, New York, and within its pages found many of the tenets by which I would judge my own life in music.

Vibrations is dedicated to Dimitri Mitropoulos, famed conductor of the Minneapolis Symphony from 1937 to 1949, and conductor of the New York Philharmonic from 1949 to 1958. A friend of the Amram family, it was actually Mitropoulios who constantly reminded David as a youth that one should never think more of themselves than their music. Mitropoulos continually impressed upon David that, above all, it should be the music that reigns in a performance. A musician on stage is nothing more than a conduit through which the music may flow and weave its magic upon the listener. Without the music, a musician has no reason to be onstage. The theatrics of a conductor, or the antics of a rock-and-roll band would look pretty silly if suddenly the music were taken from the scene.

As all autobiographies are, *Vibrations* is the story of a life, with all the pitfalls and accomplishments that abound within that life. By the time I had finished reading it, however, I had garnered from the stories set down on the pages three enlightenments.

The first enlightenment: How immense is the concept of music, from the intricate rhythms of logs being pounded together on the shores of Africa, to the single stringed instruments of the Orient;

from a 100-piece orchestra playing a Beethoven Symphony to the 3-note song of a howling wolf! It is all music, and it is all fundamental to the fabric of our lives.

The second enlightenment: How huge is the capability we have to waste time in our lives! I don't expect that, as a composer, I can spend every spare moment of my life writing music, and yet how many times do I find myself sitting in a bar or fighting a losing battle with some inanimate object when I would be far better off trying to be creative with that precious time?

The third (and the most important) enlightenment: How blessed I am to be a musician, for if music were not in my soul, I could never truly understand and appreciate the power and the significance of those wonderful vibrations that direct my existence!

Later that summer at the Philadelphia Folk Festival, I was walking by one of the smaller workshop stages. The workshop in progress was being hosted by David Amram. I remember hearing the final few words of his introduction to an instrumental piece that he was about to play on two wooden whistles: "And so, from the people of Asia to you, here is 'From the Khyber Pass.'" Just as with Brian Bowers a month before, once again I was compelled to listen. The piece of music was a gift to me from a far-away people, and for me to pass on by without taking in this gift would have made me just a little poorer.

Four years later, David asked me if I would perform a duet arrangement of "Red River Valley" with him on stage at the Kerrville Folk Festival. I played the guitar and David played a Native American flute. It was at that festival that I asked him if he would be so kind as to sign my own copy of *Vibrations*.

* * *

Late in September of 1980, Karen and I were invited to attend the opening-night party and the Cambridge, Massachusetts, premiere of a film by John Sayles called *The Return of the Secaucus Seven*. Mason Daring had been involved with much of the legal work for the film and had arranged for me to do some yodeling on the soundtrack. Guy Van Duser and Billy Novick, as well as Mason and Jeanie, were also on board for some of the music. It was a low-budget production (somewhere around $60,000), but the film would launch John Sayles into the limelight as one of the industries' most respected writers and directors.

Secaucus was released out of New York and immediately began getting rave reviews. Hollywood became jealous. There had always been a rivalry between the coasts in film production, and at the time New York had a foot up on the "hip" film releases. Hollywood responded some months later with a film that was very similar in concept and plot—and in the eyes of many, simply a remake of *Secaucus*. The movie was called *The Big Chill*, and although John Sayles' film became a bit of a cult classic, it would be *The Big Chill* that would get most of the mainstream attention.

* * *

My journal entry for September 27,1980, reads:

Sept. 27, 1980. Interstate 80 bridge at the Mississippi River.
On the road again, again in the gray morning.
Welcome to Iowa. The geese are southbound over the autumn dry cornfields.
There is music on the tape deck. Nebraska-bound today, straight out
Over the flatland plains.

It seemed to me that my life was beginning to follow some sort of a pattern. It could not have been a year since my last fall tour. Where was the time going? I had worked hard setting up the fall tour that year and performed almost every night on my trip across the country. I had been rebooked at many of the places from the previous tour but still managed to include a few new venues on the schedule. In California, I did a concert in San Diego and performed at the Old Time Café in Leucadia. When I reached San Francisco, the welcome mat was out for me at Marty and Dabris' place on Whitney Street, and I spent a week with them. Steve and Jean had scheduled another concert for me with Carol McComb, and when it was time to head home there was the usual stop at the Coffeehouse Extempore in Minneapolis.

The second fall tour was now history, and once again many of the places booked me for a return the following year—suggesting, in fact, that we might just as well make the date for them an annual routine. This was ideal for me, for much of the pressure and responsibility for booking the fall season was eased. Making these return trips and scheduling the tour seemed slated to become an annual occurrence.

* * *

I met Dan Breslaw and Judy Tharinger, along with their kids, at Passim in the fall of 1979. Dan always insisted on being called "Dog," and when they showed up for my gigs at the club, the whole family looked a bit like a vision out of the 1960s. Dog had long, shoulder-length hair which was held in place by a headband fashioned out of a bandana that was usually red, and a wise countenance, with eyes that smiled at you and made you feel at peace. The kids were always dressed in some sort of colorful clothing, and every once in a while they would send me homemade greeting cards adorned with bright red hearts, birds, and flowers of the sweetest design.

By the fall of 1980, the whole family had moved to Alaska and had been writing me that they missed listening to my music. They asked if I might be interested in doing a tour in Alaska. At the time, Alaska may just as well have been the other side of the moon, being so far away from New England, but at their insistence, I sent off some promotional materials to see if they might be able to put together a tour.

I sent the promo packages to Dog and Judy in Homer, Alaska, where they were renting a cabin adjacent to the homestead of Yule Kiltcher. Yule had left his home in Switzerland and settled in Alaska in 1940. He was living completely off of the land, land that he had cleared and homesteaded some 40 years before. Dog had lived in Homer during the 1960s and knew Yule and the Kiltcher family very well.

I reserved a five-week time slot in my schedule from the middle of May to the end of June in 1981 and sent a note to Dog along with the promo materials, asking him to get back to me as soon as possible as to whether the Alaskan tour would happen. Dog and Judy went to work and by the end of 1980 surprised me with an itinerary that was enough to make my head spin. I was booked almost every day during the time period I had given them and was scheduled to do concerts from Juneau and Sitka in the southeast to Barrow and Prudhoe Bay in the far north. The only time during the tour that I was not booked was a period of four or five days when I could visit with Dog and Judy and do a concert for them in Homer.

My plan for the first half of 1981 was to spend January through April doing performance dates near my home in the Northeast, and then travel to Minneapolis in May. From Minneapolis, I would fly to Alaska, and if all went well I would be home by the end of June.

Home? I was on the road so much that I was beginning to lose track of just what and where home really was for me. It was time for Karen and me to either find or build a place of our own. We loved where we were living in the country, but it belonged to someone else, and once again it was becoming obvious that we needed to grow as a couple. We acquired our first dog, a Springer Spaniel that we named Hallie (short for Halcyon), and it was because of Hallie that we became just a little bit closer.

CHAPTER 20

The Fall Tour, Day Nine

It is an early rising this morning, and it will be a long drive to the northern California coastal town of Arcata. The waters of Donner Lake are serene and blue in the early light. With the exception of the occasional darting flitter of a swallow and the sharp cry of a jay, at this hour all is very still.

There is a state park nearby that encompasses the spot where, in the winter of 1846-47, the ill-fated Donner party of wagons was stranded on its way west by early snows. Out of the 90 members of the party, almost half of the group succumbed to the ordeal of cold and hunger. The saga of the Donner Party is a story in itself. Not only is it a tale of bravery, it is also a testament to the fact that when we make bad choices in life, there somehow always manages to be a consequence.

Adjacent to the visitors' center at the entrance to the park, there stands a monument. Although it is dubbed "the Donner Monument," it is really a monument to all of the families that met the hardships on the trails during the western migration. The larger-than-life figures depicted atop the stone pedestal are that of a man with a young child at his side, and a woman with a baby in her arms. Their determined eyes are forever riveted on the mighty mountains to the west, and it is one of the most powerful tributes to the human spirit that I know. The height of the stone pedestal upon which the sculpture stands is 22 feet, the depth of the snows endured by the Donner Party during that bitter winter.

I stop to stand a few moments at the monument almost every time that I drive by the park, for to me it is not just a monument to the western pioneers, but a monument to all of those who strive to reach for their most cherished dreams.

I have a show to do in Arcata and little time to spare, so I take the nearby westbound freeway entrance to Interstate 80 and begin the climb up the long grade that will take me over the crest of the Sierra.

On the western slope of the mountains, my van passes the exits for Nevada City, Dutch Flat, and Colfax. We cross California State Route 49, the main road through the mother lode and the camps of the California Gold Rush. I once panned for gold along the American River. It took me all day to garner enough of the yellow metal to fit under my thumbnail. Yet, it was a prize, and to this day I still have that meager treasure salted away for my retirement.

Down past Auburn my van and I travel, into the low, hot Central Valley of the state, rich with the pungent aroma of onions, tomatoes, and garlic. As a frequent traveler, I have almost arrived at the point where, if I were to close my eyes, I could identify which of the states I was in by its scent alone. California is certainly a buffet of bouquets. Of course, I could always make a snide comment about the smog and pollution of the cities, or the greasy texture of the air in the Los Angeles basin, but beyond the pollution, there is also the Eucalyptus and the sweet Ponderosa Pine. There are the scents of the citrus trees, the oranges, limes, and lemons; and the earthy aromas of the onions and tomatoes as the trucks haul them to market along the farm roads. There is the grape smell of the wine country, heavy with the bursting richness of its bounty, and always, always the unmistakable freshness of the cool, fog-moist salt air of the northern Pacific coast.

Just above San Francisco, I hug the north shore of San Pablo Bay from Vallejo to Novato and head north past Santa Rosa along Route 101. In a few hours, upon reaching the Pacific coast at Eureka, I will have made my 20th fall traverse of the continent.

In the next six days I have performances in Ojai, San Jose, San Francisco, and Berkeley, but this afternoon my sights are set on the little town of Arcata.

Upon my arrival in town, a room is waiting for me at one of the picturesque hotels on the square. It is nearly 5:00 in the afternoon, so I grab a quick bite to eat and head to the hall that will serve as the performance venue for the evening's concert. It is to be one of those small but enthusiastic audiences that warms the heart and yet humbles the ego. Remember Bill, you are here to play music, not to be a star. It is the music only that is the important element. Over the years, how many times has that philosophy sustained me when I have come to question my own value as a performer?

Consider this response to a question that I have been asked many times. "Do you ever get nervous before you perform?" Why would a performer get nervous before a show? I expect that it is because they are afraid that in some way they will fail in the performance, that they will make a fool of or embarrass themselves on stage. Is it not then the case that they are thinking more of themselves than they are of their art? If one respects what they have to offer as a performer, then how, short of becoming physically incapacitated or dropping dead onstage, can a performer fail? Now and then every performer will have an off night, but these nights pass and should not diminish in the mind of that performer the recognition that there is an opportunity to do a great show the following night. It is when by choice an artist shows up for a show under the influence of some substance (and we have all seen it happen) that the element of respect is gone and the performance frequently fails. Truly, if one respects their art and places that art above themselves, they will not fail. Understanding this, it would seem to follow that there is no reason to be nervous before a show. You simply—as Brian Bowers' performance at the 1980 Winnipeg Folk Festival proved—get out there and "do your thing."

It has been a long day. The concert is over, and as I climb the steep stairs from the lobby of the hotel and open the heavy door to my room, my thoughts fly away from this empty hallway and alight on a far-away home.

CHAPTER 21

Northland

On May 20,1981, I left home for Minneapolis and my tour to Alaska. I would be away from home for six weeks, the longest time to that date that I had spent on the road. Before I left, Karen, Hallie, and I took a long walk in the woods near the house, past the long shed and the enclosure where our neighbor's horses grazed, and returned through the knee-high fields of winter rye. As much as I had traveled by myself around the country, Alaska was still a far piece from home, and this would be the first tour during which I would depend on others to provide for my transportation as well as a place to stay night after night. I was certainly excited about the tour, but I could still feel deep within me a gripping anxiety as to how it would all turn out. My packet of plane tickets and itinerary combined looked like a Sunday edition of the *New York Times*, and when I drove away that day, I wondered if I would ever see my home again.

In Minneapolis, the Coffeehouse Extempore was sold out for the three nights that I was there. On the Sunday afternoon of the weekend, during an interview with one of the local newspapers, I was pleasantly surprised to hear the voice of an old Texas friend coming up the double-wide staircase that led to the second-floor club.

It was Elkin Fowler. He and his wife, Aileen, had been in town the night before doing a gig and had decided to stay around for an extra day and drop in on the Extempore for a visit.

"Staines! Where's Staines?," I could hear Elkin bellowing in his thick southern drawl as he reached the top of the staircase and entered the room. He gave me a big bear hug, and I knew immediately that the night was going to be a grand affair. Knowing that the audience would love them, it would be unthinkable not to have Aileen and Elkin do a guest set to open the show. Before the night was over, we were all up onstage together doing a version of one of my favorite songs, Ian Tyson's "Four Strong Winds."

The end of the performance was only the beginning of the night, however, and after hours at the club Aileen and Elkin, Jerry and Barbara, myself, and a number of the coffeehouse volunteers sat up in the back room drinking beer, telling stories, and playing music. It was a night of laughter and freest fancy. One of the volunteers, perhaps sensing my apprehension about the long tour to Alaska, sent me on my way with a "Godspeed on your trip, Bill Staines." I certainly was not John Glenn heading into orbit on the nose of a rocket; it was only a flight to Alaska, but those words became a source of comfort for me the next morning as Jerry drove me to the airport and I boarded the plane for Seattle and the flight to "the Great North."

* * *

The final approach by the Boeing 737 into Juneau that late afternoon was from the west, banking to the right over a ridge of mountains and into a steep descent across the foggy flats to Runway 8 below. It was 5:00 P.M. Alaska Time. My body, though, was functioning on far-away Eastern Time, which meant that it felt like 10:00 P.M. With little sleep the night before, I was pretty well spent and ready to call it a day. A steady, wind-blown drizzle was falling, and the Gastineau Channel at Juneau, otherwise known as the Inland Passage, looked gray, choppy, and very cold.

After retrieving my guitar, duffle bag, and four boxes of LPs, I scanned the airport lobby, hoping to set my sights on somebody who appeared as if they were looking for me. This was to be, according to my itinerary, John Ingalls, inventor, promoter, and one of the chief characters in the Juneau folk music scene. John promoted concerts all around southeast Alaska and each year was instrumental in the operation of the Juneau Folk Festival.

The passengers on the afternoon flight claimed their belongings, and the small crowd disappeared through the doors of the log cabin terminal into the Alaskan mist. I was alone.

I dialed the telephone number listed on my itinerary, and some six miles away in town John Ingalls picked up the receiver. His voice was low and he spoke slowly, as if he had just been awakened from a deep sleep. Yes, he was expecting me but he couldn't get to the airport that day because his car had broken down. I felt a bit relieved. He suggested that I take the city bus into town from the airport and he would meet me there at the Hotel Baranoff, which was just a few blocks from where he lived.

By the time that the bus from the airport had let me off at the Baranoff, the steady drizzle had turned into a driving rain. John was waiting for me in the recess by the front door of the hotel. He picked up some of my bags and instructed me to follow him to his place. Dressed in a dark woolen shirt, overalls, and high rubber fisherman's boots, he moved quickly through the streets, oblivious to the rain, while I struggled along behind him, toting the guitar and the four boxes of LPs. I would be staying at John's for the night, with a 9:30 flight out the next morning, across Admiralty Island to the native fishing village of Hoonah. It was for the public school system at Hoonah that next evening that I would be doing my first concert in Alaska.

John Ingalls, for his part, was scheduled to promote a concert by me in Juneau on the coming Sunday. The show in Juneau would be my final concert of the tour in the southeast, but for the coming week, between Hoonah and Juneau, I was set up to do concerts in

Sitka, Petersburg, and Haines. In fact, my concert in Haines was to be the first show presented at their new performing arts center.

I walked (or more precisely, tripped) through the door at John's house, cold, tired, and now drenched with the elements of the long day. My soul was crying out for sleep, and so John showed me to my room and suggested that I take a nap. He did wonder, however, if I would be willing to do an appearance on the local folk music show on public radio. The show was broadcast at midnight, but it would be good exposure, and it would help promote the Sunday night concert. I consented, and at 11:15 that night he knocked on my door to get me up for the broadcast. I looked out the window of the room. The town was foggy, but the sky was lit as if it were the middle of the day. I looked at my watch. It indicated that the time was 11:15. Incredulous, and not remembering the radio show, I thought, "I have missed my 9:30 flight to Hoonah !". John sensed my panic and assured me that it was still Monday evening and that we had a radio broadcast to do at midnight. I just didn't realize that it hardly got dark in Juneau in the summer.

It had stopped raining, so John and I walked to the radio station, which was only a block away, and I did the interview, which lasted until about 1:00 in the morning. At the time, there was a rapidly growing and devout audience for "A Prairie Home Companion," which had recently made its way onto the national airwaves. Having made a number of appearances on the show made me somewhat of a celebrity about town. I was told that I was the first musician who had performed on the "Prairie Home Show" to visit Alaska. I played a few more songs on the broadcast, plugged the upcoming Sunday concert, and headed back to John's house, determined to complete my night's sleep without any more interruptions.

The alarm clock next to my head was thankfully vigilant in its duty, and by 8:45 the next morning I was on the city bus headed for the airport, with an arrival time of 9:10. I would have 20 minutes to catch my flight to Hoonah. At 9:15, I presented my tickets to the young woman who was manning the counter for the small airline service that carried passengers and mail to my destination, and she informed me that the flight had actually been scheduled to leave at 9:00 A.M. rather than 9:30. I felt weak. On my first day in Alaska, had I already messed up?

"Perhaps there is still time to catch the plane!" she offered. "They never take off on schedule around here." A glimmer of hope flared inside of me. She sprinted to the door which led to the tarmac and returned, only a moment later, with a smile on her face.

"The pilot is still loading the mail. He didn't realize that he had a passenger this morning. Follow me."

My glimmer of hope burst into a raging "Thank you! Thank you!" as I followed her out onto the airfield where a uniformed young man of about 20 was loading packages into a single-engine Cessna.

"I'm sorry; I didn't realize I had a passenger this morning. I need to unload a few pieces of cargo to make room for you, but we'll be on our way in a few minutes."

I was just glad to have made the flight. There was a lesson to be learned from this experience, I thought as I loaded my belongings into the space behind my seat on the plane. As soon as you arrive at a destination, always check the particulars of your departure. This was a lesson that would last throughout the years, and one that would save me over and over again.

I literally lived at the Juneau airport that first week in Alaska. A couple of the airport agents even had tickets for the upcoming concert in town. I fell into a routine. Since there were no direct commercial flights from Petersburg to Sitka, or from Haines to anywhere except Juneau, I would have to take a flight each afternoon out of Juneau to my daily concert destinations. There, I would get picked up by the people who were putting on the show, rest a bit, do the concert, and then catch the first flight in the morning back to Juneau, where I would sleep for two or three hours before repeating the whole procedure. I felt as if I had been adopted by the airport personnel. They would ask me questions about the concerts I was doing in Alaska and what it was like to play on that "Garrison Keillor show out of St. Paul."

By the time Sunday arrived, my show at the Fiddlehead Restaurant was sold out. There were a number of fine musicians about town, and a group of them played a set as an opening act. I loved playing for these people. I felt a connection with these Alaskans. I had brought my music to them and they had accepted me, an outsider, into their lives.

After my concert, I was invited over to the Red Dog Saloon to hear a late set of music by more of the local talent. Around 1:00 in the morning, a group of about 30 people, fresh off one of the large tour boats that had just docked at the town wharf, piled into the saloon.

"Here come the tourists!" one of the locals bellowed.

"Let's give 'em the song!" another offered from the bar, and the whole place erupted into a melodious ditty about "Cheechakos," those people who are new to Alaska and haven't quite gotten the hang of things yet. It was obviously a musical routine that had been enacted many times before at the arrival of the tour boats, and though I did not know the words, I found myself an eager participant in the jest. I had been in the North only a week and here I was, acting like one of the townies. It seemed as if the same spirit that I had come to know on my first trips to Texas in the early 1970s was carrying me along again, only this time it was into the heart and arms of Alaska.

The next morning, I was on the early plane out of Juneau, bound for Anchorage with a short hop down the Kenai Peninsula to Homer, where I would hook up with Dog and Judy and spend a few days at their cabin. Between Juneau and Anchorage, we had one stop to make at Yakutat, where we would unload some supplies and take on a few more passengers. As we were on our final approach and about to land, the pilot had to initiate a "go around." The concerned looks on the travelers' faces turned to smiles when he reported over the intercom that the maneuver was due to a family of bears that had just ventured out onto the end of the runway. A vehicle had just been dispatched to shoo them away, and we would be on the ground shortly. This place, this Alaska, certainly was a lot different than any other place I had ever been.

Dog and Judy were waiting as the twin-engine Otter that was carrying me touched down at the airstrip in Homer. I was to spend three days with them before catching a plane to Kodiak for a concert there. On the weekend, I would return to Homer for a show at the high school auditorium, and then head off on the rest of my tour to Barrow, Prudhoe Bay, and the far north.

We left the airport and stopped at KBBI, the local public radio station, for a short interview with the daytime host. The station was helping with the promotion for the Saturday night concert in Homer, and an interview on the air would hopefully spur ticket sales during the week. It was the first time that Dog and Judy had ever been involved with a concert promotion, and they wanted to do it right.

Dog's truck bounced down the one main street through the center of Homer, and we headed out East Road about four miles until we came to the parking area at the edge of Yule Kiltcher's homestead. Dog parked the truck, and we hiked into the nearby woods, down a steep, mossy, woodland trail for about a half mile. The trail widened into a clearing and there, beneath the bright blue Alaskan sky, on the side of the fern carpeted hill, stood Dog and Judy's cabin.

It was a two-story octagonal structure of weathered wood and glass, and when I entered I found the large, first-floor room bright, comfortable, and homespun in its décor. Off to one side of the room, and yet obviously occupying an important position in the cabin, was a tall iron coal stove. This heavy metal wonder was not only the fundamental heat source for the space, but also appeared to be the rallying point around which the family would spend the cold Alaska nights. A small cache of coal nuggets the size of softballs filled a nearby wooden bin, and a pile of newspapers and spruce slivers stood by to act as a vanguard in the creation of the warming fire.

Coal was an abundant resource in Homer, for when the winds and tides along Katchemack Bay were in the right configuration, large chunks of the black substance would be ripped away from underwater seams and deposited upon the shore. All that remained for the local inhabitants to do was harvest this unusual bounty with sledgehammers and pickup trucks. Broken into small pieces and left to dry over the summer, this unlikely gift from the deep was a perfect fuel supply for those living off the land.

That afternoon, Dog and I hiked over to Yule Kiltcher's place, where Yule was busy tending to his horses. The craggy Swiss homesteader invited us up to his cabin for tea and some of his famous sourdough bread. Sampling Yule's sourdough was like stepping back in time to the years of the Alaskan gold rush. It was easy to see how this baker's concoction, rich and tangy in its heaviness, became a staple foodstuff with the miners and merchants of the gold fields. Yule prided himself in his baking, and a wedge of his bread the size of your fist, along with a good piece of cheese, would hold you for most of a day.

We left Yule to his work and returned to the octagon, where Judy was busy putting together the evening meal. She was standing at the sink, holding a colander filled with fiddlehead ferns beneath a spigot that was spewing cold, clear water. The spigot was the terminus of a hose that ran up the side of the hill to a small stream. This hose, with a little help from gravity, conveyed water to the cabin.

Salmon was the main course on the menu that night, and as the pungent pink flesh of the fish was separated from the silvery skin and washed down with good wine, I began to feel as if there was perhaps something to be found in this wilderness living, where the land and the sea provided all that was needed to live a complete and simple life.

Inasmuch as the coal stove dominated one wall of the cabin, a second wall area was set aside for one of the true treasures of the household. This was an old upright piano, and how it came to be brought to the cabin through the woods and along the trails will always be a mystery to me. Piled high upon the top of the piano was the sheet music for a number of classical compositions, and resting on the narrow shelf over the black and yellowed ivory keys were four or five books of music ranging from "heart songs" to "popular favorites." Among these selections, I was amused to find a copy of one of my own songbooks, *If I Were a Word, Then I'd Be a Song,* which I had been working on in March of 1980 and had been released by that fall.

I was beginning to discover a depth and character to this Breslaw/Tharinger clan that I had not realized existed until I had come to spend time with them in Alaska. Dog, for instance, at one time had been just a few steps short of earning a doctorate in literature and was an accomplished classical pianist. This musical ability was put to good use when, later that evening, after all the dishes were washed and put away and the rest of the chores were completed, we sat around the piano and from those books sang some of those old heart songs and popular favorites.

It was truly a heartening experience to find that here within a cabin on a hill in the wilderness, a family could still gather together and entertain themselves in a timeless way, by telling stories, reading poetry, and singing along with music played so well on an old upright piano.

In Alaska, there seems to be no end to the characters you meet who piece together the mosaic of their lives in a day-by-day, tile-by-tile fashion, not really knowing what the final design will be, until in one moment somewhere down the line, it all seems to make perfect sense. "I was who I was," they say, "and I came to be who I am. I have lived lightly upon this place, and I know that when I leave this good earth, if there be but one person who has come to know my heart and thinks well of me, I shall be content."

The next day Dog introduced me to Findley Abbott, local jack-of-all-trades, inventor, and tinkerer who had a knack for fashioning useful objects out of junk that he came by around the town. He lived in a small shack on a thin arm of land that jutted out into Katchemack Bay that was known as the Homer Spit. It could be said that no discarded piece of machinery or abandoned bicycle was safe from Findley. He was a quiet and pleasant man, with eyes that seemed to be forever scanning the horizon for any materials with which he could work his magic.

If Findley was in his own way an artist, then his mother, Alice Abbott, was also inclined. Alice lived in Anchorage and built architectural miniatures. With the use of toothpicks, paste, and heavy paper, as well as a few techniques pioneered by Findley, she could and had transformed the two-dimensional blueprints for many of the buildings in the Anchorage area into the tiny landscapes that brought the projects into first visual life.

In the late 1940s, the Abbott family had built a homestead on Yukon Island, a small wooded island southwest of Homer toward the mouth of Katchemack Bay. Findley had invited me, Dog, Judy, and others of his friends and members of his clan over to the family cabin on the island to spend a night while I was visiting in the area. The next day, with music still ringing in my ears from the previous night spent at Dog and Judy's, we all boarded a small boat owned by Billy Dorsey, a local artist, and motored down the bay through Eldred Passage, and beyond to Yukon Island.

It was a blustery, rainy day, and the cold salt spray, driven over the gunwales of the boat, soaked us through to the skin. A flock of puffins glided overhead, while flying fish could be seen breaking the surface of the bay, their flashing silver bodies like bright sparks in the gray mist. A pilot whale surfaced on our port side, followed us for a while, and then swam off toward the south shore of the bay that followed the base of the Kenai Mountains. Having grown up in New England, I was used to seeing a great variety of shorebirds and sea life, but I was quite unprepared for the intensity and the vibrancy of these rolling waters with their abundance of sea creatures and airborne oddities.

We arrived at Yukon Island by mid-afternoon, making the boat fast with a nylon line about 20 feet from the shore. We waded in and headed for the cabin, hauling our sleeping bags and packs of food along the narrow beach. As we approached the cabin, I noticed an unusual-looking object resting on the sand halfway between the cabin and the water. It looked like an old cattle feed tank, but it had been fitted with a maze of metal piping and plastic tubing. Adjacent to the large galvanized tank was a small enclosed area that sheltered what looked like a propane tank and an old lawnmower engine. I made a note to ask Findley about this contraption and what its purpose might be, but at the moment he was busy trying to get a fire going in the wood stove that occupied a space in the center of the cabin.

The wind had picked up a bit and the waters of the bay had become even choppier, so Billy Dorsey and I went to double the line that held the boat to its anchorage. By the time we had returned, Findley had the fires of hell roaring in the old wood stove, which had by now taken on a definite red glow, and the air in the single large room was heavy with the water vapor being drawn off soggy clothing and wet people.

Melissa, Findley's cousin, brewed up a giant pot of coffee and passed out great portions of her reputedly famous coffee cake. The comfort level in the warm room was coming up for us all, and by now the tumultuous Alaskan weather that was beating at the walls of the cabin from all sides seemed very far away.

Later in the afternoon we were visited by a brief respite from the wind and the rain, and although the sun never shone clearly, the sky brightened to a glaring white. Dog, Judy, Findley, and I decided to take advantage of the moment and went to explore an ancient native burial site on the far side of the island. Above us, I caught a glimpse of a large coal-black raven as it swooped down between the tall, dark spruces, calling and calling again, perhaps to the spirits of this ancient place, or perhaps even to me as my own spirit soared above Yukon Island.

We made music together that night and once again feasted on the bounty of the northern seas, the Alaskan salmon. When the music finally came to an end, sleeping spaces were assigned. As the guest of honor (although I really felt like family), I was given a berth in what the Abbotts called "the Tea House."

Located at the far end of the beach, the Tea House was a cabin-like structure, perhaps 12 feet square, of Oriental design that was built atop a giant rock that rose 25 feet out of the waters of Katchemack Bay. Being that this rock was about 20 feet from the shore and directly opposite a bluff of 25 feet in height, an arched wooden bridge had been constructed between the bluff and the rock, which allowed access to the building. Beneath this tiny bridge swirled the gray waters of the bay. The Tea House was to be my sanctuary for the night.

The interior of my dwelling was beautifully simple, with large windows that took in the vast panorama of the Kenai Range and the Eldred Passage. The walls were adorned with rice-paper drawings in colored inks and charcoals, and located along one of these walls stood my sleeping accommodation, a simple yet comfortable cot. Placed at the foot of the cot and meant to serve as the only chair in the dwelling was a large stuffed cushion. The only other occupant of the room was a tiny wood stove set into one of the corners that now, because of an earlier effort by Findley, was emitting a warmth that made the tiny Tea House just perfectly comfortable. It would take but a little more wood to maintain the stove until morning, and that wood was stacked neatly at the side of the stove.

I drifted off to sleep that night once again thinking of time and design. The paths laid out for me in my life had brought me here to this simple space, where I was lying alone in a small and beautiful shelter atop a rock in the middle of Katchemack Bay in Alaska, listening to the timeless poundings of the waters below me, connected to land by only a small wooden bridge, and thinking to myself, how very fortunate you are, Bill, how very fortunate you are.

The lone figure on the beach stood behind an easel, working his paintbrushes quickly and methodically, staring across the bay and singing to himself. It was Billy Dorsey, and as I approached him on this gray but calm morning, he offered me a "good day" and asked me how my night had been in the Tea House.

He was experimenting with a new type of paint that morning and was busy interpreting the scene before him onto his canvas. It was a view of the Kenai Mountain Range as seen by looking across the Eldred Passage from the beach on Yukon Island. In the near distance, one of the small islands, sporting its green, grassy cap, could be seen standing sentry beneath the gray and uncertain skies. I asked Billy if he would like some coffee from the cabin, but he said that he was just about finished with his work and would be in as soon as he packed up his paints.

As I approached the front door of the cabin, I was nearly trampled by a four-person contingent led by Findley, almost in marching formation, and all headed to the shore to try out his new Jacuzzi. So that's what that thing was on the beach! Findley's creation had turned out to be none other than a saltwater Jacuzzi. I had to see how this thing worked, so I did an about face and followed the squad to the ominous contraption a few yards away.

The design was simple enough. Using an old gasoline-powered reversible pump, seawater was drawn up through a plastic pipe which was equipped with a one-way valve and deposited in the large galvanized feed tank. Once inside the tank, the water was warmed from below by a propane heater that Findley had recovered from a local fishing boat. When the tank was full, the pump was then reconnected to pipes leading to the inside of the tank. The pump, when started, would cause the water to move in a circular motion, completing the Jacuzzi effect. As the water was being warmed, a large sheet of foam insulation cut to the dimensions of the tank was placed over the whole apparatus to hold in the heat.

The concept seemed very logical, if only half proven, for by the time we arrived and were standing around in skeptical wonder, the tank had already been filled and was now being heated to a setting of just under parboil. All that remained was to choose a candidate to test the supposedly relaxing internal flow of the water. I was immediately selected as the first volunteer, so I entered the steaming waters, ready for the comforting and revitalizing effects of the Jacuzzi.

At first the effect was gained, but as the inertia of the circulating water increased, I began to feel more like a bug caught in a giant drain. I could not hold my own against the flow of the water and valiantly grasped at the rim of the tank, hoping to arrest the circular motion which now threatened to launch me over the side of Findley's Jacuzzi and halfway across the bay. Seeing my predicament, Findley proceeded to slow the pump motor, and finally the water settled back down to subsonic speed, which allowed the other folks, who were now laughing at the top of their lungs, to have a turn at the aquatic wonder. Findley allowed that he might have to make a few adjustments to the design, but that all in all he was happy with the results.

By that afternoon, it was time to leave Yukon Island and the Abbotts. The sun was beginning to peek through the thinning clouds as we clambered aboard the boat, raised the anchor, and motored back up the bay toward Homer. We passed the rock upon which was perched the Tea House, and in the distance I could see Elephant Rock, so named because the formation looked like an elephant standing on the waters of the bay. The puffins and the gulls soared over us once again, and a group of porpoises playfully leapt from the waters directly in front of us.

In a little over an hour, we were back at the spit in Homer, tying up the boat at one of the docks. As we all began to go our separate ways, Billy Dorsey gave me a small cardboard tube. Rolled within the tube I found the painting that he had been working on that morning. He told me to keep the painting as a memento of the island. When I returned home from Alaska, many of the images from the Yukon Island adventure would find their way into a song that I entitled, "Northland," and some 15 years later Billy Dorsey's painting would become the front cover art for my recording of *The Alaska Suite*.

> *"There's a raven far above me, and I've heard his call before,*
> *From the ghosts of ancient people that walked along the shore,*
> *From the herring gull and the puffin, and the porpoise in the sea,*
> *They were calling me to listen, and I was learning to be free . . . ."*

I did a show in Kodiak and then flew back to Homer for a concert, spending a few more nights with Dog and Judy. With my time in Homer at an end, the beginning of the following week I boarded an Arco Oil Company plane for Prudhoe Bay and a two-night stint in the theatre at what was known as the "Arco Hilton."

Although operated very much like a hotel, the "Arco Hilton" was really the sleeping quarters for the Arco oil workers at the Prudhoe Bay facility. In 1981, it resembled what looked to me like an artist's rendering of a moon base, complete with a 24-hour cafeteria and a theatre where musicians and other entertainers were flown in for the crews. It was a special moment when my guide at the base took a picture of me standing at mile zero of the Alaska Pipeline.

I flew to Barrow, the northernmost point on mainland North America, where I was booked by the city to do a concert at one of the local schools. While I was in Barrow, I could not miss the opportunity to visit the location of the plane crash that took the lives of Will Rogers and his pilot, Wiley Post, on August 15, 1935. I convinced the young Eskimo woman who was the city entertainment director that it was important to me to see this place, so she loaded me onto the back of her motorized, balloon-tired three-wheeler, and off we drove to the site. A small marker had been placed by the lagoon at the actual site of the crash, but being that it was in such a remote area, a larger memorial was erected within the city of Barrow itself. It was here, though, at this very small patch of earth by a lagoon located at the farthest reaches of North America where once again I found that old connection to those who are truly the threads in the fabric of our history.

I was booked for one more weekend on that first tour to Alaska. It was at a place in Fairbanks that had opened and closed so many times that its most recent and final name was to be "Chapter 11." I played three or four sets each night and finished at 3:00 in the morning, when I would venture out into the bright sunlight of the northern late spring and back to my room for a few hours of sleep.

The time had arrived to leave this place that would eventually become such a big part of my life. In Fairbanks the following day, I boarded my plane back to Seattle and Minnesota. As we passed over Mount McKinley in Denali National Park, my mind was inundated with thoughts and images of this wild and wonderful part of the world.

I questioned, being that it is so big and beautiful, whether anyone could ever feel as if they are truly close to Alaska, or whether they could ever come to understand its nuances. Certainly Alaska is a place that demands respect from all of those who come to be held within her arms, whether they be a visitor, a cheechako, or a lifelong resident. She can, in one moment, bless you with the sight of a grizzly bear mother and her cubs frolicking amidst the high country wildflowers, and in the next breath sweep you away forever into the current of a wild river. It is Alaska that ultimately holds the cards, and it is she who has the final word in your relationship with her.

I felt old in a sense, because everyone that I met on that first trip seemed young—not necessarily in years, but in actions. Nobody that I met was spinning their wheels. Everyone was in motion. Perhaps that is because Alaska is no place to be unhappy. The weather is too hostile, the nights are too long, and there is just too much to do in order to survive. Obviously, not everyone is happy there, but it seems that in Alaska one is given three options.

The first option is to anesthetize yourself with alcohol, which will eventually kill you, or leave your troubles behind and do yourself in, making short work of the whole thing.

The second option is to leave Alaska and settle someplace amongst all of the others who feel as lost as you. Perhaps as time passes you will find your passion again, but in a common world it is very easy to become old in your heart while you are still young in years.

The third option, and the one which is perhaps the hardest, is to move on in Alaska, rise up out of the muck and mire of what is commonplace, and live out your dreams in a place that is so beautiful and so full of profound opportunity.

* * *

Jerry Rau met me at the airport in Minneapolis and I spent two nights in town, reliving my adventures for anyone who would listen. When it became time to leave and drive the 1,500 miles back to New Hampshire, I began to realize that this road that I had just traveled had taken me very far, and that it might just take all that I had within me to find my way back home again.

CHAPTER 22

The Fall Tour, Day Ten

It is unusual for me to have a Friday night off on a long tour. Given that the reason for being on tour in the first place is to play music, I try to keep as busy as possible when I am gone from home. I'll take this Friday for myself, however, because I am doing 3 shows in the next 2 days, and 9 shows in the next 11 days. This one-night break in the tour also gives me the opportunity to stop along the coast and revisit Mendocino. The last time I had been to the little seacoast town was back in 1984, when I traveled through from San Francisco to do a concert at Humboldt State College in Eureka. I am looking forward to seeing the village again.

The morning coastal fog lies heavily across the road as I head south on Route 101 out of Arcata. It is one of those gray California mornings that brighten around 10:30 A.M. and admit what seems like the inexhaustible supply of sunlight that blesses the state. I am thinking that if I can make Mendocino by noon, I will be able to take advantage of a whole day at one of the hotels in the area, and this might offer me the opportunity to do some songwriting.

It has been a while since I have written a song, and I suppose that down deep inside of me I have begun to have doubts as to how my creativity seems to be holding up. I ask myself at times, "Is that all there is at my wellspring? Have my creative reserves run dry?". There is an intense fear that takes hold. "Will I ever write another song? Do I have writer's block?" Contemplating this dilemma, I exit from Route101 at Leggett and join Route 1, which takes me west across the short distance to the coast and down through Westport and Fort Bragg to Mendocino.

"What is writer's block anyway?" I ponder as I reach the coast where Route 1 turns to the south.

It seems to me that there are two reasons for which a writer arrives at a point when their craft becomes very difficult, if not impossible. The first is simply that they have nothing to say, and the second is that they have something to say, but that the words emanating from deep within for some reason just do not want to materialize. It is the second of these scenarios that, to me, is the essence of what amounts to writer's block.

"Do I really have this 'writer's block'," I question as I pass through Fort Bragg on this Friday morning and gaze out at the blue Pacific, "or just nothing to say at this particular point in time?"

There are those writers who write a hundred songs a year and keep ten of those songs. There are those who write ten songs a year and keep them all. It is of this second school that I have always felt that I belong. I want to write great songs—not in a good, better, best, sense—but songs about great things, things that matter. I will write songs about living and dying, and songs about work; I will write songs about home, family, and love. These are amongst the great things in this world. It is not often that I have something to say that I feel is profound enough to be conveyed to people by way of a song, but I do know that it is those songs that I have written, hopefully because they have some sort of insight into life, that will survive as my slightest legacy to the immense realm that is music.

Will a writer lose his craft if he doesn't write each day?

I am reminded of a story of a painter who did little else but paint all day long. He had created hundreds of works. A friend of the artist asked him why he spent so much time at his easels. The painter's response was that he was truly afraid that if he put his brushes aside, even for a short time, he would never pick them up again.

I think that, as a song craftsman, I will always be in search of material, but as a creative person, I will wait until those materials offer within them something of substance.

It is late morning, and under the now bright sun I take the exit off of Route 1 for Mendocino. It is a short loop road into town and it leaves most of the hotels and motels behind at the main highway. I descend a small hill to the main street of the town, take a right turn, and search for a place to park the van along the oceanfront row of shops. A parking space materializes across from the Mendocino Hotel, the only hotel on the street, and I immediately take advantage of my good luck. The hotel is a yellow, box-like building, and its three-story structure dominates the rest of the street-side shops.

I have always been intrigued by the businesses that manifest themselves in small seacoast villages. Nowadays there is, of course, the mandatory collection of expensive art galleries. These galleries present supposedly fine works in oils and other media, which usually portray seascapes of various forms, from those that are bright and almost surrealistic to those that are genuinely wondrous to gaze upon.

There is the small seaside restaurant, with its fully complemented wine list, and a host of bed and breakfast homes which have been restored by people with the financial resources, people who have moved in from other parts of the country.

What I enjoy the most is discovering and exploring the occasional emporium that I run across in these towns. The shop is usually run by some curious old local character who has lived his or her life beside these same waters, and will probably come to die amidst the cigars, buoys, anchors, old records, and dusty antiques that line the shelves of the shop. Adorned in tank top jersey, khaki shorts, and well-worn old leather sandals, the owner usually radiates the fact that he couldn't care less whether a customer enters the shop or not.

I go in search of two such shops that I discovered on that first trip into Mendocino some 15 years earlier. One, a small corner store that sold everything from old decks of playing cards to 78 rpm records, and the second an antique store, complete with a wine bar at the rear of the shop. One could buy a glass of a blush zinfandel and a bowl of cheese goldfish for not much money and spend the afternoon sitting on the front patio deck of the place in the warm, comfortable sun, staring across a cliff-top field of high grass and wildflowers to the tumbling surf assaulting the beach below.

Inasmuch as these waves are timeless in their endeavors, and one hopes to hold onto a moment in that time, the years still pass above our heads, as out of reach as the odd-numbered groups of pelicans that I behold winging their way south along the sweep of the coast until they vanish into the subtle mists. Upon their backs, they carry my memories and the essences of the two shops that are no longer here.

I book a room at the Mendocino Hotel, a top-floor room with a balcony that faces west, and spend the afternoon writing in my journal. I pick up my guitar and strum a few chords, but the time just does not seem right for a new song. Perhaps it is another abandonment of responsibility, or perhaps it is simply a day that is just too beautiful for anything but memories.

In the early evening, I take my meal while sitting at the bar at the hotel. The menu is the same as that of the restaurant on the premises, and I figure that the staff at the restaurant could use the extra place at a table set for two. With the exception of a few words to a gas station attendant and the hotel counter clerk, I have not spoken to anyone for the entire day, so I strike up a conversation with the bartender, a young woman who seems to know everyone who walks through the door. The attractive young blonde in her 20s has just returned to California from Colorado, where she had fallen in and out of love, and she is now putting her life back together and reevaluating her future. We talk about music and dreams until there doesn't seem as if there is much more to say to each other, so I leave her with a couple of my CDs and make my way out of the swinging front door of the hotel and onto the street, which now seems very empty.

Returning to my van, I retrieve a cigar from the glove compartment, light it up with a flashing match, and walk to the far end of the street to catch the last pink remembrance of the sun before the long Pacific horizon becomes nothing more than a black void. It is for the bright burning lights of the hotel to remain in defiance of the passing hours.

Back at the high east end of the street, the last of the hotel dinner patrons, a group of six, exits the hotel in a boisterous clamor. Once they depart in two separate vehicles, the street becomes quiet again, with the surf crashing below at the base of the cliffs the only sound in the now dark California night. Crushing out my cigar, I quietly walk back along the length of the street towards the hotel, passing a couple linked arm in arm and whispering to each other as they gaze into the dim light of one of the galleries. They move as ghosts past the windows and are gone. The street is silent and empty. A sense of finality overtakes me. There is nothing more to do this day, and yet I feel as if I should hold onto the time, grasp it tightly, and never let it go, for once gone, the hour shall never come again.

I have been provided with a small half-bottle of red wine in my room. I uncork it and carry it, along with one of the two clear plastic wine goblets, to the balcony to view the street from aloft, this time with a higher perspective. It is late, and now there is a cool night breeze blowing from offshore. I am aware of the dark night, and I am aware of the weariness that is now upon me like a warm blanket. I surrender to the wine. I surrender to the warmth, and last of all, I surrender to the future.

CHAPTER 23

Freest Fancy

I was in love with Alaska. I was in love with the road. I was in love with the attention being showered upon me by my audiences, and I was still miles away from home when I pulled into my driveway that last week in June of 1981. Karen seemed distant, and my own emotions were in an upheaval. My marriage and home were in real danger. I called Jerry and Barbara to talk about my feelings, but they were also going through tough times and had no real answers for me.

In July, Karen decided to take two weeks to visit with her folks in Virginia. I traveled to Saratoga Springs to perform at Lena's, visit with Logan English, and try to get my heart back in working order. I felt as if I were on fire and was being consumed along all fronts, with no place to go.

Logan allowed that in all matters of the heart, he referred to Shakespeare's Sonnet Number 116.

"Let me not to the marriage of true minds
Admit impediments. Love is not love
Which alters when it alteration finds,
Or bends with the remover to remove:
Oh no; it is an ever fixed mark
That looks on tempests, and is never shaken;
It is the star to every wandering bark,
Whose worth's unknown, although his height be taken . . ."

To Logan, Sonnet 116 defined all that is love, and he recited it as we sat at the bar of The Parting Glass Pub that weekend, drinking "Irish Flags" after one of my shows at Lena's.

The Parting Glass was opened as an Irish pub in 1981 by Bob Cohan and Joan Desadora in a building on Lake Street that was formally occupied by Rocco's Italian Restaurant. Logan had been spending a good deal of time in the place, reading and doing the *New York Times* crossword puzzle while he contemplated new verses for his poetry or new scenes for his plays. I think that in many ways he had found a family in Bob and Joan, and a place to ease whatever loneliness came into his life. Logan raved to me about the pub, and when I came to visit that July, we took to The Parting Glass after my shows for the late night company of many of the musical and late-night characters from around the town.

". . . Love's not Time's fool, though rosy lips and cheeks
Within his bending sickle's compass come;
Love alters not with his brief hours and weeks,
But bears it out even to the edge of doom.
If this be in error, and upon me prov'd,
I never writ, nor no man ever lov'd."

"*. . . That looks on tempests and is never shaken . . . .*" That line from Shakespeare reached deep into me and moved my foundering feelings off dead center. I did not want my marriage to end. What would that bring? A life on the road? The road is not and could never be a home to me. I knew that I needed foundation in my life, and that foundation was not to be gained by a shiftless existence.

When Karen returned from Virginia, we decided to make a go of our marriage and began to talk about the future. We needed a home of our own. By summer's end, we had purchased a small piece of land half a mile from where we were living. With the arrival of the fall that year, and with plans to build a new home, we were fragilely on our way into the next stage of our lives.

* * *

After a September of doing concerts in upstate New York, I found myself back on the road for the 1981 fall tour. Until now, I had spent a lot of time traveling by myself, so for this West Coast swing I decided that it would be fun to have some company.

I called Jerry Rau to see if he might be interested in splitting some of my gigs, or doing an opening set at others, and he jumped at the chance to get out of Minneapolis for a few weeks and get back out on the road again. I had not traveled with anyone since the California trip with Walter Spinks and Bill Cade, but I figured that I could easily survive with Jerry as a traveling partner.

Before leaving home on October 5th, I took a walk to our land with Karen and our dog, Hallie. It was another of those beautiful, crisp New England fall days, and we shared some cheese, crackers, and apple cider together on a blanket set out on the tall fragrant grass. I knew that the road would always be a large part of my life, if for no other reason than the fact that it was from the road that I was making my living. Nothing could change that. Music was still all that I knew. There was, though, a change that had taken place within me. Now I felt as if I had set down real roots in the world. A sense of family and place had grown up inside of me, and an appearance by my rainbow on the day that I left for the tour was sign enough for me that my life was once again on track.

As I headed out along the pine-tree-lined road that had seen me leave home so many times before, I slipped a cassette into the tape player. The music was by a group called Banish Misfortune, and I had brought the tape back with me from my trip to Alaska. The title song was "Freest Fancy."

The cover art was a drawing of three musicians sitting in a colorful flowered field, playing music together. Over the musician's heads, appearing in a faint cloud formation, one could make out the figures of two dancers laughing and swirling in a wild abandon. It was the freest of fancy, moving but for a moment amongst the clouds, clouds that would soon change and evolve yet again into a different, but always beautiful and grand, design.

That fall, Jerry and I traveled west in my little blue car. Behind the driver's seat, on the rear side window, we placed a hand-lettered sign which read:

The Staines-Rau
Fall Tour
1981

If the stars could have their flags and banners, then certainly so could we have ours. The sign wasn't much to look at, but people did stare as they left us behind out on the long, interminable highways.

We crossed gray and rainy Nebraska, following the Platte River with its willows rich in the golden hues of fall. Roll on, big blue river!

We listened to a recording of Stan Rogers singing "Northwest Passage," and it struck me that only two months earlier I had been to Prudhoe Bay, Alaska, and stood with both of my feet in the Beaufort Sea.

We drove through Kansas and over the high plains to Denver.

We headed southwest to Cedar City, Utah, where we drank a little too much in a bar and had to spend the night in woeful recovery.

We arrived in San Diego and performed for the local folk song society. Afterwards, Jerry told me stories from when he was in boot camp after joining the Marines. He pointed out some of the familiar southern California hills and told me of how he had been made to run up, down, and over some of those hills, day or night, with heavy packs and little rest, all to keep America strong. Jerry loved the Marines. I could tell it just by the timbre in his voice when he told me these stories, and I could tell it by the intensity of the light in his eyes as he gazed across the dry sandy ridges to a distant mirage. It must have seemed like only yesterday to him when he was a soldier, and yet still so far away in the living scheme of things.

We returned to Ojai, where we had first met a little over six years before, and played a concert for Tom and Becky Lowe, who ran a music series in town. We celebrated later that evening in one of the local saloons and once again spent the night in woeful recovery.

We stopped in Tarzana, just north of Los Angeles, where we were booked for a house concert at the home of Clark and Elaine Weissman, founders of the California Traditional Music Society, and where we met Howard and Roz Larman, the legendary folk music radio hosts. The Larman's radio show on Pacifica Radio had lasted for many years, and the couple knew or had interviewed just about everyone in the world of folk music.

We stopped to visit with our old musician friends Jim Ringer and Mary McCaslin in San Bernadino, and after we had spent the night with Jim and Mary, we headed north to the Bay Area, with shows in San Francisco, Palo Alto, and Davis.

In San Francisco, Dabris and Marty once again played the roll of innkeepers to the restless of the road, and when our time by the Bay was over, we headed back across the great West, scheduled to do a concert in Denver for Swallow Hill.

The Swallow Hill Association was currently presenting their concerts at a restaurant in Denver called the Sanctuary, an old decommissioned church with an atmosphere that was something akin to that of the Spanish Inquisition. The concerts were held in the large sanctuary hall at the rear main part of the building, while the food was served in every other conceivable space by waiters and waitresses that resembled the Ghost of Christmas Future out of Dickens' *A Christmas Carol.* Shrouded in cloaks and hoods, they made their silent way amongst the tables with the demeanor of dark apparitions.

If the staff was a little bizarre, the audience for the concerts proved to be one of the warmest and friendliest of the tour. Jerry and I each did individual sets, and then we finished the evening together with a version of "Pack Up Your Sorrows." I certainly had traveled a good number of miles in the 15 years or so since the night that I watched Richard Fariña play the song at the Barn Coffeehouse with the lyrics written on the knees of his blue jeans.

We traveled back across Nebraska, with a stop in Lincoln to do a house concert for Paul and Dixie Moss, and finally returned to Minneapolis in time for Halloween and to attend a concert, sponsored by the Coffeehouse Extempore, by Gordon Bok, Ed Trickett, and Ann Mayo Muir.

I left Minneapolis the next day, looking forward to being at home again, but also knowing that my life was rich with the friendship of so many people and the ever-present music that so filled my heart.

The third fall tour was over, but the rest of 1981 was still a mesmerizing series of weekend or week-long trips to Connecticut, New York, Montreal, and Houston.

Toward the end of the year, I was invited to perform at a folk festival at Wilson College, Karen's alma mater, so both of us traveled to Chambersburg for the event, visiting some of our old haunts while we were in town. While sitting in a side room waiting to perform at one of the evening concerts in the school auditorium, I casually picked up an old student yearbook and thumbed my way through some of the yellowed pages. There was a short entry adjacent to one of the photographs in the book, inscribed to the owner by the smiling young woman in the picture.

> *"God gave us all memories so that*
> *we would have roses in December."*

It was one of those lines from which songs are born, and some weeks later, in the dead of winter, I penned the song, "Flowers in the Snow."

It was a period in my life when I was doing a good bit of songwriting. The songs were the fruits of the miles and emotions that were constantly unfolding in front of me along the path of my existence. I was writing songs about Alaska ("Northland") and songs about riding horses in Texas ("Just for Lov*e*"). I was writing about home ("Where I Live"), and I was writing songs about life and the faith that we sometimes need to face that life, even when it means letting go and trusting that somehow things will all work out for the best ("The Quiet Faith of Man").

Into the early months of 1982, I kept up a good writing pace, while at the same time Karen and I began putting together tangible plans for building a house.

In March, I was back on the road, performing all over Michigan, Illinois, Wisconsin, and Minnesota. I did a spot on the *Prairie Home Companion Show,* and once again appeared at the Coffeehouse Extempore in Minneapolis with Aileen and Elkin Thomas doing an opening set.

Inasmuch as I was rich in friends and music, there were still times when I felt very much alone on the road, with nothing more than some sort of undefined inner strength that kept me going. Often late at night, after one or two drinks at a hotel bar, I would write in my journal and try to understand just who I was in this world and what I was looking for in my life. On March 16, 1982, I wrote:

> *"I am alone, looking for the beauty in music,*
> *looking for light in shadows,*
> *looking for dreams on the earth and in the sky,*
> *And looking for peace, wherever I may find it.*
> *Play on, actors and poets!!*
> *Recite your lines and inform the world of the strength of the heart."*

Once again at home, as the days of late March slipped away one by one, I realized that my life had become busier than ever.

With plans for the new house progressing steadily, I was also beginning to think about a new record. I had just written "Eyes to Eyes," and with that song I now had enough material to go back into the studio. In early April, I called Mason to talk about the album and to see if he would like the role as producer on the project.

It was also a busy time for Mason. He had been working with John Sayles, who had critical if not popular success with *The Return of the Secaucus Seven* and had followed that with *Lianna* and *The Brother from Another Planet.* Mason had put together the music for *Lianna* and was now working on the new film, but he agreed that we should do my project together.

Mason suggested that we use the talented Glenn Berger (who had worked on the film *All That Jazz* and had recorded with Paul Simon, as well as many of the other top names in music) to serve as engineer and to help with the production. Along with Kenny White, a true wizard on the keyboards, we gathered together many of the musicians who had worked on my previous albums and in May of 1982 went back into Blue Jay Recording Studios in Carlisle, Massachusetts, to record *Sandstone Cathedrals.*

It was a wonderful experience. The musicians played to the heart of the music, and the energy that every one of them brought to the sessions came shining through as each of the final mixes was put to bed. Not only was I happy with the music, but *Sandstone Cathedrals* also came in on time and under budget. It had taken two weeks to do the recording, and by the end of May I held the completed master tapes in my hands, ready to be shopped to any label that would take them. This time, however, I wasn't so sure that I wanted to shop the project around. I loved the album, and I had put up my own money to get it recorded. After some thought, there seemed to me little question that I should simply release it on my own Mineral River label and thereby be in control of its destiny.

With one of Karen's photographs of the Chisos Mountain Basin at Big Bend National Park taken during our 1975 western trip as the front cover art, and an original title poem inspired by the Big

Bend area on the back of the album, *Sandstone Cathedrals* was released at the end of the summer of 1982, in time for my annual fall tour.

On June 28th, we broke ground for our house. That day, Karen and I watched as the roots that we had put down together began to rise out of the earth.

CHAPTER 24

The Fall Tour, Day Eleven

Juggling the morning *San Francisco Chronicle* and a tray with a large cup of dark coffee, a small cup of orange juice, and a raspberry and cheese Danish, I unlock my top floor room at the Mendocino Hotel and head for the glass door leading to the balcony. The sun is just now rising above the trees and ridges on the east side of the building, but the white wrought-iron chairs and table in front of me are completely enveloped in the cool shade. It is a quiet and golden October day. The early fog that usually blankets the coast in the morning seems to have forgotten to appear this Saturday, and the vast china-blue Pacific Ocean is at peace with both of its neighbors, the land and the sky.

Placing the newspaper and the tray on the dewy tabletop, I collect the wine goblet and the empty bottle from the previous night and return them to the room to be discarded.

I am drawn to a bright flash of silver about 50 yards from the shore, and I watch as the dark head of a seal emerges from the water, carrying with it a large fish. The shimmering mass of the fish's body dances back and forth as it catches the bright sunlight.

A host of gulls circles and dive bombs the seal, hoping to pull off a heist, but the seal is too quick and dives for the bottom, hauling with it the tender treasure. This development leaves the gulls bobbing about on the surface and crying out in great disappointment. Some minutes later, the seal resurfaces and the gulls resume the attack, but nothing is left of the fish. They soon depart, leaving the satisfied seal to bark once and then continue along its jovial way.

I finish my Danish, scanning the skies above for the marauding gulls (although they seem uninterested in my meager fare), and discard the newspaper, with its usual olio of politics, mayhem, and murder.

In response to a question about why the news that is reported in the media always seems to be so bad, a friend of mine, one of the news anchors on a major radio station in Boston, once commented that news by definition is the reportage of things that are not supposed to happen.

For example, a bank is not supposed to be robbed, therefore a bank robbery is news. A visitor at the zoo is not supposed to be mauled by a tiger, therefore a mauling at the zoo is news. People acting in a kind and appropriate manner, completing the small, menial tasks that keep the world running is the way that things should be, and therefore it is not news.

There is, of course, the person who does the right thing and returns a purse containing $10,000 to its rightful owner. This becomes a "good news" story. Why? Perhaps, sadly, because nowadays returning a large sum of money is perceived as something that is not supposed to happen.

It all seems to make sense to me, so just before I toss the paper, I check the sports section to see if the New England Patriots managed to win the previous week's game. That would be news!

With the morning and Mendocino behind me, I leave coastal Route 1 at Albion and head up the Navarro River along California Route 128. Passing through the redwoods near Yorkville, I continue east to Cloverdale and the junction with Route 101, where I turn south to Santa Rosa, San Francisco, and finally San Jose. It is in

San Jose that I am scheduled to do an evening show for the Fiddling Cricket Folk Music Concert Series.

I leave Marin County and cross the Golden Gate Bridge, orange and immense with its 746-foot towers reaching for the heavens. Quickly now, so many memories, so many years on the road, so alone. Now through the Eisenhower Tunnel and past the Presidio, I follow Route 1 to 19th Avenue, and then 19th until it empties into Interstate 280 south for a straight shot down the peninsula to San Jose.

Off to my left, through the haze of South San Francisco, I can see jets as they lift off the runways at the San Francisco International Airport. The still, shallow waters of the Bay serve as the backdrop for their departures.

I am 52 years old. I am still young. I am one of Kerouac's *Dharma Bums* on this perpetual journey along the roads of America. I am traveling to where the music is waiting for me. I am rich with Steinbeck in my veins, a cohort to his Doc and the colorful, calamitous inhabitants of *Tortilla Flat*. They are my friends. I know them as my brothers and my sisters, and they are living within me, simple in their existence and yet profound to my heart. They are a part of the everlasting soul of California, and they are with me now as I journey through the hills and valleys of this time and place.

On the side of a hill adjacent to the interstate, a large statue of Father Junipero Serra levels his finger at me as if he is warning or perhaps reminding me to slow down as I travel through this world. After all, it took him most of a lifetime to establish his nine missions along El Camino Real, the aorta of old California, and it is not how fast or how much we create in our lives that is important, but the quality, goodness, and truth that is contained within our legacies for which we shall be remembered.

The traffic increases as I enter the northern outskirts of San Jose and begin my watch for the exit to Bascom Street and the Valley Medical Center. A few blocks down Bascom, I take a left and pull into the small parking lot for three or four storefront businesses and the Espresso Garden Café.

In 1997, the Fiddling Cricket Concert Association began holding concerts at the café, and this will be my third year doing a performance for the club. I am met at the front door by Dick Brundle, a Britisher with a wide, toasty smile and a direct demeanor that is in full gear as he hustles to get the café's tables and chairs aligned in the correct configuration for the night's performance. The café closes for a short period of time between the afternoon coffee customers and the evening concert-goers so that the sound system can be set up and tested, and the interior of the place rearranged for the show.

Fiddling Cricket Concerts is the result of a merger between two house concert series, one run by Dick Brundle out of his home in San Jose, and the other presented by Dvora Yanow in nearby Santa Cruz. Dick, who is drawn to bluegrass music, and Dvora, a fan of traditional music of the British Isles, decided to get together and offer a variety of folk and acoustic music performances to the people of the area. They combined their two house concerts, and it all came together in 1997 with a performance by fiddler Laurie Lewis at the Espresso Garden Café.

Calls have been coming in all day, and it looks as if the café will be sold out for the show. Placards have been placed on many of the tables indicating that they are reserved for those who have already purchased tickets. I notice that one of the tables is marked for Toby Roodman and his wife, Nita. Toby, a real estate agent, had recently fallen in love with the world of folk music, and when we met at the Kerrville Festival in Texas in the spring of 1997, he offered to do the footwork to set up a fall concert with the folks at Fiddling Cricket. It has now become an annual stop for me, and as I watch the people begin to gather in the small flower-filled patio enclosure outside the front door, I recognize a number of old friends and familiar faces.

A little yellow-haired girl of about nine or ten, accompanied by her parents, waves to me through the window of the café and giggles when I return the wave. I think to myself, "Right there; there it is—job security!"

"Crossing the Water," "Ol' Pen," "The Roseville Fair"—there are the smiles, there are the voices, there is the music once again. And there is the reason that I am who I am, the reason that I have come to this place and, in the end of ends, the reason that I have been put upon this earth.

"Sing with me, my friends, and in the music we shall find each other and all that is around us. Sing with me tonight, for in the morning I shall be very far away, and then it will be only the memory of your sweet voices and the promise of tomorrow that powers my fragile journey."

It is late. The lights of downtown San Jose are nothing more than a blur as I search for a hotel sign above the headlights of the oncoming traffic. It has begun to rain a little, and it strikes me that, although I have driven almost two and a half million miles in my life, it is still driving through a late-night storm in an unfamiliar city that remains one of the toughest challenges of the road.

A sign emblazoned with the familiar orange, yellow, red, and black which identify one of the national hotel chains cuts through the watery blur on the outside of my windshield, and I swerve across two lanes of traffic and into the driveway of the fortress-like compound that will serve as my dwelling for the night. The surrounding trees block out the lights of the city, and the high walls separate the hotel guests from the local residents. Within this semblance of security, and beneath these heavy starless skies, I walk from my van along warm, humid, covered concrete pathways to a door with a number posted upon it that matches the number on my key. I am home.

CHAPTER 25

The Parting Glass

". . . But since it falls unto my lot
That I should rise and you should not,
I'll gently rise and softly call,
Goodnight and joy be with you all."

Late September of 1982 found me and Karen busy working on the design and building of the inside of our new home. The exterior of the structure was done, but by predetermination the builders had left us with little more than a weather-tight barn, finished on the outside and empty within. It was up to us to complete the interior living space. Fortunately, we were friends or acquaintances with people who could either set up the plumbing, wire in the electricity, or do the carpentry. I confess I never provided much of the brainwork for the project, but I was good at following directions, and during the construction I managed to hit a nail or two with a hammer without destroying any of my fingers.

For the carpentry, we hired my good friend Dennis Rabe, a gentle giant of a man who took the daily design changes and decision making in stride. Years later, Dennis would save my son's life when the younger was involved in a freak accident that had him running through a glass door.

I will never forget the day that water arrived at our house. The pipes were in place, the well had been pounded deep into the earth, the pump was lowered into the metal casings and hooked up, and Ken Warren, the blowtorch and copper-tubing wizard from South Berwick, Maine, came to me and announced in his heavy down-east accent that everything was set up and ready to go.

"Just turn on that thaya faucet, Bill, and we'll see what happens."

I turned on the cold-water valve at the kitchen sink. There was a hissing and a popping, and something that sounded as if Gene Krupa was doing a jazz drum solo deep within the vitals of the house. A few seconds passed, and then the water came spurting out from the faucet like it couldn't wait to get out of the dark depths of the ground.

It was if a newborn baby had just been smacked on the backside. It seemed that the whole house just swelled up, took a deep breath and came alive. At the same time, some other valve, one inside of me, let go, and my own tears sprang from within.

Since that moment, I have never judged a house to be merely building materials. There is something of a soul in each one, guided by those who dwell within, to be sometimes rich in love or sometimes sadly abandoned in apathy. I have tried over the years to respect my own home and to hold it dearly, for out of that humble wood I know that I can find the reflection of my own character.

* * *

Just before my fall tour that year, I spent a weekend in New York state, performing in Albany and staying at Logan's apartment in Saratoga. He had been working for some time on a long poem about his home state of Kentucky, which he entitled, "No Land

Where I Have Traveled, a Kentucky Poem," and it had been recently published in a 56-page volume by the Kentucky Poetry Press. It was a masterpiece—but I expected nothing less from Logan.

Beginning with a description of the death of his father, a Baptist preacher, and a history of the family farm outside of Paris, Kentucky, the poem moved along a stream of consciousness that depicted life along the Ohio river, the distillation of Bourbon whiskey, the cultivation of tobacco, and the years when the Civil War touched the heart of the South. There was love and the season of spring, and the merging of the two, told in the language of the true poet, consumed in subtle yet burning lyrical fire. There was a conclusion, with a return to thoughts on the life and death of his father in the form of a letter to his mother which ends:

> *Sixteen years. And now it is spring again in Kentucky.*
> *If one longs for Kentucky all year—one aches for her*
> *in the spring. No land where I have traveled is more fair.*
> *Your loving son,*
> *L.*

I read Logan's poem during one of the afternoons that I was staying with him that September, and when I returned to Saratoga late in the evening after my final show in Albany, we spent the remaining wee hours of the morning at The Parting Glass, talking about writing and music, and our lives and our dearest dreams.

It had been a while since Logan had done any recording, and with the exception of a few poetry readings and an occasional date at Lena's, there had been little outlet for his songs and his writing. He told me that one of his biggest fears was that he would die and his work would be lost forever. He was 53 years old. It was late. Bob and Joan had given last call at the bar, so we all rose and sang the old song about the parting glass. Logan and I walked back to his place, and although the new day was well upon us, still we talked some more about what it meant to be a writer.

October came, and with it the time for the annual fall tour. This would be the busiest so far with stops in Ashland, Wisconsin;

Minneapolis; Calgary; Seattle; and Spokane. Then it would be down through California to Davis and San Francisco, then back again across the Rockies to Denver; Lincoln, Nebraska; and another spot on Garrison Keillor's show in St. Paul.

The first snows fell early that year while I was outbound through Minneapolis, and the Canadian high plains bore a brilliant blanket of white as the Trans Canada Highway led me into Calgary and a concert for the Calgary Folk Club. Then it was down to Lethbridge for a show, and a drive over Crow's Nest Pass the next day for a swing through Idaho, and finally the end of the journey west at Seattle. Once in Seattle, I was to meet up with Heidi Muller, who had just moved from Boston to the Pacific Northwest to check out the music scene. Heidi had arranged for me to do a concert for the Seattle Folklore Society, and it would be my first time playing in the area.

She introduced me to Steve Gouda and Kat Eggleston, a young couple that sang on some of the ferries that shuttled their way back and forth across Puget Sound. They billed themselves as the Ferry Boat Musicians and were well known by those who traveled the ferries. It was actually a reintroduction to Steve, for some 20 years before I had given him his first guitar lessons when the Gouda family lived four houses up the street from me in Lexington, Massachusetts. I think that those were the only guitar lessons that I ever gave to anyone in my life.

Steve and Kat came to be for me in Seattle what Marty and Dabris were in San Francisco—my family away from home. Eventually, the Ferry Boat Musicians would split up, going separately along their own musical and personal ways, but for a time in the early 1980s, we were all together in the great Northwest.

I left rainy Seattle and headed south through Oregon. I have come to understand that a northwestern weather forecast of a 50 percent chance of rain ultimately means that at any one time, it will be raining under 50 percent of the skies above you. I have stood on a downtown Seattle sidewalk in a watery deluge while the opposite side of the street was bathed in sunlight. Once I walked out of a restaurant in Portland, Oregon, and into a shower, while overhead the skies were completely blue. Isolated showers simply means that it may decide to rain on your address alone. It is always raining in the Northwest, but then a good deal of the time it is sunny.

In the fall of 1982, I entered California from the north for the first time and caught my first glimpse of beautiful Mount Shasta, snowcapped and shining in the distance. Winding down out of the high country beside cathedral-like rocky escarpments, I followed the highway past Weed and Black Butte, and over the bridge at Shasta Lake. Now it was into the long Sacramento Valley, past Reading and Willows, and on to Davis where I was booked at the Palms Playhouse. I left Davis after my show and drove to San Francisco, finally pulling up at Whitney Street for a late-night reunion with Marty and Dabris and a weekend concert at Plowshares. The lights of the Oakland Bay Bridge shone silver and pretty in the distance as I knocked upon their door, but the light from the lamp in what they called the Bill Staines Memorial Bedroom was even more dear.

By 1982, Steve Nerney had accepted a job teaching math and astronomy at Navaho Community College in Tsaile, Arizona, and I expected that I would not see him that year. True to form, though, Steve—never one to miss a good time—arrived by plane from New Mexico on the morning after I arrived in San Francisco from Davis.

We were all together again, and the music flowed. One night we all traveled over the Oakland hills to a house under the great redwoods near Moraga, and we sang and drank wine until the warm, shining, golden beams of the sun invaded the canopy of the giant trees and roused us from our places on the far side of thoughtlessness.

Later, Marty, Dabris, Steve, and I made the drive back over the hills and valleys from Moraga to San Francisco. Steve flew back to New Mexico that afternoon, and the next day I began my trip back across the country, bound for Denver, Lincoln, St. Paul, and home. On November 11th, I pulled into my driveway, the long road behind me.

I was looking forward to working on the house and spending time with Karen and Hallie. There was still a lot of work that would have to be done on the building before we could move in ahead of the full brunt of winter, but Karen had been busy while I was on tour and had worked miracles with the place.

On December 9, 1982, Marty Robbins died. I had always enjoyed his music. On the same day we moved into our new home. We would be living on plywood flooring, surrounded by walls of open insulation and a mile of electrical wiring, but for the first time Karen and I would spend the night together under our own roof. It was a good feeling, and the warmth of the wood stove, our only source of heat at the time, rose through the floor and the timbers beneath us; I knew that the house was strong and secure, that the morning and the new year would come, and that we would be together.

* * *

January of 1983 was a snowy month. The pines sparkled with their icy feathers in the morning sun. If I wasn't trying to write a song, I was trying to get my booking schedule together for the spring and the fall. During the evenings I worked on the house. I was beginning to think that we would never get the place finished, and that Karen and I were doomed to live amidst boxes, drywall, and insulation until the end of our days.

I traveled to Saratoga to perform at Lena's that January and again stayed at Logan's apartment. My latest recording, *Sandstone Cathedrals,* was doing relatively well, and the shows at the café were sold out for both nights.

It was good to see Logan again. It had only been since September that I had last stayed at his place, but still the time we spent together was special, and I was always inspired to write something after our late-night sessions at The Parting Glass.

It would be the last time that I would see my dear friend, the man who had come to be my literary and musical mentor, the man who had become my second father. On March 9, 1983, while

I was in Minneapolis for my late winter tour, I received a phone call from Karen.

Lena had called her early that morning to say that the weather had been icy and bad the previous night, and that while walking home Logan had slipped in front of an oncoming car and been killed. It was really nobody's fault, but simply one of those unfortunate and tragic occurrences that make life so uncertain and so incredibly precious.

It was as if a light in my life had gone out. There was a period of profound darkness. Then, after a few days, much as when one's eyes adjust to the lack of light in a darkened room, I began to see and hear those things around me that meant so much: the new day, the brightening sky, the music of the March wind over the snowy city, the sound and feel of my own breath as it filled my chest and exited as a song. It was "Way Out There," a song that Logan and I had sung and yodeled together so many times at the festival in Kentucky or onstage at Lena's. There was only one voice now, but in my mind there would always be the memory of two.

A memorial service was planned for Logan the following weekend at Lena's. Karen flew to Albany in a snowstorm, and I cut my tour short by a few days to meet her at the airport and drive up to Saratoga.

The theatre at the café was filled, and many of Logan's friends and acquaintances reminisced about his life through music and poetry. I sang a song that we had written together entitled "Going Back Where the Wheatfields Wave." I had recorded it years before on the *Miles* album, and Logan had always been fond of the song. Bob and Joan were there from The Parting Glass with their combined families. For many years afterward, they took over Logan's role for me in Saratoga, always with a place to stay at their home or a hot meal at the pub.

So many friends have come and gone,
So many joys and tears,
So many miles upon the road,
So many long, long years.

As Karen and I made the trip home across the mountains of Vermont after the memorial service, I couldn't help but think about the importance of family and friends in our lives, and how no matter where we are or what we are doing at the moment, there are always those times when we have to put our immediate plans on hold and tend to the things that really matter. The births, the deaths, the sudden tragedies—they belong to all of us, and when they happen we must always try to be there to see them through.

Logan was brought home to Kentucky and buried in a small cemetery outside of Paris. Months later, Karen and I visited his grave and spent a day with his mother. On that occasion, she told me that she felt that Logan would want me to have his guitar; she gave me the instrument, which I kept for many years. Logan's writings were collected and accepted as a permanent part of the library at the University of Kentucky in Lexington, and the hills and lands of the Bluegrass State became a richer place the day that he was softly and quietly returned to her bosom.

The echoes of The Parting Glass remained:

> "*. . . But since it falls unto my lot*
> *That I should rise and you should not,*
> *I'll gently rise and softly call,*
> *Goodnight, and joy be with you all.*"

CHAPTER 26

The Fall Tour, Day 12

The traffic on the Nimitz Freeway is relatively light on this fall Sunday afternoon, the 12th day of the tour. I'm on the short trip up from San Jose to Berkeley for an evening show at the Freight and Salvage Coffeehouse, one of the legendary West Coast folk music venues. I pass the exits for Freemont and Hayward, San Leandro, and the Oakland Airport. I pass Jack London Square, and I think of my bookshelves at home and how one of them is heavy with the novels and writings of this extraordinary man known as "the Sailor on Horseback." I think of his wonderful stories of the North, of Alaska and the gold rush, and my thoughts are gone again to that far off world of grizzlies and wolves, frozen silence, and the warmest of friends.

I travel past downtown Oakland and the exit for the Bay Bridge, with San Francisco visible across the span, bathed in the late afternoon sun. My van knows the way, and we act as one and take the exit for Berkeley, stopping at an intersection to let a host of colorful characters cross the street in front of us.

Berkeley, or "Berzerkley", as it was known in the 1960s, is home to the University of California at Berkeley, one of the real hotbeds of political turmoil, drugs, and alternative culture, and with that distinction comes all of the excitement and unbridled energy that is generated within such an environment. The streets are lined with bars and pizza parlors, clothing boutiques and copy centers, music stores, and used book shops. Circling through the back streets for a minute or two, I pull into the parking lot at the side of the Freight. After knocking a few times on the heavy wooden doors and getting no answer, I step around the corner onto the main street and begin a quest for something to eat before the show.

Two doors down from the corner, a shirtless young man of about 20 with long, dark, matted hair and sinewy arms, sits on a wooden box the size of a milk crate. He is surrounded by a collection of drums, beautifully crafted out of wood and hide and ranging in size from six inches in diameter to a large kettle-like drum that surely measures two feet from side to side.

Eyes closed, and flailing away with his hands, fists, arms, and elbows, he is bent upon beating out a series of intricate rhythmical patterns designed, it seems, to either awaken the dead or at least register on any nearby seismograph. He is lost in the ecstasy of his own drumming, all the while nodding his head in time. I can't help but think that this is a person whose soul must surely be made up of pure rhythm.

In the great realm of music there are two types of people: those whose musical souls have at their epicenter rhythm, and those whose musical souls have at their epicenter melody. This is not to say that a rhythm-centered person does not have melody, or that a melodic person does not have rhythm; it is simply that the core of the being is centered on one or the other.

Take two circular, colored but transparent disks of the same size: one blue and one yellow. The blue disk represents those who have a rhythmical center to their being, and the yellow disk represents those with a melodic center. Place the disks so they are directly aligned, center over center, and hold them up to the light.

The configuration will be green. This is the world of music. Now move one of the disks slightly off center. At one end of the configuration you'll find a fingernail area of blue, and at the other end a thin arc of yellow. In the middle, there is a large area that shows up green. This green area, the area that is the combination of rhythm and melody, is where most everybody resides in music, yet their core *center* still belongs to either rhythm or melody.

Those people who are moved by blues, jazz, or rock tend to be rhythmically centered, while those who enjoy classical music or folk music tend to be driven by melody.

Over the years, it has always been the melody that first attracts me to a piece of music. It has always been the melody that first fires my emotions when I hear a song. Today, though, as I watch and listen in fascination to this drummer of the streets, I can hear the rhythm of his life and feel the pounding harvest of his hands as it echoes all around me and then fades away into the distant alleys and streets of Berkeley, and I am moved. It is the beat of the city, it is the pulse of the passage of time.

Later, the people are there again at the Freight and Salvage. For 20 years I have played in the Bay Area on the same weekend in October. Why do they return, these people? Why do they come to hear the songs over and over again? Why do they take the time from their days to come and see some wandering troubadour?

Does the music bring them answers to some of the questions that they have in their own lives? Does it carry them away to some far-off place? Does the music soothe them or comfort them? Does it lift them out of themselves for just a little bit and set them down upon some high place where the view is long and clear? Does it bring them together for a moment and open their eyes to each other? Does it matter? Is it lasting? Do the notes remain when the troubadour is well upon his way to some other town?

Do they feel the magic that drives him to be the musician, the song maker, the king and the clown, all rolled into one, belonging to everybody and yet to no one at all?

Do they feel his heart as it breaks upon the stage and falls before them in little pieces at their feet? Do they feel his joy as the music of his entire being floods into the hall, eddying between the chairs and tables as it searches them out and enters their hearts and minds? Do they listen? Do they understand? Do they comprehend this moment of all sadness and all joy?

An artist may become thin in body for lack of food, but it will not matter to him when he is nourished by even the slightest appreciation of his work.

A woman steps up to me after the show and says, "I know you hear this all the time, but your music has meant a lot to me over the years."

Does she think that telling me this is such a trivial thing? Sometimes it is the knowledge that I have reached someone which is the only thing that keeps me going. Thank you, fair lady. Thank you for your time and your thoughts. Thank you more than you will ever know.

A friend of mine on a whim once wrote a letter to John Steinbeck expressing his appreciation of Steinbeck's work. Not expecting a reply, he received a letter from the author which he framed and hung in his hallway.

> *Dear Friend,*
>
> *It was good of you to take the time to write to me.*
> *Thank you for the letter, but even more,*
> *For the impulse to write it.*
>
> *Yours,*
> *John Steinbeck*

It is late, and once again I am on the road. I shall not see San Francisco or the rest of the Bay Area again on this trip. My tour now takes me south to Ojai for a show two nights from now. At this moment though, at this 11:00 hour, I have no thoughts other than to be in motion until my energy fails me and I find some hotel to shelter me for the night.

"Doesn't it get lonesome on the road, traveling by yourself all the time?" someone asks me at one of my performances.

Yes it does, my friend, when it is dark and late, and you feel as if you are driving at the edge of the universe and that if you should happen to disappear from this galaxy of bright and circling stars, no one would ever even notice.

CHAPTER 27

Bridges

In April of 1983, Steve Alarik, who was managing the Coffeehouse Extempore at the time, contacted me with the idea of recording a live performance album at the club. The entire concept was for the coffeehouse to record a number of the artists who performed there and release the recordings on the Coffeehouse Extempore record label. Sales of the recording would bring in some extra money for the coffeehouse and provide me with the opportunity to do another album.

I jumped at the offer, but knowing that the club was loosely run by musicians and their friends, I did so with the understanding that, should the coffeehouse happen to close down at some point, all of the rights to the recording would revert back to me. This was acceptable to Steve, so we set up a weekend slot in July of 1983 to do the project.

I invited Guy Van Duser to drive out to Minneapolis with me, and we arrived in town on a Friday afternoon, five hours before the concert and the recording were to begin. Steve Smulian, the sound wizard at the coffeehouse, would be the engineer for the recording.

The album would be edited from the tapes of three nights of performances, which was fortunate, because when we got up onstage for the Friday night show, with the place filled to the brim with people, I just couldn't seem to do anything right.

I began the first song, "Pretty Boy Floyd" by Woody Guthrie, with the second verse, and it was all downhill from there. Halfway through the first set, I broke a string on my guitar, and from then on it seemed anybody's guess as to when the instruments were in tune. By the end of the evening, I was resigned to the fact that the album was going to have to be edited from the tapes of the remaining two nights.

In preparation for the recording, I had put together a list of perhaps eight songs of my own that were going to comprise the core of the album. I figured that the remaining content would just serendipitously fall into place out of the performances. Certainly, out of the three concerts, there would be enough material for the project.

By the end of Saturday night, I wasn't so sure. A review of the tapes later that evening left me with the feeling that maybe four or five of the songs might be usable, but most of the album was going to have to come from the Sunday night performance.

It wasn't that the shows were off on Friday and Saturday, or that the audience wasn't responsive, it was just that for one reason or another, technical or artistic, I knew something was missing, some bit of magic wasn't quite there. Perhaps it was a producer's ear, perhaps it was my ego, perhaps it was the position of the stars; I couldn't be sure. I simply knew that the pressure was on, and that we had one last night to make the thing work.

I suggested to Guy that we take Sunday afternoon and record the songs that I wanted on the album at the club without any audience. The room sound would be nearly the same, and we could edit in the audience response in the final mixes. In this manner, we would have the album recorded and in our pockets even if we fell short during the Sunday evening concert.

By late Sunday afternoon, we had the album recorded. As it turned out, however, we may as well have spent that afternoon at a ball game or a movie, for the evening concert, with the house full and everybody singing, had all the magic I could have wished for and more. Maybe it was because the pressure to get the album on tape was no longer there. Now it was just fun to play. Now Guy and I could just relax and joke around onstage. Now we could just be ourselves. Now, it was just the music that mattered.

I never did use any of the songs that we recorded without the audience that afternoon. The album was eventually edited from the tapes of all of the performances that we did on that hot summer weekend in Minneapolis.

Guy and I drove home that following Monday, feeling pretty good about the weekend. In the spring of 1984, *Bridges* was released on the Coffeehouse Extempore record label.

* * *

That summer of 1983 seemed to pass very quickly. There was still a lot of work to be done on the house, but it felt as if Karen and I were finally closing in on the light at the end of the tunnel. I was still writing at a good clip, and it seemed that life that summer had begun to take on a new meaning for me.

It began with a sense of great fragility. Logan's passing had been a blow, and that past June had seen the untimely death of Stan Rogers during a fiery emergency landing of an Air Canada flight in Cincinnati.

I had been with Stan at the campfires at Kerrville the night before his flight home and had then traveled to Houston for a weekend at Anderson Fair. While I was at the Fair, Nanci Griffith called Tim Leatherwood, who ran the club, to break the news to all of us. I found it hard to believe that someone with such an energy about him, and such a profound grasp on all that was life, could have possibly had that life taken from him in such a way.

That summer I thought about the uncertainty and the fragility of it all, and life was very precious.

As fall approached and the brilliant colors began to creep across New England from the north, I knew that it was once again getting to be time for the annual long trip West. I also knew that life was very special to me and that it was getting harder and harder to leave my home. If it were not for my friends, those dearest of souls that I knew along the road who cared for me and understood me for who I really was, I would not have been able to drive another single mile.

On the first day of the 1983 fall tour, I drove from New Hampshire to Toledo, Ohio. There, in a hotel on Route 23, I made an entry in my journal.

"Stopped here on my way to Minnesota. I left Karen and Hallie early this morning but talked with them later. Karen was not feeling well and I felt bad leaving her. This year I am so much closer to my wife and home and dog. I know that I must be on the road, though. It is my life. Karen said that Hallie was waiting for me to come home today. I love life. When I get home again:

I will chop wood for warmth,
I will build my fire for light,
I will savor the smoke on the cold autumn air, and unpack sweaters and dress in wooly red,
I will wax skis and clear the woodland trails, preparing for winter once again with love and hope for the new year,
And while I am doing this, I will sing, and my voice shall arise from out of the depths of my heart.
When I get home again all of this shall be,
When I am truly home again."

* * *

I returned to Alaska in the fall of 1983, visiting Dog, Judy, and Yule Kiltcher in Homer, where I played a concert at the new high school auditorium. It was good to see my Alaska friends again, and when 600 people showed up for the show, it was hard for me not to feel as if I were sitting on top of the world.

Sometime after midnight that night, just before I climbed

into bed at Dog and Judy's cabin, I walked outside for a short distance along the trail that traversed the field below. I watched as one of Yule's horses quietly grazed about 50 yards in front of me in the bright moonlight. A light dusting of snow had recently fallen, giving the slope of the field, the dark spruces, and the distant Kenai Mountains visible beyond the shining waters of Katchemack Bay a crystalline, fairy like appearance. The scene in front of me and the world around me this night were silent, cold, and immense in their beauty. I felt incredibly small. Taking a long deep breath and feeling the icy air invading my body, I turned and headed back toward the dim lantern lights of the cabin, a tiny figure on the vast landscape of all that there is in this world.

It would be the last time that I would stay at Dog and Judy's at the far end of East End Road in Homer, for not long after that they became disenchanted with the development of the town and the selling off of large tracts of land to speculators in places like New York who had never been to Alaska, and they moved back to New England, settling in Vermont in a quiet rural place of their own near Chelsea. Occasionally they would return to Homer, visiting friends but never quite getting used to the road bypass built adjacent to the McDonald's restaurant, carrying the traffic out to the spit and the boutiques that had replaced the old fishing shacks that had stood their ground for so long against the many long and wild Alaskan winters.

I dreamed of writing a novel set in Alaska, but I only made it as far as the title: *Beneath the Moon and the Morning Star*. The novel died in its infancy, but I did use the title, derived from that late evening walk in a field near Homer, some ten years later for a song recorded on the album *Going to the West*.

Kodiak, Sitka, Ketchikan—I played them all again in the fall of 1983, returning to the lower 48 and a week of concerts on the West Coast. By Halloween, I had worked my way back across the country and was booked into Passim for a weekend of shows with Nanci Griffith.

A product of the Texas music scene, Nanci had grown up as a singer surrounded by the likes of Jimmy Dale Gilmore, Lucinda

Williams, and Butch Hancock, playing on Sunday nights at a little bar called the Hole in the Wall on Guadalupe Street in Austin. When I came to know her in 1977, she was living in Houston and married to songwriter Eric Taylor, performing at Anderson Fair and making trips back to Austin to perform at the Alamo Lounge or Emma Joe's.

Not only was Nanci a gifted songwriter, but as a solo performer her vocals and musicianship were enough to fill a coffeehouse or any concert hall with a full-throated richness of sound that could be matched by few others. Nanci brought to the stage an intelligence of lyrics and melody, and a kinship with musical tradition that was deeply inspirational and moving. I loved listening to her sing. I loved feeling the energy that emanated from her music, and I tried to breathe in that energy as I watched her onstage in hopes that some of that energy might find its way into my own music.

I could see only one drawback for Nanci. Inasmuch as I loved Texas and all of my musician friends playing around the scene, something inside of me kept saying that she should be out on the road, out away from Texas. She should be touring around the rest of the country, not just in and about the Lone Star State. Nanci would certainly be able to hold her own in any of the venues that I was playing, and with a little exposure I knew that the rest of the world would be waiting for her.

By the early 1980s, her marriage with Eric had come to an end, and with a bit of encouragement she seemed ready to take to the road and bring her music to the rest of the world.

We did a few shows together at the Coffeehouse Extempore in Minneapolis. Now, in the fall of 1983 and fresh from her appearance on Austin City Limits, Nanci and I were doing a weekend together at Passim in Cambridge.

We split one more show together on Valentine's Day in 1984 in St. Paul. I've seen her only briefly over the years, at one folk festival or another, but I have never faltered in my admiration for her, or for the fire and passion that, through her music, she has brought to so many others.

CHAPTER 28

The Fall Tour, Day 13

With my concerts in the Bay Area completed for this year, it is about time to head up to the Northwest for a week. I have always scheduled my own bookings, so I never have had anyone to blame but myself for the routing on a tour. It would seem only sensible that after playing in northern California, I would start north for the next shows, but true to my booking techniques I have one more date to do, two nights from now, in Ojai, just east of Santa Barbara and six hours to the south.

It would figure that after so many years in the business I would be able to do a better job of scheduling my tour dates; however, one fact remains: for the road musician a booking is a booking, and short of driving yourself insane, you take them as they come. Wherever they take you, that is where you go. A trip down the coast is not out of the way, it is just part of the tour. Besides, it will be good to see Tom and Becky Lowe and do their concert series for the first time in about 15years.

My immediate plan for this particular night is simple: find a hotel by the ocean, perhaps near Avila Beach or Pismo Beach, buy a bottle of good wine along with some cheese and bread, and do nothing but stare out across that vast expanse of ocean that is oh so far from my home.

By the middle of the afternoon, I've booked a room at a small motel on Pismo Beach. It is one of those tiny courtyard Shangri-las that looks as if it was built in the early 1950s and in its heyday some ten years later might have been a stop over for Annette Funicello and Frankie Avalon on their way to some beach blanket bingo bonanza.

The main building—a flat-roofed, two-story affair of white stucco and turquoise wooden trim, festooned with white wrought-iron curlicue railings—is built perpendicular to the beach, facing south. Directly across the court, which is half parking lot and half neatly mowed lawn, and beyond the fenced in swimming pool, a row of seven small cottages, all facing north and also lined up perpendicular to the beach, form a parallel to the main building and complete the cozy enclosure of the motel complex.

I enter my room on the second floor of the main building, take a breath, and find that the room is delightfully imbued with the smell of sea salt and fog, and rich with the fragrance of the winds that have constantly blown in over the years from the coasts of some unseen, far-off western islands.

I inhale deeply once again and savor the sustenance of the low-angled sunlight as it fills the room. Tossing my suitcase and guitar onto the sagging but spacious bed, I scan the room to see if it offers up any secrets, any surprises uncommon to any other hotel room that I have ever visited. Usually there are none, just the usual bar of soap on the sink, the thin plastic cups encased in their crinkly wrappings and, if one is lucky enough, a coffee maker primed for that early morning jolt necessary for a swift wakeup.

This afternoon though, my attention is drawn to the bed. Near the base of the pillows where the top quilt is tucked under is a small book, perhaps three quarters of an inch thick, and journal-like in its appearance. Obviously placed there with some intention as yet unknown to me, it is striking and compelling in its presence.

Opening the unmarked cover of the book and examining the title page, I read:

> *"The Sea Court Motel, Pismo Beach, California*
> *Room 217 Diary"*

It is a room diary, a volume of thoughts and feelings of the people who have stayed in my room at the Sea Court Motel during the last six months. The book is almost full, with entries ranging from a single line to a few pages.

Replacing the book on the bed, I exit and start toward my car in the parking lot below in order to bring up the rest of my belongings. Once moved in and comfortable, I set one of the chairs in the room outside my door, open a bottle of wine that has been traveling with me for the last three days, and under the late afternoon sun begin to peruse the journal.

> *August 5, 1999*
>
> *The ocean is in much upheaval tonight, with wind and pounding surf. We decided to take a few days and come over to the coast from Bakersfield. It has been a long time since I have seen the ocean. Tonight, it is spectacular.*
> *Kevin ______, Bakersfield*

I take another sip of wine.

> *My name is Tom _____. I am a musician, a songwriter, traveling up the West Coast from L.A. to Seattle. This is my first tour and I hope to make my living playing music. Eventually, maybe someone will know who I am. Right now I am mostly playing for friends that I know along the way, but it beats the day job that I had.*

I fill my cup and hold the rich, blood-red liquid up to the sunlight.

"Here's to you, Tom. Maybe someday someone *will* know who you are. Just stay at it. It is a fine road out before you. Just be careful that it doesn't take you so far that you forget from where you started, and who you are in your deepest soul."

The latest entry is by a new bride who writes of her young husband:

"This man takes my breath away."

I am envious. It has been a long time since I have taken anyone's breath away. Perhaps that power is only for the young. I know that I love my family, I know that I love my home, but to be able to take someone's breath away—that surely must be an incredible experience.

I am reminded of a line written by British humorist Jerome K. Jerome in an essay on love that, "Cupid spends no second arrow on the same heart."

If this be so, I would hope that Cupid's arrow would not be one that delivers love alone, but would deliver with it the simple ability to learn how to love. Then would that one arrow from Cupid's quiver be sufficient.

"This man takes my breath away."

I reread the entry and take another sip from my cup of wine.

"I hope that you may also take his breath away," I whisper to the writer, "and that the one and only arrow that you may receive flies true into the depths of your heart."

I am dozing now, with the high sounds of shorebirds all around me and the crescendos and diminuendos of the somersaulting surf, a simple and sweet music, plying its way across the courtyard of the hotel, up the stairs, and then far down into the spaces of my sleepy soul.

Later, after some dinner at one of the local beachfront bars and an attempt at some songwriting back at my room, I return to the diary to make my own entry.

"I love the ocean. I come to its vast watery spaces and it brings me solace and peace. I know that it is the one place where I can turn my back on my troubles and take a deep breath in order to clear my mind. Its song brings me strength, its constancy brings me hope. I know that when I turn once again to face the land, my troubles will not have disappeared, only my perception of them, and that they are small and inconsequential things, that now I am resolute and have the strength of the ever-present tides to carry me forward again, until somehow I will find a way to prevail. Bill Staines, October 1999"

CHAPTER 29

Red River Valley

In May of 1984 I was out on the road again, a Texas tour this time, with stops in Mesquite for the Mesquite Folk Festival, Houston, and Kerrville. At the time, I was driving a Toyota station wagon, a funky looking thing that I had bought new in 1983, but with 115,000 miles on it by the time I left for Texas that spring.

On the afternoon of the first day away from home, I was driving just east of Rochester, New York, on my way west, when the alternator light on my dashboard began to glow, indicating that something was amiss in the charging system. The battery was being drained, and when the power was gone, the car would stall. I knew that if I turned off the radio and all of the other accessories, I would probably have enough juice to fire the sparkplugs for a few hours, and so I decided to push on to Buffalo, where I could stay with my friend Jim Dombrowski and deal with the problem there.

Jim allowed that there was a large used parts store right around the corner from his house, and that they would probably be able to replace the alternator in the morning.

The next day I was up early, eager to deal with the situation and get back on the road. I had only a window of one day to spare on the trip south; after that I would have to start canceling some of my concert dates. At 8:00 A.M. the doors of the parts store opened, and there I stood with my alternator in my hands, desperately seeking to purchase another beast of the same species. The store clerk examined the part, took down some numbers, and vanished into the back of the store with reassurances that he would return shortly.

After a good 20 minutes, during which time a sense of trepidation began creeping into my life, the parts man returned with the news that I had somehow been expecting. Not only did they not have a rebuilt alternator, but no other parts place or dealer in western New York could come up with one either. The explanation was simple: integral parts for 2-year-old cars with 115,000 miles on them simply did not exist out in the field. Sure, they could be ordered and delivered from the parts depot in New York City in three or four days, but out here on the road there were none to be had. Two-year-old parts had not had the time to go bad, and because of this there were none around to be rebuilt and sold.

A second check on my alternator determined that it was definitely not charging, and therefore I was left with few options other than canceling some dates and waiting for a part to arrive from the Big Apple. The clerk suggested that I buy a couple of car batteries, order the alternator to be delivered to a town somewhere along my route, and just drive through the day on battery power, recharging the batteries at night at a service station.

The plan seemed complicated, but it appeared as if it was the only option available. Of course, the parts store didn't have a battery that would fit the car, so it looked as if even this option was not going to fly.

Ready to pack it in and start canceling gigs, I took the old alternator, reinstalled it in the car, reconnected the wires, and prepared myself for the worst.

I don't know what made me do it, other than perhaps sheer

desperation, but I put the key into the ignition, placed my hand on the dashboard, and uttered, "Darling, you have never let me down; don't let me down now." I turned the key. The car sprang to life, the alternator light flickered for a moment and then went out. Lo and behold, everything seemed to be acting normally. I ran back into the store to see if the clerk would put a meter on the charging system, and sure enough the alternator was putting out a charge.

I drove on that same alternator for three more years before selling the car with 284,000 miles on it in 1987.

It was not the only time that my cars would respond to me after a gentle word or some positive thinking. Once I returned from a month-long tour in a car that was leaking oil badly from all of the seals and sounding as if a group of gremlins was sawing wood in one of the front wheels and bowling a game of ten pins in the transmission. I have made it over steep mountain passes in blizzards and made it across deserts with duct tape holding radiator hoses together. In one of my cars, I set aside an area above the sun visor where I pinned small pieces of ribbon signifying the times when I blurted out, "Baby, if you get me through this situation, I'm going to give you a medal."

I will never doubt those noble machines that get me here and there around the country. Now and again I have been left in a bind, but I know that it was never because the cars did not try their best to make it through.

* * *

My first stop that spring was in Mesquite, Texas, just east of Dallas, for the Mesquite Folk Festival. Rod Kennedy, who had taken on the role as coordinator for the festival, as well as running Kerrville, rounded up many of the performers who were appearing at the latter festival that year and brought them to Mesquite for the weekend happenings.

There were Friday and Saturday night concerts, as well as an afternoon show on Saturday which featured a yodeling contest with me, blues lady Marcia Ball, and Patsy Montana, the yodeling cowgirl, as judges. Patsy was credited with being the first woman to have a million-selling record when back in 1935 she had a hit with her song, "I Want to Be a Cowboy's Sweetheart." Each of us had a favorite entry that day, but in the end the prize went to a young cowboy from California who had driven all the way to Texas to enter the contest.

The Saturday night concert included sets by Patsy Montana, Marcia Ball, and Leon McAuliffe, the legendary steel guitar player for Bob Wills' band, the Texas Playboys. I did a set, and I was followed by David Amram, who invited Patsy and me up onstage to do an impromptu arrangement of "Red River Valley."

After the concert, a few of the performers at the festival headed over to Poor David's Pub, the local Dallas-area folk spot, to catch the last set by Townes Van Zandt. As a final tune for the night, Townes, somewhat in his cups by this late hour, was coerced by the audience to do an encore of his song, "Pancho and Lefty." The song had been recorded by Emmylou Harris and was doing well on the national music charts. Even though Townes' version of the song was a little ragged in those early morning hours at Poor David's, it was still delivered with the heart of a poet, and the audience cheered in response.

At the end of Townes' set, I looked over at David Amram, who was sitting next to me, and heard him humming something quietly to himself. I asked him what the music was, and he answered that he wasn't quite sure, but that it was the tune from one of the pages of sheet music that had been plastered all over the walls of Poor David's as wallpaper. I admired the depth and command of the music within this man's soul. What a great ability, what a wonderful gift, what a blessed thing it is to be endowed with the essence and the glory of the music that is all around us.

Two weeks later, we were all together again at Kerrville. It was at this festival that I came to know and respect the music of John Ims and Chuck Pyle. It was at the late night campfires, surrounded by the dearest of friends, that I met Steve Gillette for the first time, even though I had known his songs "Darcy Farrow" and "Back on the Street Again" for some years.

What a wonderful place to be. I played "Red River Valley" again onstage with David Amram while (I was later told) a teary eyed Guy Clark looked on from the VIP seats. In hindsight, maybe it was the idea of a classical composer from upstate New York and a yodeling Yankee from New Hampshire doing a version of such a beloved Texas song that really fired Guy's emotions. I'd like to think, however, that it was just the power and magic of that simple song that carried the moment, for that is the true essence of the music. I camped that year at the festival, sleeping under the Texas skies, kidnapped by a western wind, and hostage to the sounds of the scorpion-black night.

After the Kerrville Festival, I returned to New England, driving almost the entire way without stopping to rest. When I could travel no farther, I stopped for a night at a hotel in Allentown, Pennsylvania. Figuring that I would hit the hotel lounge for one drink before I went to bed, I sat down at the bar and realized that I had taken a seat in the middle of a local version of the "Gong Show."

The original "Gong Show" was a network television production which featured contestants strutting their talents, which included singing off-key, reciting very bad poetry while standing on one's head, or any one of various other lame-brained antics, until one of the three or four host panelists could not take it any longer, arose from their chair, and began to beat upon a huge Chinese gong, signaling the end of the routine. Amidst all of this craziness, now and then a performer with real talent would do their thing, vying for the prize money that was given away at the end of each of the shows.

True to the American penchant for crazy entertainment, live local takeoffs of the show started showing up around the country in comedy clubs, nightspots, local bars, and wherever else people gathered to get crazy. And it was here that I found myself, after driving for 25 hours, seated at a bar while people took to the stage in their underwear and sang, "Danny Boy," or blew themselves blue on a nose flute while twirling a hula hoop.

I began to wonder whether I may have missed a turn on my journey and had actually gone "round the bend." I thought perhaps I had fallen off the edge of sanity, when a young woman took the stage with a classical guitar draped from her neck, legs stiff, heels together, and introduced the piece she was about to sing.

"I'd like to do an Emmylou Harris song."

She proceeded to launch into an operatic soprano rendition of "Pancho and Lefty."

That was it! I think I started to cry. I had now seen and heard what must have been all that could happen to a song, from its origin and Townes' late-night version at Poor David's in Dallas, to the Metropolitan Opera version performed by a stiff-as-a-board wisp of a woman on a classical guitar during a "Gong Show" at a hotel in Allentown, Pennsylvania.

It was definitely time for bed. In only another ten hours of traveling the next day, I would be home and away from all of this craziness on the road. I longed for the ocean, my wife, and my dog. I was ready for summer and the days that I would spend at the shore.

It was a fine July and August. Karen and I traveled to Quebec City and camped along Wild River in the woods of western Maine. Other than a brief weekend trip to Minneapolis, most of my performances were in the northeast, which allowed me time to write at home and gather wood for the fall and winter. There was always something to do, whether it was clearing a trail through the woods, working on the house, painting the interior trim, writing a song, or booking performance dates. I wrote "Last Margarita at Monterey," "Stone Face," and "October Winds." Then I received a call from Mason Daring who informed me that Rounder Records was interested in doing another album.

We also had a visitor that August. Athena Varounis, one of Karen's college friends, called and said that she would love to come and visit us for a few days. Karen had hardly seen Athena since they had graduated from Wilson, and it would be a great opportunity to catch up on old times. A brief inquiry over the phone as to what Athena had been doing with her life for the last ten years led to the disclosure that she had become a special agent for the FBI.

It seemed incongruous to me that this petite, pretty, dark-eyed woman with a constant wit and a sense of humor about her should arrive at my house toting the three pistols that she had named "Killerette," "Killer," and "Boomer," but here she was, little Athena, a trained law enforcement officer assigned to the Washington, D.C., office in the murder and extortion division.

It was a joy to see her, and true to the old Athena, she was a walking library of stories culled from the years that she had spent with the FBI. We listened to her tell tales about everything from serious drug busts to hilarious rescues of biting parrots out of the arms of the unlawful. She and Karen had a lot to talk about, and during her stay that summer they reminisced about their days at Wilson and what had become of their lives since those college years.

We kept losing touch with Athena until we received a letter from her a few years later, telling us that she was on a special assignment as a consultant for an author who was writing a novel about a female FBI agent. In the end, it would be Athena who would become the model for agent Clarisse Starling in *The Silence of the Lambs.*

* * *

I stood with my dog at the top of the hill just above our home that late September and took in the colors of the maples and oaks that border the fields around where I live. I was savoring the smell of the smoke from our wood stove and watched as it lofted above the ridge behind the house. Down deep in my heart, though, I knew that I was preparing for the fall, and the highway that would once more take me so far away.

CHAPTER 30

The Fall Tour, Day 14

The sun is warm overhead, and the brilliant blue Pacific lies serene in its immense majesty, the sky and water horizon broken only by the oil rigs standing at a distance off the coast. The trip down from the Sea Court Motel at Pismo Beach to Santa Barbara has been uneventful, and now I take the Las Positas exit and head west to the beach for my annual stop at the Brown Pelican restaurant. It is early in the afternoon, and I have only 30 miles left to go until I get to Ojai. I feel as if I can relax, have a glass of wine and some lunch, and enjoy a sweet respite at one of my favorite places.

The yellow sandy cliffs that surround this sheltered cove are a favorite spot for hang gliders, and occasionally the bright rainbow patterns of a delta-shaped sail can be seen overhead, a splash of color sweeping across the sky, a giant kite riding the warm updrafts rising from the beach. I am rewarded this day with a demonstration. As I watch, I think, "Ride upon the wind, my friend, twist and turn to your heart's contentment. You brighten my world with your silent, colored wing, and you lift me up in my soul until I can see the farthest forever."

I am making an entry into my journal when the waitress arrives with the check, and within a minute or two I am back on the road, bound over the California hills to Ojai and my evening concert at the Ojai Women's Club.

Inasmuch as I have changed on the outside over the years, on the inside I have remained much the same, and as I pull into town it feels as if Ojai and I have been growing old together, at about the same pace and in the same way. There are the changes—the new shopping mall, the crowded streets, the increase in people and traffic downtown—and yet there is still something of the same little town that I came to know in 1975 with the candle factory adventure.

Now, late in the afternoon, I head straight down the main street for the Women's Club and find Tom Lowe setting up chairs for the night's performance. It looks as if it is going to be a good crowd judging by the presales, and I begin to get my head together for the show: load in the boxes of CDs, change the strings on my guitar, put together a loose set list, and check the settings on the sound system. I can do this all in my sleep: rearrange the monitor speakers, listen to the equalization, and alter the frequencies so the vocal and guitar sounds are bright and clear in the room. Then we are done and everything is ready for the audience to arrive.

At 7:15, the hall is filled to overflowing. People have driven up from Los Angeles and Santa Barbara, and even up the coast from San Diego, complaining to me that I rarely get to their part of California. All I can do is thank them for their time, and tell them that I appreciate that they have come so far. I really do appreciate them, for they are my life's blood and the reason that I am here.

"Actually," a young woman confesses, "we have family in the area, and it seemed like a good time to visit them and catch your show while we were here."

I feel a little better, relieved of the total responsibility that someone has driven six hours to hear me sing. I am grateful, of course, that they would have—but then, I have driven 3,000 miles to play in Ojai; so in the end, it all seems to average out.

It is time. There is the introduction, the first half of the performance, the intermission, and then the second set. There is the energy again, and the identification with the songs that brings us all together. The songs are not mine, they belong to all who will listen. The night is not mine, it belongs to all who have come for the music. Then it is over, the final applause and the emptying out of the hall.

I hope that perhaps a little of the music has found its way into the being of the place, that it has permeated the plaster of the walls and found a home in the remembering soul of the building. I hope that somehow it will come to enrich the fabric of time in these hills, and that the sound of the music will linger lightly within this space and never die.

It is midnight, and California Route 33, the winding mountain road that transects the Los Padres National Forest, comes at me as if I am driving a course in some electronic video game. Watch for deer, slow down, turn hard to the left; now hard again to the right, brake, speed up, and then stop for just a bit, get out of the van and gaze at the myriad stars above my head. I am very alone, almost spookily alone. It is 1:00 in the morning. I feel as if I am the only person awake in the world. The air is dry and cool up here. The tan-colored embankments on both sides of the road and the double yellow lines down the middle will direct my existence for the next hour.

And now I am winding down out of the hills with my left wheels holding close to the center lines and my eyes intent upon the future unfolding before me in the bright headlight beams of the van.

Around 2:30 A.M., some 80 miles north of Ojai, I descend out of the national forest (which is hardly a forest in my opinion) and enter the Great Central Valley of California. Passing through Taft, I decide, for no particular reason, that I will hold to Route 33 and follow this western parallel to Interstate 5 until I reach Avenal, where I can slip over to the main highway.

At the junction of California Routes 33 and 46, I pause for a moment to recall that just 27 miles to the west, at the junction of

Routes 466 (which is now 46) and 41, near Cholame, the actor James Dean made the final decision of his life: that the approaching car driven by Donald Turnipseed would not make the turn onto Route 466 and cross his path. Dean's final words to his friend and mechanic, Rolf Wutheric, were to the effect that Turnipseed was bound to see them and that he would stop. He did not. Wutherich was thrown clear, but severely injured. Turnipseed was injured slightly. For Dean, it was the final scene, the last curtain for a young Hollywood legend.

Not far from the fatal intersection, a V-shaped monument of shining chrome and steel partially envelopes the base of a shade tree and commemorates the existence of the actor. Its inscription is simple.

JAMES DEAN
1931 Feb8—1955 Sep30pm5:59—OO

Nineteen fifty-five to infinity. Will we remember him for that long? Perhaps we are all born for infinity. It is an interesting concept, infinity. Is it not infinity that is the ultimate destination for everything that is set in motion? Is it not only that the journey along that path is thwarted by either the heavenly pre-planned or the purely scientific interaction of all of the other forces that occupy, shape, and maintain the universe as we know it? Gravity, friction, aging, chemical reactions in our brains that lead to wrong decisions, drugs, cars making left turns in front of us—they all strive to pull us away from that true path to the greatest of unknowns.

I am reminded of that old quandary concerning an arrow that is loosed in the direction of a tree. If the shaft continues to cover half the remaining distance to the tree at any point, then how will it ultimately ever arrive?

If, for the purpose of discussion, we eliminate gravity and all of the other forces except friction, and accept that the ultimate and only goal at the launch of the arrow is infinity, then the tree becomes only a molecular barrier which interacts by friction with the molecules which make up the head of the arrow. The shaft, happily on its way to infinity, now becomes sapped of its energy, and its forward motion comes to a halt. The truth of the matter is that the arrow has never reached its ultimate destination, that of infinity.

In essence, one cannot aim the arrow at the tree. Upon its release, it is aimed solely at the point of infinity determined by the straight line vector upon which the arrow is traveling. The tree simply gets in the way and the true flight of the shaft is suspended before its completion.

Of course, one can manipulate the initial course of the arrow so that it is predetermined that the tree will interfere with its flight and call that "aiming for the tree." Regardless, the true destination of the shaft will still be infinity, and it will never arrive.

If we transcend our earthly bodies upon death and continue somehow to another place, or in some other space, then perhaps our infinitesimal journey continues. James Dean will always be that young man of 24, suspended along his path in our world in time and image, but certainly by now he is much farther along on his true course to infinity.

I believe that the monument out there beneath the tree at Cholame is correct in its portrayal of time. In a sense, it is not just a monument for James Dean—it is a monument to the life journeys of all of us.

I need to get some sleep; all of this late-night, homespun philosophy has taken the last measure of my endurance and flung it out into the emptiness that is all around me.

At Avenal, I turn almost due north, cross over the Kettleman Hills, and join Interstate 5 for my trip up to the tri-city area of Kennewick, Pasco, and Richland, Washington. The time spent in Ojai just seven hours ago has become a blur in my consciousness, and the night is ever so slightly beginning to merge with the coming day.

There is little worse than the tension of trying to stay awake when one is driving. The stress itself is exhausting, and at the first rest area along the interstate I pull in, shut off the engine, and let go of the reins, oblivious to the sounds of the passing semis and the very first inkling of dawn. It is the beginning of the third week of my tour, but I will be unaware of its arrival until the warm morning sun is shining brightly once again upon the valley of the San Joaquin.

CHAPTER 31

Wild, Wild Heart

In the early days of November 1984, I received another phone call from Mason Daring, reaffirming the fact that Rounder Records was interested in doing an album with me. I had just returned from my annual trip out West and was planning to be home for a while, with performances booked almost entirely in and around the Northeast. With almost enough original material to do another recording, I called Mason back, and we set up a timetable for the project. If I was a little short on the number of my own songs that I could use for the record, it wouldn't matter; I knew that I could complete the program with a couple of songs written by my newfound friends, Jon Ims and Chuck Pyle.

I was particularly fond of one of Jon's tunes called "Two of a Kind." The song really spoke to me about life as a guitar picker on the road, with its cheap hotels and late-night hours of driving.

I was also taken by Chuck's song, "The Other Side of the Hill." I guess it was that same feeling of recklessness and the ways of the rodeo-riding vagabond that touched me this time.

The title song for the album would be "Wild, Wild Heart," a tune about an independent trucker and his travels around the country. I got the idea for the song when, on my return trip from the West Coast that fall, I was passed on the New York Thruway by an 18-wheeler. Painted on the doors of the cab of the truck were the words "Wild, Wild Heart." Inasmuch as my car was rocked by the turbulence of the passing semi, so was I moved by the sentiment of the driver. As I was writing the song, I used my own CB handle in the verses to bring the tune home.

> *". . . I've got no steady address,*
> *They call me 'Pony Express,'*
> *And my rig is the "Wild, Wild Heart."*

We did the recording sessions at Blue Jay Recording Studios during January and February of 1985. Karen took the photographs of Hallie and me for the front and back covers, and by that summer "*Wild, Wild Heart*" had been released and was in the stores.

Near the end of 1984, Tom Rush phoned me with an invitation to be a participant in one of his New Year's weekend Club 47 Reunion shows at Symphony Hall in Boston. Performing onstage at Symphony Hall would be an exciting experience for anyone, but what was even more special to me was an invitation to participate in an event that featured so many of the performers who had been my heroes and influences in the early years of my involvement with folk music.

The Club 47 had been my coffeehouse home in the 1960s and the place where so much of my musical soul had come into existence. Now, here were so many of those names and faces, together once again, for a three-night reunion. Some attending were folk music "stars"; others had become architects, surgeons, chemists, record producers, and recording engineers. Some were writing novels, while others were writing for television shows.

Joan Baez and Mimi Fariña were there. Bill Keith and Jim Rooney were there, along with the Charles River Valley Boys. Jonathan Edwards and Jackie Washington were on the show. Dick

Pleasants, New England's most enduring folk music radio personality, emceed one of the nights, and there was, of course, Tom Rush, who put the whole thing together. As I was watching Tom onstage introducing Keith and Rooney, it struck me that here were two of the acts that made up the first show that I ever saw at the Club 47, one night so many years before.

Mark Edwards, the owner of the by-then-defunct Sword in the Stone Coffeehouse, caught up with me during one of the intermissions. Once at his club some 15 years earlier, Mark had commented that he knew that someday I would get to play Symphony Hall, and that when I did he would be there in the audience. I had long forgotten that passing comment, but I was glad to see him and moved that he would remember his promise after such a long time.

There were some performers who had never set foot in the Club 47 and knew the place only by its reputation, and then there were the musicians who had played at the club but hadn't picked up a guitar, for one reason or another, in ages. Above all of this, and throughout the hall over the entire weekend, there remained the glorious, resurrected, and undying common spirit of a brief time and place, and a special musical moment in our lives, that we all still shared together.

* * *

By the end of February, "*Wild, Wild Heart*" was completed, and I was back in the Midwest for a tour that would last almost a month. After stops in Ohio and Illinois, I traveled all around snowy Wisconsin and Minnesota, at one point performing 18 nights in a row. It was during this tour that I began to have some concerns about my voice.

One night in the middle of a show at the Coffeehouse Extempore, I felt a sudden catch in my throat, and although I continued, it was irritating and uncomfortable. My voice had suddenly become husky and hoarse. I was confident that the problem was nothing serious, probably just overwork, but still I was concerned. I had never smoked cigarettes, and only occasionally would I indulge in a pipe or a cigar. One thing that I was doing almost every night, however, was yodeling. It was only one or two songs each evening, but if the audience was in the mood, I would gladly cater to their requests and yodel, whether I felt that my voice was up to it or not.

There are two types of yodeling: good and bad. Any yodeling less than good yodeling is aural torture. The process is simple. Yodeling is a controlled crack in one's voice whereby the yodeler alternates between the vocal chest tone and the falsetto. The "crack," or the break, in the voice occurs in both directions, up and down. The vocal needs to be relaxed and loose and the tones need to be clear, musical, and on pitch. Somebody yodeling either flat or sharp is likely to lead the listener into believing that they would rather be anywhere else having a car wreck.

When everything is working well vocally, it is relatively easy, like rocking back and forth on a seesaw. If the voice becomes tired and hoarse, however, the action becomes more like shining shoes, where the voice begins to erode and can be damaged.

This, I was sure, was what was happening to my voice, so during that tour I decided that it was time to be more discerning as to when I would yodel in concert. Although the yodeling was memorable and could be used as a show stopper, I knew that my musical future was not going to depend on my yodeling. It would be more important to for me to pay attention to the health of my voice.

April was slow, and by May of that year my voice was back to normal. I was writing a fair bit, but mostly I was enjoying a brief respite from a very busy schedule that would pick up again in the summer.

Karen and I began talking about having a family. We both knew that it would be difficult, raising a child with me being on the road so much, but the time seemed right for both of us, and there was a whole other side of the human experience that we each wanted to know and feel—that of being a parent; that of opening your life up to a small soul totally dependent upon you; that of finding emotions within yourself that you never knew existed until, in one moment, a veil is drawn away from your being, and a whole world of discovery is laid out in front of you in the form of a child.

What would it be like, becoming a parent? It would begin with a small step and continue with an immense journey down a completely new road—experienced by so many, and fathomed by so few.

* * *

I spent most of the month of July in the Midwest, performing at the Winnipeg Folk Festival and doing a number of shows over a two-week period in Minnesota. I performed at the Owen Sound Folk Festival northwest of Toronto where, late one night, I sat with John McCutcheon, Johnny Cunningham, and Canadian singer Owen McBride, drinking single-malt scotch and writing what in our own minds surely must have been the most beautiful Celtic air ever created. The later the hour and the lighter the bottle of scotch got to be, the more beautiful the melody became, until it got to be so beautiful that the heavens decided that it belonged there. In the morning there wasn't a soul among us who could remember how the tune went.

Gone then is the tune, along with the bottle of scotch, but held forever in the heart of at least one is the memory of a time when four souls created music together in a hotel room on the shores of Owen Sound, by Georgian Bay, in Canada.

At the end of August, Karen and I returned to Quebec City along with our old friends, John Synnott and Vicky Prescott. It was nice to have the time together with Karen, and in September, we found that the small step had been taken and in the spring we were to become parents.

It was not to be an easy pregnancy for Karen, and as I traveled around the West that fall, through Kansas and Oklahoma, through Colorado and Wyoming, night after night my heart kept telling me that where I should really be was on the road back home. Why was I driving around the country when I should be with my wife?

How many musicians have asked themselves that very same question, and how many times has it been answered: because it is what you do, and if you are a dyed-in-the-wool musician, you simply do not have a choice.

CHAPTER 32

The Fall Tour, Day 15

Someone is screaming in my car! I am slowly opening my eyes, expecting an impact, and realizing that the scream is the sound of my own voice. I am sure that I have fallen asleep at the wheel and it is about to be all over. The sun is warm upon me, and now slowly I come to the realization that the van is parked in a rest area along Interstate 5. It is morning, and the night's drive from Ojai is just a few hours of sleep behind me.

When is it that I started talking to myself all the time? Is it that I am so alone? I am not dead. I can still feel my legs, even though they are a little stiff and cramped. Reclining seats never offer up enough legroom to allow a comfortable night's sleep on the road.

The last time I spent the night in my van was in South Dakota. That night seems like a long time ago. It was a long time ago—nine days to be exact, maybe not a long time in the great course of history, but a long time when you are traveling by yourself.

The facilities at the rest stop are well maintained, generally the exception to the rule, and a splash of water across the back of my neck and on my face chases away the gauzy curtain that seems to be affecting my brain.

There is a small, shiny aluminum trailer parked adjacent to the cream-colored cinderblock restrooms. One side of the trailer opens and folds down, forming a countertop where coffee is being offered by a local veteran's organization. Depositing a dollar in the donation jar, I acquire breakfast: one cup of coffee and three Oreo cookies. I feel guilty about taking the third cookie, but after all it is breakfast, and we all know that a good breakfast is important when it comes to a healthy body.

The tour now becomes a grand journey north through the counties of California: Fresno, San Benito, Merced, and Stanislaus. I enter Sacramento and leave it behind, its governmental heart pumping the automotive corpuscles along the winding arteries of the town. North and north again, into a long valley and the counties of Yolo, Colusa, Glenn, and Tehama.

They are names long whispered upon the breaths of the old native peoples: Siskiyou, the "Bobtailed Horse." They are the names celebrated by the Spanish: Santa Clara, and Mariposa, the "Beautiful Butterfly." They are also the names of the late arrivals: Kern; Glenn; and Lassen, named for Peter Lassen, the Danish immigrant who arrived and explored the area in 1840. They are the names given by or for those who plied the brushstrokes of our history, and now they have been laid upon the maps and atlases of the place in order that we not forget its storied past.

I love this land—this land, my country. I love it from coast to coast. Never shall I tire of its wonders and its people, and along every mile I travel, I shall always be in complete awe of its absolute splendor.

Once again I cross over the bridges at Shasta Lake, old friends now after so many tours. I pass the elegant 14,000-foot volcano, also known as Shasta, and marvel at its presence.

The origin of the word "Shasta" is often debated. Some historical accounts indicate that the name of the mountain is derived from the Shasta Indian tribe. Early variants of the name of the tribe include Sasti, Sasty, Shastl, and Shastika.

Other sources contend that the name is of Russian origin, stemming from the years between 1812 and 1838, when a Russian colony was maintained at Fort Ross on the northern California coast. It was claimed that Mount Shasta could be seen from the summits of the Coastal Range, and the Russians referred to the peak as "Tchastal," or the "White Mountain."

Nonetheless, in 1850 the current name, Shasta, was adopted by the California legislature as the name of the county and the mountain. The letter "a" was added to the end of the moniker to enhance the Spanish flavor of the word, and thus it remains today. Along with its smaller nearby cousin, Black Butte, Mount Shasta is one of the most recognizable landmarks along the trail through northern California.

The shadows begin to lengthen now as the hours of the afternoon and the mile markers slip behind me into oblivion. Oregon is just ahead, and soon California joins the daylight hours and is gone. Once over Siskiyou Summit, I am now alternately coasting and braking down the long, winding grade toward the sparkling lights of Ashland. I have entered Oregon, the "Promised Land" of the American pioneer.

In the dusk of the dying day, a song finds its way to me and I begin to sing.

> *"On Jordan's stormy banks I stand,*
> *And cast a wishful eye,*
> *To Canaan's fair and happy land,*
> *Where my possessions lie.*
> *I'm bound for the promised land,*
> *I'm bound for the promised land,*
> *Oh, who will come and go with me,*
> *I'm bound for the promised land."*

The lyrics were written in 1787 by Samuel Stennett and were set to music in 1835 by M. Durham. Sung often by those who traveled west over the Oregon Trail, the song affectionately became known as "The Pioneer's Hymn," the optimism of its message bringing heart and courage in times of hardship and doubt to those along the trail.

> *"There generous fruits that never fail*
> *On trees immortal grow;*
> *There rocks and hills and brooks and vales,*
> *With milk and honey flow.*
> *Soon will the Lord my soul prepare*
> *For joys beyond the skies,*
> *Where never-ceasing pleasures roll,*
> *And praises never die."*

In the darkness now, the melody and the memory of when I first heard the song on a recording of American Folk Songs by the Norman Luboff Choir linger with me. It was many years ago and I was much younger when I checked the recording out of the library in Lexington, Massachusetts. It was the same day that I first heard the recordings of John Jacob Niles and Richard Dyer-Bennett. How simple and profound this music was to me, and how rich were these stories of the human experience.

Now in the early dark of the Oregon night, it seems that it is only a simple hymn that keeps my lurking loneliness at bay. Stopping at a trucker's hotel just north of Roseburg, I think about calling home to make some sort of connection, but it is three hours later on the East Coast, probably too late for talking, and nowadays the phone calls home never seem to be good for much more than collecting messages or carrying on some sort of domestic business. It is a cold communication. It was not always this way, but so often now the words are never enough to bridge the distances and miles, even though they are so ultimately digital in their clarity.

Far from home, and long out of touch with those that I hope still care, I stare at the walls of this latest hotel until I can stand it no longer and head out across the parking lot, noisy with the din of the diesel engines, to the truckers' lounge and perhaps a barmaid or a bartender who might feel like a little conversation.

It is dance night at the saloon, complete with live country

music provided by a four-piece band set up in the corner. As the truckers and the local guys and gals gather on the floor for a line dance, I can't help but notice that more than half of the men are wearing big black Stetson hats and black-and-white striped shirts, complete with neatly pressed jeans and shiny boots. A colorful bandana is tucked halfway into the right rear pocket of each of the men's jeans, and it strikes me that I have either walked into a bar full of dancing football referees on their night off, or this is the place where all of the Garth Brooks look-alikes are cloned in some sort of a country version of *The Invasion of the Body Snatchers.*

Sitting at the end of the bar, the excitement of watching these prancing stencils has become overbearing. I am about to leave when I pick up one side of a heated conversation between a trucker and whoever is at the other end of his cell phone. It sounds domestic to me and is soon terminated when the trucker, holding a drink in one hand, launches the phone over his left shoulder with the other, causing it to careen off the wall behind him.

"Bitch, bitch, bitch! I never will understand her. I try and do right by her and all I get is bitch, bitch, bitch!"

"Whoa there, Vance, eashey on the rezt of us!" one of the other truckers interjects, slurring his response. "I got one fur ya!" Raising his glass into the air, he searches into the depths of a hole far back in his mind and happily comes up with what he thinks is an applicable ditty.

"Here's to liquor so amber and clear; it's not as sweet as women's lips, but it's a damn sight more sincere!"

Expecting a rousing cheer from at least the male company present, the poet is mystified by the relative silence in the bar. The band is on their break, and only the murmur of 20 or so voices can be heard. He raises his glass again in vain retaliation, then thinks better of it and returns to his seat to graze on the popcorn set out before him in a paper bowl.

I am out of here. I have a show tomorrow in Kennewick, Washington, and a long drive in the morning. As I pass Vance, who has now retrieved his phone from the back corner of the bar, I notice the forlorn look on his face. It is the look of someone who is very tired of everything in his life. It is a look of someone who has not known any sense of victory in a long time and now feels nothing but desperation as each hour of dark time passes before him. He knows nothing else. He has not chosen this life; it has chosen him. Only in the morning will he feel better when he pulls out onto the highways of America, once again in control of the big, loud, smoky machine that he knows so well, searching for some distant glory, the temporary conqueror once again of the dark loneliness that abides within him and slowly eats away at his soul.

It is not a look that I would want to see on my own face as I gaze into any mirror.

I have always believed that there is a reason for what I do and a purpose for the songs that I create. I know that what guides my heart in this life is the presence of family, home, and friends, but I also know that the reason that I was put here upon this earth, what guides my soul and keeps me going, is the creation of music.

When I began to write songs as a teenager, it was rumored that one of the ways that a writer could copyright a song was to record it and then mail the tape of the song back to himself in a sealed package, registered mail. When the package was received back home, it was left unopened and stored away as copyright protection, the premise being that the writer would then have a sealed copy of the song with a dated, government postmark. This dated postmark would be the earliest official confirmation of the existence of the song and would supposedly hold up in court as proof of ownership by the writer. Whether or not this was actually the case, I never did find out for sure, but I did begin a collection of these unopened tapes of this earliest original material and stored it away for safekeeping in what I have come to call "my cabinet."

As the years passed, I began to record albums of my songs, and as each of these recordings was released, I stored two unopened copies of each in the cabinet. When I began to write my journals, and as each of the volumes was completed, they were also stored away. Any incidental music for films or videos would go into the collection. Poetry, lyrics, outlines for long-forgotten novels—they all found their way into the pile. It became, and is to this day, the legacy that I will leave behind in this world.

I consider myself very fortunate, for if I were told that I had ten minutes to left to live, family feelings aside, I could wrap a ribbon around the "cabinet" and say, "Here it is folks, my purpose, my life. I am ready to move on now. It is all that I could do. It is all that I had time for on this good earth. Do with me what you will now, I am finished here." How many are able to place their arms around their own lives and say, "This is who I am and why I am here"? I am truly very fortunate.

I have no delusions of grandeur. What I have created in my life is likely to amount to little more than two dead bugs in the whole of the world. I do know, however, that when I leave this truckers' lounge and go back to my room to make an entry in my journal about the loneliness of the road or where all the Garth Brooks clones have come to dance, my "cabinet" will have grown by just a few lines, and no one can take that away from me. Barring flood or fire or act of God, that cabinet can only grow until my last spark is cold and I am no more.

The music fades now behind the loud diesel din of the parking lot, and it has begun to rain. It is a soft Oregon rain, and I jump to the left and then to the right over the oily puddles that are forming in the low areas of the truck stop. Once back in the room, I shed my boots, sit back on the bed, and write down a few thoughts in my journal. My mind keeps slipping back to the scene at the bar and Vance, the lost soul of a trucker.

Will he call back and apologize to the wife or the girlfriend for hanging up on the conversation, for becoming angry when he should have just reasoned out a response? It seems unlikely. He has done that before, and the reasoning that he gathers in his mind for such a response has never amounted to much more than a finger jammed into the hole of a dam that is collapsing all around him.

"What's the point?" he asks, "Nothing will ever change."

Perhaps he will just have a few more drinks and forget that the conversation ever happened. In the morning, he will find the road there waiting for him, like some enduring masseuse, consoling him with her cool fingers, working him over until the frayed ends of his fragile existence lie easy once again, gathering strength for the next communication with home.

It is almost midnight when the entry into my journal is complete. I have written more than I expected I would write at this late hour. Placing the volume and the pen on the table next to the bed, I turn off the light and wrap my arms around both of the pillows, hoping beyond hope that sometime during the night they will turn into a lover. I fall asleep, feeling very alone—and yet very satisfied. What a strange and fickle existence it is that I have come to know along this road; what a strange and shining star music must be, that I have followed it for so long.

CHAPTER 33

First Lullaby

The year 1986 was ushered in for me with the news that Ricky Nelson had been killed in an airplane crash in DeKalb, Texas. It had been only three weeks since I had gone to see him perform at a nightclub in Buffalo, New York. He was the first legendary rock star that I had ever seen in concert. He sounded as smooth as ever, and his band at the time was one of those old-time rock ensembles that, when they did "Milk Cow Blues," sounded like a train running through the place, with a big driving rhythm and a purity of rock-and-roll soul that was profound. I never knew the man, but his passing, like that of so many other musicians before him, left me with a sense that I had lost a brother or a friend, or someone that I had known very well. He played music. That is all that we had in common in our lives, but that is a strong connection, and I felt a cold emptiness inside of me when the news came of the plane crash.

It was the seventh year of the January All Stars show at Passim, and the club, as always, was full. I spent most of the month doing concerts around the Northeast, but on the morning of Monday the 27th, I, like many people around the country and almost everybody in our small state, was home in front of the television set to watch the launch of the space shuttle Challenger, with New Hampshire high school social studies teacher Christa McCauliffe on board.

It was just not a day to fly; high winds around Cape Canaveral and Launch Pad 39B forced NASA to delay the launch. Everyone would have to wait another 24 hours to cheer on their favorite teacher. I don't know whether it was pride in the fact that Christa McCauliffe was a teacher from New Hampshire (my wife also being a teacher), or some deep-down intuition that had been affecting me, but for weeks, whenever the Challenger flight was mentioned, I would feel a surge of emotion rise up out of my insides, and I would come to the brink of tears. I have always been emotional about such things, but this seemed out of the ordinary.

Tuesday the 28th of January was a cold, clear day in New England. I had been out running errands and arrived home at 11:45 A.M., immediately turning on the television to pick up on the status of the flight. A local newscaster was on camera reporting that counselors had been dispatched to all of the schools in the area. That same welling of emotion churned up, and I knew before I had even heard the news that the Challenger had gone down, and that all souls were lost.

So many of us complain about what we as humans have done to this planet. We pollute our environment, we are constantly at war with each other, we have overpopulated, over-consumed, and ignored many of the forces that keep this world in its natural balance. All of this is true. Yet if this is the human experience at its worst, then it must also hold true that there is another other side to us, a side that sets forth what is the best that we can offer, a side that demonstrates what we can accomplish when we put our minds to it, an example of what we are in our best moments. There are those who dedicate their lives to cleaning up the messes that are the result of the wasteful side of humanity—the poverty, the disease, the hunger—and there is nothing more admirable than this. What I have always been drawn to, however, when I see us in our shining hour, is the dream and the dedication that we may someday reach out and journey to the stars.

On January 28, 1986, one lunging paintbrush stroke to the blue sky—the brilliant orange of exploding fuel, the dark oily smoke, and the bizarre, frenzied little white trails darting from the pieces of a dream—once again reminded us that we are only human, that we are not born to the sky, that we had paid the ultimate price once again in order that we may step beyond ourselves and follow some marvelous path that leads to the unknown edges of the universe.

The crew of the Challenger little knew that day of the dimensions or scope of their journey. They little knew that day that, by the time the sun had set upon this Earth, they would be at rest among the stars.

Some years later, I was fortunate enough to see a space shuttle launch from Cape Canaveral. How could I ever forget the incredible presence of power, or the shock waves as they buffeted my body? As the shuttle reached the same altitude as the Challenger when it left us, I closed my eyes for a moment, waiting for some sign that the danger had passed. When I opened them again, it was just in time to see the tiny speck disappear into the deep blue of the Florida sky. My last inclination before turning to leave the Cape was to ask myself, "Where did it go?" It was an unsettling feeling, to see gravity defied, and so once again I found myself asking, "Where did it go?"

I shot an arrow in the air,
But it did not return,
Instead, it fared across the bluest sky,
And disappeared, a higher place to earn.

* * *

In May of 1986 my son Bowen was born. The labor took 20 hours, and by the end of the delivery, I was prepared to bestow upon my wife the title of bravest woman in the world. We were now parents. I was now a father. What a bundle of emotions this new being was, with his infant's vocabulary of gurgles and coos, charming chortles, and unfathomable screeches. I took to singing the old song, "Pretty Saro" to him as I held him in my arms and walked him around the house. I had always been told that becoming a parent would bring about new awakenings, but little was I prepared for the actuality of the changes.

I developed what I came to call a "heightened sensitivity," and became in my own mind something of a father to every other child in the world. Until this time, watching the evening news was merely an exercise in keeping informed of world situations, but after my son was born, seeing the devastation and the terrible events wrought by wars and the suffering of so many children in the face of poverty and violence became almost unbearable. I found myself unable to listen to many of the stories or look at many of the pictures that were broadcast. Before my son was born, I would shake my head at these daily images and wonder how people could do these things to each other. Now, I could see the face of my own child in the faces of all of the children. It wasn't so much that I feared for Bowen's immediate safety, but now I could look into his face and see the promise and the potential that is inherent in every child. To see this potential destroyed without a chance to flower was something that I could not watch anymore without being deeply wounded in my own heart.

This heightened sensitivity was not limited to children. Early in that summer of 1986, I was scheduled to do an evening outdoor concert at a park in central Massachusetts. It was a warm night, and I arrived an hour early to set up for the show. Shortly after my arrival, there was a commotion in the nearby bushes, and some youngsters came running over to their parents to tell them of some sort of a find. Before long the police arrived to investigate the discovery of the body of a young man. An empty bottle of liquor was found at his side, and he had apparently died of alcohol poisoning. A crowd had begun to gather and curiosity was rampant. Standing at a distance, I found that all I could do was weep—weep for the lost promise and the lost future of a child, everyone's child perhaps, somebody's child for sure. It was very difficult for me to do the concert that night. My mind kept flashing back to the last time that I had seen Bowen, just a few hours before, asleep comfortably in his crib, and probably oblivious to everything around him except the nearness of his mother.

I had a conversation about this experience some weeks later with a friend. We were talking about life in general and the responsibilities that we all must learn to shoulder when it comes time. It struck me then that the young man found in the bushes, although not very old, had certainly reached an age where, barring mental incapacity, he should have been able to make decisions for himself. Choosing to take to the bottle was not a decision made by an innocent child, but by someone who had probably made many bad decisions over the course of an unfortunate life. We have all been children, but we are only children for so long. Bowen will always be my son, but he will not always be my child.

As a parent, what was it that I wanted for my new son? I was asked that question once out of the blue. My immediate response was that I should want him to be truly happy and contribute something to society. That was all. I paused then, wondering whether my answer was adequate. Was there more that I should want for him? When I had time, I thought about it again and concluded that my answer was a good one, and as the years would come to pass it was a response that would never change.

I was performing on the average of three to four nights a week during this period of my life and writing a fair amount of music. I wrote "First Lullaby" for my son, and although I think that people expected that I would write a number of songs about him, "First Lullaby" was the only one that was truly specific. There were a good half dozen songs that came into existence from this period on, however, that I could not have possibly written had I not been a parent. Songs like "Spirit Song," "The Little Cowboy's Lullaby," and "Child of Mine" were all garnered from the experience of parenthood. That experience, one which I have shared with my wife and son, I have always cherished as one of the greatest gifts given to me on this earth.

* * *

In October of 1986, I left for the West Coast with concerts in Chicago, Denver, Fort Collins, Jackson, San Diego, Los Angeles, Ashland, Corvallis, Portland, Seattle, and Alaska. While in Alaska, I was scheduled for a Wednesday show in Ketchikan, a Friday show in Wasilla, and a Saturday night show in Homer.

My flight from Seattle settled reluctantly down onto the rain-soaked runway at Ketchikan, fighting a determined crosswind and braking to a stop with little of the landing distance to spare. From my window on the left side of the plane, I could see beyond the small terminal buildings to the choppy waters of Tongass Narrows, cold and metallic gray, reflecting the hue of the cloud cover over our heads. Once inside the building, I claimed my guitar and bags and followed the signs to the tiny ferry that would take me across the channel to the city of Ketchikan. Descending the steel gangway out of the terminal to the water's edge, I boarded the craft and took a seat, one of a dozen or so passengers bound for the village that receives an annual rainfall of 162 inches. I had been told that Ketchikan was the rainiest place in North America, and one look at the weathered buildings as we approached the city landing supported the fact that it was a well-placed claim. There was that old familiar smell of wet wool again as we all rose to exit the heated cabin of the ferry, and memories of my time on Yukon Island some five years before bounded briefly through my mind. I wondered how Dog and Judy were doing, and I wondered if I would ever see the island again.

A blast of cold, wind-driven mist caught me square in the face as I left the boat and valiantly looked around to see if I could spot my contact. This was a woman who worked at the local public radio station which was sponsoring the concert. In only a few minutes, the connection was made.

Our first stop was at the radio station, where I did an interview with the afternoon host and where there was a message waiting for me concerning the show at the Windbreak Restaurant on Friday in Wasilla. The message was from Patricia King (who also worked for a public radio station in Big Lake), who had done the footwork for the concert in Wasilla. The Friday show had sold out, and she wondered if I would be interested in adding a show on Thursday, the open night between Ketchikan and Wasilla. She also mentioned that if I could get into town for a Thursday night show, there was a pilot who would like to take me flying Friday morning for a few hours.

My flight out of Ketchikan was on Thursday afternoon anyway, and although the 7:00 arrival time in Anchorage and the 45-mile drive to Wasilla from the airport was going to be cutting it a bit thin, I figured that with a 9:00 start, we could probably do the second show. I called Patricia, and we settled on a second show at the Windbreak for 9:00 on Thursday, the next night.

It was a small but responsive audience that evening in Ketchikan. It didn't matter to me. I was just glad to be back in Alaska; the only drawback was that I was missing my family terribly. It would be a feeling that would follow me through the years—so very glad to be here, so very hard to be away from home.

The next day I was at the airport in Ketchikan at 2:00 in the afternoon, waiting to board the plane when it came in from Seattle. As the time slipped away, I became concerned and checked with the gate attendant. There had been an air inversion in Seattle, and all of the flights had been delayed. In fact, my plane had not yet even departed for Alaska. In a bit of a panic, I called Patricia and told her what was happening. She informed me that, amazingly, in the short time since we had last spoken, the second show had sold out. I was at a loss. I could never make it to Anchorage in time to get to Wasilla by 9:00 that night.

It was then that Patricia called into play something that I will always remember—something foreign to me, but something so typically Alaskan. Perhaps it was a spirit, perhaps it was just a mindset—but whatever it was, it worked. She told me to sit tight and that she would monitor the progress of the flight and let me know what to do. As information made its way to the passengers, we were informed that the plane was on its way from Seattle. Even if all went well, I knew that it would be midnight before I could get to the Windbreak. I called Patricia. She said that she would have someone waiting for me at the airport in Anchorage and that the concert was still on. A group of local musicians would fill in until I could make it.

Shortly after midnight, following what seemed like one of the longest days of my life, I walked through the back door of the Windbreak. To my amazement, the place was still full, and everyone cheered. They were ready for a show. The energy came back to me, and I ended up playing until 3:00 in the morning. It was that old energy that never fails when music and good people come together.

When the show was over, Patricia brought me over to one of the tables where a few people were still hanging around and introduced me to Doug Geeting, the pilot who had offered to take me flying the next day. Doug was a big man with a broad face beneath a head of tousled sandy red hair, and he had smiling eyes that betrayed what seemed like a cross between a twinkle and outright laughter. Doug also loved music and was a fine picker in his own right. There was not much time left that night to get to know each other very well, but I had a sense that I was going to like this bear of a man. As far as what kind of a pilot he was, I would just have to wait until the next day to find out.

At 10:00 the following morning, I showed up at the airstrip in Willow. Doug had flown in from Talkeetna where he operated an aviation service specializing in everything from flying grizzly bears out into the bush to conducting moose counts, from depositing hikers up onto the glaciers of Denali to giving wayward folksingers a God's-eye view of the roof of North America. Dressed in a heavy insulated flight suit, obviously well worn, he was in the middle of doing a last-minute walk-around on his bright red single-engine Cessna 185, and he greeted me with a reassuring handshake. After all, I was not particularly accustomed to flying into some of the most extreme mountain areas in the western hemisphere in a little red airplane with a musician pilot that I had known for only six hours.

His walk-around completed, we climbed into the plane and buckled ourselves into the seats. I gazed at the cockpit control panel, trying to decipher what the indicators and switches were all about, and gave up after recognizing only the fuel gauge and the face of the ammeter. Doug handed me a set of earphones, complete with a voice-activated microphone, and told me that this was going to be a great day to fly.

Then Doug began to mumble things to himself and punctuated each set of syllables by either flipping a switch or adjusting some dial. I had no idea what he was rambling about and figured that maybe this was some sort of pilot's prayer or Alaskan Zen ritual. Every once in a while, my ear would catch a word that made sense to me: transponder, flaps, mixture. Suddenly, as if announcing some great "Amen!", Doug yelled out, "Clear!" The propeller began to revolve, slowly at first, and then disappeared visually at the front of the plane as the engine came to life with a roar like a grizzly bear and a blast of wind that rattled the windows. Easing in on the throttle, Doug gave me a wink, and the little Cessna began to taxi toward the far end of the airstrip. Following a brief communication on the radio, he gunned the engine, kicked the rudder over so we wheeled into the wind, and in no more than five seconds we were hurtling down the runway. The tail came up, lowering the nose, and with an ever-so-slight rotation on the yoke, we were up and above the airstrip at Willow. I fell in love. I fell in love with the air. I fell in love with the wind. I fell in love with the little red airplane that was carrying me off on an adventure that would leave me forever changed. I released my breath—which I had been holding for some time—and when I did, a sense of pure joy came over me. I looked down at the winding Susitna river beneath us, its channels like braided tresses lying upon the landscape. I gazed up into the empty blue bottomless sky and when I looked directly ahead, I was immersed in the image of our destination, the snowy ghost-white, ice and granite massif known as Denali. Even from the distance I could feel its spirit—timeless, immense, and howling with the winds that caressed its summit.

In 1896, it was named Mount McKinley by prospector W.A. Dickey after Senator (and by then President) William McKinley of Ohio, a mere mortal who had never set foot in Alaska. The

Athabascans, natives of the Alaskan interior, had a different name for the mountain and had traditionally called it Denali, "the High One." Over the years there were many attempts to change the official name to Denali, all of which were unsuccessful until 1980, when the United States government compromised by changing the name of the surrounding national park to Denali but keeping McKinley as the official name of the mountain. For Doug, and for most Alaskans, it is Denali.

The plane's engine droned and the propeller bit into the frigid air as we approached the mountain over the Peters Hills. Then it was through One-Shot Pass and the assent up the Kahiltna Glacier to an altitude of 10,000 feet, the tiny shadow of our plane a mere mote against the walls of the mountain. I looked up and above us to the spiraling, dizzying heights of the place and knew then what it must be like to be a ladybug making its way through this world of giants. We entered the Don Sheldon Amphitheatre, a bowl of blinding white snow and granite walls, named for the legendary bush pilot who pioneered the procedures for glacier landings in these mountains. We flew across the crest of a ridge, invisible currents of air rocking the plane, and I saw and felt the whole floor of the world fall away from us as we circled down and scooted by the 6,000-foot sheer rock walls of Mount Dickey just a few feet beyond our wingtips. I felt as if I could have reached out and touched the mountain—when in reality the mountain was reaching out to me, touching me and telling me that its spirit was within me, and that we were all a part of the same great music of things.

Then it was out of the heights and onto the Ruth Glacier, our little red plane feeling its oats and willing to carry us anywhere we wished. Doug turned on the FM radio, and music filled my earphones. Peter, Paul, and Mary were singing "Early Morning Rain." It had been a long time since I had heard the song, but I found at this moment that its power over my heart had not diminished through the years. I closed my eyes, thinking about all of the miles I had traveled since those youthful days of driving to Logan Airport in Boston and listening to the planes as they landed there, thinking of far-off places, and it all came home to me.

Descending then, a few hundred feet above the Ruth Glacier, slowly but constantly moving downward on its quest for the sea, I was overwhelmed, and it was then that I could not hide my feelings.

We followed the Susitna back to Willow, and by late afternoon I was again on the ground and getting ready to do the evening show at the Windbreak in Wasilla. My mind and heart, however, were still someplace else. They were soaring over the glaciers and snowfields of a dreamlike world of white, gray, and ice blue. I had felt the magic of the place and now it lived within me.

It seemed that every time I traveled to Alaska, I somehow felt touched by its magic. After the performance that night, Doug mentioned that on my next trip north, I should visit Talkeetna and do a show. There was a little lodge in town called the Latitude 62, and he thought for sure that he would be able to line up a concert date for me at the place. It would be a down-home audience, and given that my tours were in October, most of the audience would be locals. They were great people and loved all kinds of music. I told him that I would see how the bookings for the following year fell into place, but I already knew that nothing was going to keep me from visiting Talkeetna, the little town with such a big reputation.

Doug Geeting flew back home that night, and in the morning I was on my way to Homer for my final Alaska concert that year.

I flew back down to Seattle at the end of that October and started driving east, with only one stop in Minneapolis before heading home to my family. Once back in New England, my thoughts kept returning to the mountain, and by the end of November I had written the song "Redbird's Wing" for Doug and his little red plane. I had also written another tune about Alaska entitled "The Shores of Prudhoe Bay." I knew at the time that the song might raise a few eyebrows in the folk music world, being that it was a celebration of shipping oil out of the north slope, but my life was about people, and the oilmen and the crews that worked at the Prudhoe facility deserved to have their own unique story told. If I was going to write songs that were rich in the human spirit, then by golly I would write songs that told the stories of *all* of the different types of people that I came to know in my travels.

I spent much of that December around home, watching Bowen become an even bigger bundle of energy and responsibility. I knew that it was hard on Karen, having me on the road so much, but now I was almost 40 years old, and time appeared to have carved a groove in front of me, a groove along which I was always meant to travel.

We spent New Year's of 1987 in the hills of Georgia, visiting Karen's grandparents, Vernon and Myrtle Smith. They were a couple of the old South, and I loved to listen to the drawl and the music of their language as they talked about the years of their lives in and around Dahlonega.

Vernon's parents, Ben and Bessie Smith, had opened the Smith House in Dahlonega as a restaurant shortly after buying the building in 1922, and they developed it into what is today a Georgia landmark for home-style dining.

From Georgia, Karen and Bowen flew home, and I continued farther south to do a brief tour in Florida, and then back up the East Coast, with stops in both of the Carolinas.

I turned 40 that February of 1987, and on that day I made a brief entry into my journal, quoting from one of my own songs.

February 6th, 1987
Turned 40 today.
"I am a climber in my soul, in search of everything."

CHAPTER 34

The Fall Tour, Day 16

From Roseburg, Oregon, to Portland, it is approximately 170 miles, and I am well on my way by middle morning, away from the trucker's motel and the dancing football referees. Vance, I expect, is well on his way, too, and I am curious as to which direction he might be traveling. Are we both headed into the same storms, or at the close of the day will our destinations be far apart? Is it really important? What does it matter? I suppose that even a thought of the trucker is just a way to pass the time on a rainy morning in Oregon.

I am scheduled for a concert tonight in Kennewick, Washington. Kennewick, along with Richland and Pasco, is one of the so called Tri-Cities, located at the junction of the Snake, Yakima, and Columbia Rivers. From this junction, the Columbia continues west through the Columbia Gorge to Portland, where it makes an easy turn to the north, and then west again, until at Astoria, amidst the forests of firs and spruces, it finally empties into the Pacific.

By noon, I am just south of Portland. Here the highway splits, Interstate 5 continuing straight ahead to the north and downtown, and the bypass, Interstate 205, skirting along the east side of the city. I steer off onto the bypass. Nearing the airport, I make the connection with eastbound Interstate 84 and begin the second half of the day's journey up the Columbia.

The Columbia River begins its 1.200-mile journey to the sea in the lake country, between the Selkirk Mountains and the Great Divide in southeastern British Columbia. Although dozens of tributaries empty into the Columbia, there are ten major contributors to its flow: one in Canada—the Kootenay; and nine in Washington—the Spokane, Wenatchee, Okanagan, Yakima, Deschutes, Willamette, Cowlitz, Lewis, and the largest, the Snake, which itself is 1.100-miles long.

Once one of the wildest rivers on the continent, with waters leaping over rocky islands and careening down canyons, the Columbia is now one of the most environmentally controlled rivers in the world, with a drainage area that is governed by more than 400 dams that provide most of the electrical power to the Northwest.

Nonetheless, it is still a beautiful river, wide and impressive in its geological legacy, creating a gorge with bluff-like walls hundreds of feet high, carving its way through lava flows and the basalt layers of the Cascade Range.

I pass Hood River and the Dalles, named by the trappers working for the fur companies in the 1800s. Based on the French word "*dalle,*" meaning "flagstone," probably because of the layers of basalt in the area, this narrow stretch of the river was an important arrival point to those traveling the Oregon Trail. For them, it was the end of the overland passage. Here the wagons were roped to barges and transported down the river that final 100 miles to the Willamette Valley and "the Promised Land." It was not an easy transport down the river, but after months on the trail, the end of the journey was now finally on the near horizon.

I am in the great river gorge now, climbing ever so slowly eastward, past John Day and into the bright sun, leaving the western rains behind me. Growing up thinking that the entire northwestern part of the country was shrouded under the cover of thick, dark forests of evergreens, perpetually wet and dripping with cool rains, it was certainly a surprise to find, on my first trip to the area east of the Cascades, that the land was a high, semi-arid plateau, poor with trees, but striking to view with its rolling hills, valleys, and sky that at night becomes a cauldron of stars.

It is the middle of the afternoon. At Hermiston, I head north, crossing over the Columbia at Umatilla. It is a long gradual ascent out of the river valley, the shadows of the sage-covered hills of Washington growing longer in the declining sun. My concert this evening is for the Three Rivers Folklore Society, and it will be good to see my old friends John and Micki Perry, the guiding lights of the organization. John and Micki are of that rare breed of diehard folkies that have managed to keep folk music alive in an area of the country that is a bit off the beaten path for most touring artists. It is also another testament to the durability of this music and the dedication of those who have made it so much a part of their lives.

Just before 5:00 in the afternoon, I pull up in front of their house in time to find John loading up the back of his car with supplies for the concert. The venue, a local Grange Hall, is only a few blocks from their home, and on a good weekday night by 7:30, there should be an audience of around a hundred in attendance for the show.

I have never been a performer who likes to sequester himself backstage before a concert. I *do* need a few minutes to tune up and make sure that I'm not going onstage with my fly down or some such thing, but other than that, it is being there to greet my audience and get a sense of their demeanor that is a far better use of my time. Besides, it is boring backstage when you are a solo performer. I spend enough time alone. I would much rather get to know the people in front of whom I am about to convey my innermost feelings through song. Some of the faces I will recognize, some will be new to me, but in the end it is my hope that in some way we will have all become friends.

This night it looks as if the place will not be full, but for a Wednesday the size of the audience will be respectable. Already a number of familiar faces have entered the hall through the double doors at the front of the building. I see that the Tolars, Mick and

Suzi, have driven up from Irrigon, Oregon. (I always thought that the name of the town had a ring to it.) Before he retired as a school principal, Mick was always willing to promote a concert through his school system whenever I was in the area. I would stay in their home, and after the shows we would always have a few glasses of wine and talk about Alaska, one of his favorite places.

It is time for the first set. I begin with "Crossing the Water" and follow it with the story song, "Ol' Pen." Then it is a slow ballad, then a lively piece about black flies. I read the faces; I watch for the lost and quiet eyes. It is hard for me to look into them, for that would be prying and personal. If during the evening there is a change in those eyes, I am glad, for I know that it is because of the music and nothing else.

It is time for the break, and I am at the table in the back, selling my CDs so the music might remain long after I am on my way to the next town. Once, during an entire weekend of shows at a college in West Virginia, I played to a total of four people. Between those four people though, I managed to sell eight or nine recordings, and that was enough to make the weekend worthwhile. Certainly it wasn't the money that I took in from the sales, it was the fact that through those recordings there was a chance that someone else might be introduced to the music, that somebody else might be moved by listening to a song.

Now the first tune of the second set. It is a piece about many of the rivers that wind their way across the landscape of this country. The song is entitled, "So Sang the River." I sing my songs "The Roseville Fair" and "Coyote." Then it is a silly song about the moon, and a story about growing older. I have sung these songs hundreds of times, and the performance of many of them has become second nature to me. Yet when I listen to them, I can still feel their soul, and I know that it is my soul, and I become aware all over again of who I am as a person.

And then it is over. Another show. The microphones are turned off. The people file out, except for a few who linger to talk awhile, and the Grange Hall in Kennewick is once again silent. John and Micki have invited a few of the local musicians over to their house for a small get-together, but by a little after midnight, the house is quiet again, and I am comfortably ensconced until morning in the folds and pillows of their living room sofa. I pray softly that my family is safe, and I pray that the sun will once more shine upon me at the coming of the new day.

CHAPTER 35

Redbird's Wing

Rounder was ready to do another recording, so in April of 1987, with Mason Daring producing, I went into the studio to complete my 13th album. The title song would be "Redbird's Wing," the piece I had written for Doug Geeting and his plane.

I had sent a tape of the song to Patricia King, my contact at KABN Radio in Wasilla, and the person who had promoted my show at The Windbreak that previous fall. I asked her if she might play the song over the air as a surprise for Doug. She agreed.

The way the story was related to me was that Patricia called Doug and told him that she had something for him to listen to, and that she would play it for him over the air at noon on a specific day. Evidently, it was not easy for Doug to pick up the signal from KABN Radio at his home in Talkeetna, so at the appointed time he climbed into a truck with his friend Sandy Norbert, and off they drove to the top of a nearby hill where the signal was stronger to listen to Patricia's show. I had no idea what his reaction would be, for writing a song about another person's life is a dangerous thing. I could only hope that he might be pleased with the spirit of the offering.

I did not talk to Doug for some time, so for a while I was in the dark about his reaction upon hearing the piece. One day, I received a copy of the Anchorage newspaper. I believe it was the Sunday feature section, and it contained an article about Doug and his life as a pilot in Alaska. In response to a question about why he chose a life of flying around in the mountains, Doug responded with the same lines that I had entered into my journal on my 40th birthday, "I am a climber in my soul, in search of everything."

I knew then that the soul of the song "Redbird's Wing," written so many thousands of miles away, like some tiny bird had found its way back home.

With the recording of the new album completed by the end of April, I took two weeks off and returned to Quebec City with Karen and Bowen. Quebec City in the spring is one of the loveliest places that I know. It was warm that year, and the Plains of Abraham were green with the new grasses of May. We walked along the wooden esplanade that hugs the bluffs and overlooks the lower town. Bowen, almost a year old, became intrigued with an old man sitting on one of the benches and playing music sprightly upon a violin. As he played, his feet moved in a quick step dance to the rhythm of the piece, tapping away against the wide boards of the walkway. With the turrets of the Chateau Frontenac towering above us, we wandered along cobblestone streets, gazing through the windows of the art galleries and admiring the flower boxes, now brimming with springtime colors and new life.

We spent a week in the city that spring, and some two years later the memories of the streets, the old man, the ever-present flower boxes, and the white birds that flew above us in the warm wind would become inspiration for a new song entitled "The Streets of Old Quebec."

It was a happy time. Bowen celebrated his first birthday, the new album was done, and the days of late spring were upon us. Why is it that so often at these times, the great balance of things shows itself, and we are reminded once again of our mortality?

At the end of May, I received a call from Steve Nerney informing me that Dabris had passed away after suffering a heart attack in San Francisco. Marty flew back to the East Coast, and on the last day of that month I attended a memorial service in Boston for my good friend.

Marty's plans, of course, were up in the air, but she expected to return to San Francisco and stay on for at least a while. I would always be welcome at her place. The day after the memorial service, I made an entry into my journal.

Mon. June 1st, 1987
It is warm and beautiful today.
If we were to treat each of our days as a lifetime,
Then we would never have to worry about tomorrow.
I love life.

The summer of 1987 passed quickly. In July, I made a short trip to Minnesota, where I played for one night at The Extempore and finished out the weekend with a spot at a folk festival in Lutsen, farther up along the shores of Lake Superior. It would be my last performance at the coffeehouse. A few months later, the Extempore, after many years of being a musical home for so many, passed into history. Its final location was a block from the original building in what was formally The Cedar Theatre, but I think that my heart always remained at the old space. Now a retail sports outfitting store, the upstairs concert hall was being used as a storage area for canoes, skis, backpacking equipment, and mountain climbing gear. Because of some sort of a city ordinance having to do with altering building facades, the sign for the old coffeehouse still remained for some months, protruding proudly above the passers by on the sidewalk—unnoticed by most, but to those who cared a poignant reminder of a marvelous era of friends and music.

As the month of August waned, I found myself back on the road for eight days with a concert on Cape Cod at the First Encounter Coffeehouse; shows at Musikfest in Bethlehem, Pennsylvania; and a concert in Wilmington, Delaware, set up by my friends, Stephanie and Bill Speakman. There was also an appearance at the Philadelphia Folk Festival. While at the festival, I hooked up with my old Texas buddies Aileen and Elkin Fowler. We were all staying at the same hotel and got together each night after the concerts, playing music just like old times back in the South.

There is a saying to the effect that when a musician is home they miss the road, and when they are on the road they miss being at home. I guess that this could not have been more true at the time, for with each passing note of the music, I still longed for that place which had always been my strongest foundation: home.

CHAPTER 36

The Fall Tour, Day 17

It is Friday, the 17th day of my tour. By now I have driven almost 5,000 miles and traveled through 16 states. John has long been up and gone, off to his job as a training engineer at the nearby Hanford Power facility. Because it is a relatively easy hop down to Corvallis for my evening concert, Micki and I have a bit of time this morning to read the paper and catch up on what is happening with other musician friends.

"So, what is Dan Maher up to these days?" I query Micki as I gobble down one of her chocolate chip cookies left over from the concert.

"Oh, Dan still has his show. I heard that he was off in Ireland or Scotland or someplace like that, doing research and gathering material to use on a Celtic music project that he has in the works."

Dan Maher, one of our mutual friends, is the long-time host of a public radio show out of Pullman called Inland Folk. A versatile performer and musician in his own right, Dan has promoted a number of concerts for me over the years in and around Pullman, Washington, and Moscow, Idaho. It was because of Dan that I came to appreciate the long rolling hills and wide-open country of eastern Washington known as the "Palouse."

It was out of this area, around the Palouse River, that the Nez Perce tribe bred wild mustangs with European breeds. The result of this breeding was the spotted horse that would become legendary for its devotion and its stamina, the horse that would take its name from the land itself, the Appaloosa.

It was also because of Dan that I came to know the pleasure of unfiltered Trappist Ale, and often after the shows we would sit at Rico's Bar in Pullman and talk about music until the early morning hours. Fortunately it was only a walk across the street to my hotel. Still, those Trappist Monks from Belgium on more than one occasion managed to turn that short walk up the hill into a mighty adventure.

By 11:00 in the morning, I am on the road again, back down across the Columbia River into Oregon and on my way west. It is a beautiful day, and the river is wide and flat and bright blue. Suddenly, the droning sound of my tires against the road is almost muted when two Air Force fighter jets swoop down out of the sky with a tremendous roar and skim along the broad river channel only a few hundred feet above the surface. Then in a flash they are gone, once again climbing steeply into the hollow depths of the sky above. I am amazed at their power and agility, and I am excited by the experience. Perhaps the hotshot pilots were breaking some sort of rules; I don't know. I do know that I am drawn to their shenanigans and the freedom of their spirits. Now the planes are nothing but two dark specks, and then they disappear for good toward the north.

I enter the great river gorge and retrace my journey of only a day before, down past the John Day Dam and then past The Dalles. In front of me, the sky is beginning to darken, a sure sign that when I get to Portland it will be raining. By 2:00, I am on the city bypass and heading south to Corvallis. The days just seem to slip away when you are constantly on the move. Prospecting for a cassette amongst the dozens amassed between the two front seats of the van, I decide on some music by John Stewart, a classic recording of his *The Phoenix Concerts.*

I have always admired the music of John Stewart, ever since the early 1960s when he became a member of the Kingston Trio, replacing Dave Guard. I suppose it is because his music has always been steeped in tradition, history, and the human spiritual energy that is such a guiding force for us all. I sensed this when he was with the Trio and I heard the songs "Run the Ridges" and "The New Frontier," then later as a solo artist or with Buffy Ford doing "Lincoln's Train," "Cody," "Armstrong," and "Spirit." Here is a person who had traveled with Bobby Kennedy and written "The Last Campaign." John is much more than a songwriter, he is a chronicler of time, events, and the human experience. Never will I forget sitting in front of the television set at my home in New Hampshire on an early July evening in 1976, watching a bicentennial special hosted by the Smothers Brothers. John Stewart appeared on that show, and amidst the headlines of the times and a recent presidential resignation, he sang a simple song entitled, "Survivors." It was a song to America, a song that assured us that no matter what happens, as a nation we will survive. Here within lies the essence of Pete Seeger, of Woody, and of Leadbelly, of all of those who have stood up to their knees in history and felt in their guts that it really mattered.

I am lost now, lost in the music that I fell in love with so long ago. I am a sailor again in John's song, "The Pirates of Stone County Road." I am adrift on a course to the south, steadily making headway against the wind and the traffic on Interstate 5, just north of Corvallis. It is a golden afternoon, the rain now behind me to the north. The low sun highlights the leaves of the aspens and maples as I take the exit for my destination and head west into town. I will sing tonight. I have been inspired by that old flame that is deep within me, inspired by the soul of music.

The concert space in Corvallis is almost full. It is in the sanctuary of one of the churches in town, and the volunteers for the Corvallis Folklore Society are busy setting up tables and chairs for the show. Anna Ellendman, a former president of the group, is concert coordinator for the night and is busy at the ticket table sorting out presales, reservations, and anything else that might need her guiding hand. It is Anna who introduced me to Carleen and Mike McCornack, the couple who are doing the opening set. Over the years it has come to be a tradition that do a tune or two together to close the concert.

As their set begins, I quietly settle into one of the seats at the back of the hall to listen to Mike and Carleen weave their way through the rich and soothing harmonies of their songs. I think it is often difficult for a performer to relax enough to enjoy an entire set by the opening act, no matter how talented the musicians may be. I know that frequently I am able to listen to the first few songs, but then I find that it is time to retreat to the backstage area to immerse myself in my own music, to feel the touch of my own guitar, and to catch the rhythm and the groove that is the heart of my own performance. This night, however (as it is always with Mike and Carleen), I am able to close my eyes and enjoy all of their time onstage. They are not the opening act. They are an integral part of the evening. Their music is as important as mine, and to watch the audience respond to them gives me an immense amount of pleasure. They are my friends, and as they finish their show, I find myself applauding as loudly as anyone else in the hall.

The energy is good this night, and as the three of us close the show with a version of Tom Paxton's, "The Last Thing on My Mind," I am again reminded of a thought from David Amram's book *Vibrations*: onstage it is not any one individual, but the soul of the music that is important.

It is late now, and after a few glasses of wine back at Anna's Home for Wayward Musicians, Mike and Carleen have left to drive back to Eugene. I close my eyes, and in short order I am asleep on the living room couch. I will be on my way early in the morning, not so much because I have a long distance to travel, but because my time in Corvallis is done. I have seen my friends. I have played my music. And in all of this, I have lived another day of my life. I will never have this time again. I may come close, when in a year or so I return to do another show, but it will never be the same moment. I am a road musician, and all that is left now in this town is an early morning disappearance and the last faint whispering notes of a song.

CHAPTER 37

Sky Dancers

On the last day of September I began the first day of my 1987 fall tour. It was the eighth year of the seasonal trip, and during the first week I stopped to do shows in Buffalo, Ann Arbor, Dayton, and Louisville. Three days later, after a stop to visit Old Bent's Fort in southeast Colorado, I was driving all around California, performing on consecutive nights in Atascadero, San Luis Obispo, San Diego, Los Angeles, Davis, and San Francisco. While in San Francisco, I met up with Marty and spent a day or two at Whitney Street. It was good to see Marty again, and she seemed to be holding up as well as could be expected after Dabris' death. We went out for dinner one night at the Cliff House and watched the seals just offshore on Seal Rock, frolicking in the late afternoon sun. It was fun, but it felt a little strange without Dabs.

Then I was off to the Northwest with shows in Portland; Corvallis; Seattle; and Moscow, Idaho. I was beginning to fall victim to the old scenario of waking up in a hotel room and not knowing where I was. I loved it, though. Except that it was time away from my family, I still felt that every bend in the road held the possibility of a great new adventure.

I was scheduled for three concerts in Alaska in 1987. On the morning of October 20, I flew out of Seattle. By early afternoon, I had landed in Juneau, been picked up by Mike McCormick (who was the promoter for the show), and was settled into the Baranoff Hotel, two days early for my first concert and glad to have enough time to do a little exploring. It had been six years since I had been in Juneau, and with no concert that night my first stop—of course—had to be a few doors down the street at the Red Dog Saloon.

The place had not changed much. There was the same sawdust floor (most likely the *very* same sawdust floor), and over in the corner there was the same table, the table that I had sat at after my concert in 1981 as a newcomer to Alaska, a Cheechako making fun of all of the other Cheechakos that ventured into the Red Dog that night from the tour boats anchored in the channel.

There was to be a big event at the Red Dog that week. Unfortunately—or fortunately, perhaps—I would be gone by the time of the event. A grand sign with all of the gruesome details, painted in brightly colored, old-timey lettering, adorned the top of the bar.

> A CHALLENGE HAS BEEN ISSUED
> At 10:00 P.M. on this coming Saturday, October 24th
> At this very Red Dog Saloon
> Tom___, will attempt to break the Oyster Shot Eating record, that record being 64 oyster shots in 183 seconds.

The sign went on to present the parameters of the competition, including the fact that upon the completion of the challenge, the participant must maintain his dignity for at least 20 minutes. The concoctions would consist of one raw oyster, covered with about a quarter of an inch of cocktail sauce, served up in a shot glass.

To me, this event reeked with the ingredients of someone's last meal, and I was glad that I would not be in Juneau to witness the festivities. It was beyond me that anyone could have succeeded in downing 64 oysters in just over 3 minutes in the first place—unless they happened to be a Silkie, part human and part seal, straight out of Irish mythology.

Out of curiosity, I did order up two shooters, and then counted myself among those who would never attempt such a thing. I reminded myself that this was Alaska, where, as the old saying goes concerning a woman's quest to find a man in this part of the world: "The odds are good, but the goods are odd."

As the hours of the afternoon waned, I left the Red Dog and made my way along some of the streets in this small and seemingly quiet town. It is not really a town, though. It is the capital city of Alaska, and as the governmental buildings emptied between 4:00 and 5:00, the streets became alive with state workers, mostly in casual clothing, all of them hustling against the dampness and the wind that had picked up off of the Gastineau Channel. Some I supposed were headed for home, while others headed for the Red Dog or one of the other many bars that lined the adjacent streets.

I entered one of the local native craft shops on a search for something to bring home to Karen and Bowen but found nothing to my liking, so I headed back to the Baranoff for a nap. Climbing the steep, dark wooden stairway to my second-floor room, I couldn't help but overhear a couple arguing behind one of the closed doors along the hallway. I thought, what a shame it is that people have to argue so much. I was tired. It was only a little after 5:00 in the afternoon, but it already felt as if it were the end of a long, long day.

The following noon, Katy McCormick, Mike's wife, dropped by the hotel to drive me over the bridge to Douglas Island, where I wanted to explore the Treadwell mining site, now a public park and historic walking trail. I had read a magazine article some three years before about the mining operation, which closed down in 1922, and had written a piece about a character working the Treadwell site called "The Miner's Song." I backed it on the *Wild, Wild Heart* recording with an instrumental entitled "Sourdough." Most of the background material for the song was garnered from the article, but now I wanted to stand next to "the Glory Hole" and experience the ghostly essence of those about whom I had written.

It was all there in the remnants of the past that lined the trail to the diggings. There were the old buildings that once housed the company miners as they toiled their way into history. There were the iron skeletons of the machines, rusted and silent, and finally there were the diggings themselves, cut down 2,000 feet into the veins of Alaska, bleeding out the yellow wealth that would find its way into the coffers of so few.

They were company men, those miners, glad for the meager comforts offered by the Treadwell Company: showers, hot food, entertainment, and at the close of the day, a two-dollar steady wage. Of course, as it has always been along the passage of mining history, much of that wage went straight back to the company through the profits from the company store and all of the other expenses incurred by the workers as they carried on their daily lives.

What a time it must have been, I thought as I backed away from the precipitous drop and followed Katy back along the path to the car. A thick fog had moved in over Douglas Island, and the deep green spruces shed droplets of cold moisture onto the thick groundcover at our feet. It could have only been love or riches that would have brought those people here, so far from home, to toil away their lives in this slippery mud, cold rain, and constant danger. Yes, what a time it must have been, I thought again as I climbed into the warm confines of the car.

Katy drove me back over the bridge to Juneau and the Baranoff Hotel. Later in the afternoon, she and Mike returned to take me to the concert venue for the show.

I loved being in Alaska again. Close to 200 people showed up for the music that night, including an old friend by the name of Gary Chamberlain who had worked at Caffé Lena in the late 1960s.

Gary had started a communications company in Alaska, become a pilot, and was currently operating a guide service based in Gustavus. We all went out for drinks after the show, and in the morning Gary drove me out to the Juneau airport to catch the "milk run" up to Anchorage and my second concert in the north at a club called Grand Central Station. I had one show remaining after my concert in Anchorage, and that was at the Latitude 62 in Talkeetna, home base to my pilot friend Doug Geeting.

I had arranged to meet Doug at the concert in Anchorage. After the gig, he and I would drive over to Merrill Field in the car that he kept at the airstrip, hop in his plane, and at midnight or so fly the 135 miles north to the little town that he called home.

The concert in Anchorage was a great success, with close to 500 people showing up at the door. I wanted to take each and every one of them with me on the rest of my tour. As planned, I hooked up with Doug, and with the excitement of the evening still raging inside of me, we scooted over to Merrill Field, climbed in his plane with all of my gear, checked the instruments, and were soon airborne, with the city lights of Anchorage rapidly falling away behind us.

We followed the lamp-lit Glen Highway for a while, heading east, and then veered north over Wasilla, where we were soon engulfed by the black curtain of night sky above and wilderness below. Doug set his directional finder and distance-to-go indicator, and after he had switched on the automatic pilot and settled back into his seat, told me to relax and enjoy the scenery; the plane would take care of the business of flying. Scenery? I thought, what scenery? All I could see was blackness, one immense world of blackness, and it was all around us.

"Are you sure you know where we're going?" I asked, feeling a little foolish, but still wanting to be very sure of our circumstances.

"Oh, yeah, no problem," he answered, pointing to the dim light emanating from a single cabin some 3,000 feet below us. The flash of a distant strobe caught his eye and he made an ever-so-slight course correction, explaining that the bright flashes were from one of the radio towers on a far-off mountain.

"As long as you can see a distant light in front of you at night, that means there's nothing between you and that light to worry about."

I wasn't worried at all. I was just remembering that, as a boy, I would stop what I was doing when I was outside at night and listen intently to a plane passing high over me in the darkness, wondering what it was like up there for those invisible people in their little world so far beyond my reach. What did they see? What were they feeling?

Suddenly Doug sprang into action, reached for the microphone belonging to his radio, and clicked the talk button a number of times. Below us and just ahead, as if by some sort of magic, two bright parallel lines of runway lights appeared out of the blackness.

"Tax dollars at work!" Doug quipped, as he throttled the engine back a bit and lined the plane up for a straight-in final approach. He reached between the seats for the lever that controlled the flaps and tugged back a notch. The plane responded easily, slowing and dropping a bit until we attained the correct slope along the flight path.

"Yeah, the state took control of our little airstrip recently and now we're real uptown, kinda like landing in L.A." With a few more adjustments to the flaps and the throttle, Doug brought us down as if we were a milkweed spore settling upon a carpet of soft earth. The plane rolled to a stop, swerved about, and we back-taxied toward the collection of metal buildings that, aside from his own cabin, were the center of Doug Geeting's world. It was 1:00 in the morning.

"You're staying in my guest house tonight. Tomorrow I'll take you over to the Latitude 62 and introduce you to Nancy and Mack, the folks who run the lodge. You'll be playing in the side room. Talk about town is good so we should have a fair number of people at the show. One thing's for sure though, we'll have a good time. You must know Ramblin' Jack Elliot. He was up here not long ago."

We climbed aboard his truck and drove the half mile down the road from the airport to his home on the banks of the Susitna River. A small A-frame, only a few feet from his larger wooden house, would be my home for the next two nights. Doug opened the door, turned on the lights, turned up the heat, and pointed to the loft.

"You can sleep up there in the loft. There are plenty of blankets, and I'll see you in the morning. If you have time and the weather holds, maybe we can go flying again tomorrow. Oh, by the way, welcome to Talkeenta."

I climbed the ladder to the loft, empty now of all energy, but again filled with the magic that is Alaska. I did not rise until the middle of the morning on the following day. After washing up in the tiny bathroom of the A-frame, I headed over to the main house and knocked on Doug's front door. He was already up and about and had been over to his office at the airport to read his mail and check on his plane. He asked me if I was up for breakfast, which seemed like a plan to me, and so off we went in his truck, a distance of some 200 yards down the road, and turned into the driveway of the Latitude 62, a piney log building that from that morning on would become my Alaska home.

The first sense one has of being greeted at the Latitude 62 is from the wooden sign posted on the front door. It is a sign which has been branded with the word "Welcome" in about seven different languages, obviously meant to make the climbers who show up in the spring and early summer to climb Mount McKinley feel at home. We stepped inside, out of the crisp, cold air of the Alaskan fall, and were instantly enveloped in the warmth of the cozy room and the smell of fresh coffee and frying bacon. Although I had never set foot in the Latitude 62 before, almost at once something within me awakened, and I had the strong sense that I had played in the place many times before. Perhaps it was simply my state of mind that day, or perhaps it was the ambiance of the lodge, with its bar, fireplace, and two rooms off to the side that served as dining areas, but I recognized and felt the same spirit that I had always known at Anderson Fair in Houston. I immediately felt a strong connection to the Latitude and knew that it would invariably find its welcomed way into the depths of my life on the road.

"Hey Doug! What's up?" came a call from the door of the kitchen area. I closed my eyes. Not only did the Latitude 62 remind me of Anderson Fair, but the voice and accent of the woman now approaching us was the same as that of Francie Files, one of the original Anderson Fair ladies. I immediately felt at home.

Doug introduced me to Nancy Trump, a tall woman with long hair and a commanding presence that might have even been intimidating were it not for her warm and sincere smile. As we struck up our conversation and I listened to her talk, again I felt the spirit of the place. I couldn't help but blurt out to Nancy that she sounded just like a good friend of mine in Texas, and that I felt as if I had played at the Latitude 62 a hundred times before. She laughed, and I knew that from that moment on we would be friends.

Nancy explained that I would be performing that night in the larger of the side rooms, and that it looked as if the show would probably sell out. Selling out at the Latitude meant only about 60 people in attendance, but it didn't matter to me; these would be 60 special people, 60 people who would become a part of my great Alaskan dream.

And so it happened, the concert stage, the new friends, and the experience of a new place to play. I suppose that for those who came to the show, I was the focus of the evening, but for me it was the sharing of the music and the coming together of people willing to listen to that music that was of true and lasting significance.

At the conclusion of the show, more than half of the people stayed and began to party the rest of the night away at the bar, which would remain open until the very wee hours of the morning. Nancy, Doug, and I sat at one of the large round tables at one end of the room and talked about flying, music, and life in Alaska.

"How has your Alaska tour been going?" Nancy asked.

"How could it be anything but great?" I responded. "Something new and magical happens to me every time I come here."

"So what has been new and magical about this trip?" she inquired, ordering another round of drinks for the three of us.

"I'm not sure yet. It's my last night in the north and I usually don't comprehend what that magical thing is until I am long gone from here. I know though, that there is magic here and something will happen. It always has."

At that very moment, a chorus of hoots and cheers began to filter through the front door from the parking lot outside. My first inclination was that perhaps some sort of a brawl had broken out, and that everyone was about to adjourn to view the happenings.

There was no brawl, but there were happenings, for all one had to do was to look straight up into the Alaskan night sky. There above, weaving, circling, and cavorting with the stars, were the brilliant blue, green, orange, yellow, and red fires of the legendary sky dancers of the north, the Alaskan *aurora borealis*, the northern lights.

Starting out in blues and greens, the strands of light circled around each other, braiding themselves and tightening like coiled springs until, with a chorus of cheers from the parking lot, they burst apart in trailings of bright yellows, oranges, and reds, filling the sky with color, and filling the night with magic. I looked at Nancy.

"We always see northern lights up here," she said, "but I have never seen anything like this. This is incredible!"

"You see," I said, "There *is* magic in this place. It is always here for me."

She smiled. We stood for a while, the two dozen of us, half frozen with the cold of the night, watching the dance, and hanging onto the next colorful pirouette of light. My eyes were moist. This was Talkeetna. These were my friends. And beneath these beautiful sky dancers, on this last night in Alaska, I knew that I would return.

* * *

The Alaska Airlines 737 from Anchorage touched down in Seattle early in the afternoon of Sunday, the 25th of October, 1987, and I began my drive back to the East Coast. My last string of concerts for this tour were in Jackson, Wyoming; Durango, Colorado; Denver; Lincoln, Nebraska; Minneapolis; Milwaukee; Rhinelander, Wisconsin; and Valparaiso, Indiana, all on consecutive nights. I was beginning to think that I had truly lost all of my marbles. Sleep had become optional, available to me only when I had time for it. I wrote out the lyrics to the Joni Mitchell song "Both Sides Now" in my journal. Those verses spoke to me of how we gain great treasures in our lives and at the same time lose a little of ourselves each day in repayment. How much of my own life was slipping away from me without me ever noticing it?

I missed my family. I had gained new friends and played my music for a lot of people, and that was great; yet I had lost another month of time with my wife and son. Should I question this balance? I didn't know. I put the thoughts behind me.

The hardest and longest part of my fall tours has always been the last 500 miles across the New York Thruway and the Massachusetts Turnpike. The last homebound day of 1987 seemed to go on forever. My wheels appeared to be turning, but the miles passed ever so slowly beneath them. Finally, late in the afternoon of Thursday, the fifth of November, I arrived home. That night I wrote in my journal:

My wife, my son, my dog Hallie,
All of the wonderful people, all of the miles,
All of the beauty of the country, all of the friends,
All of the music, all of the special times,
I am rich; I am oh so rich with all of these.

CHAPTER 38

The Fall Tour, Day 18

Anna is still asleep in her room. I check my watch, throw back the blanket, gather my things together, and do what is commonly referred to as the "disappearing folksinger" routine. It is expected. It is not impolite. It is the road. Goodbyes are spoken the night before. On this morning in Corvallis, when the sun is just a little above the horizon, I am on my way quietly out the door, ready for the possibilities of the new day.

It is a golden morning: cool, clear, and fresh. Tiny, ghostlike wisps of water vapor are rising off the streets, dampened by a brief shower during the night but now warming in the arms of the brilliant October sun. In places where many of the trees have lost their leaves, the ground is covered with a slick carpet of the yellow droppings, reflecting the morning light and brightening the rest of the world.

I stow my guitar and bag in the back of the van, climb in behind the wheel, and take a deep breath of the cool Oregon air. With a slight turn of the key in the ignition, the engine leaps to life. I believe that the van is impatient and telling me that it is about time that I am back behind the wheel, and that we should be off and on our way.

I drive a few blocks, then turn left along one of the one-way streets through the center of town, heading east, where in 10 or 15 miles I will cross Interstate 5. I turn north on the interstate, following the arrows for Portland, only a little over an hour away, and accelerate down the ramp, merging into a space between two semis that are hell-bent for speed and trying to annihilate any four-wheeler that gets in their way.

They can have the road this morning. I am in no hurry. I glance across my left shoulder to the west and the low-lying mountains in the distance. Oregon is strikingly beautiful at this time of year. I suppose there is nothing like New England when it comes to fall color, but if fall is one's favorite season, there is beauty to be found all across this vast and magnificent country. I am fortunate to have been able to see so much of this land, from Portland, Maine, to San Diego, California; from Point Barrow, Alaska, to Key West, Florida; and I have performed in every state except Hawaii. I know that I will get there someday; it is just a matter of time and half an ocean. Hawaii will always be there. The ocean will always be there. It is only the time that I worry about.

Some 16 years ago, I looked up to Logan English as a father figure and a literary mentor. Now I realize that I am almost as old as Logan was when he died. How could that have happened? Inside of me, there is still something of a little boy in search of the great thing that is the experience of life. I don't think that will ever change. What may have changed, perhaps, is the perception of greatness and what is truly important to the process of living.

Once I did a concert in Johnstown, Kansas. Johnstown is seemingly miles from any other place in the universe, and I arrived in town one April afternoon to do a performance that evening at the high school auditorium. After registering at the one motel in town, a 12-room traveler's delight, I drove over to the school to check out the stage setup for the night's show.

It was a breezy day—although I don't believe that there are many days on the Kansas plains that aren't visited with an incessant wind—and being that it was spring, the surrounding farm fields had just been fertilized. What was blowing in the wind, however, was not the acrid odor of chicken droppings or fish meal that is sometimes used on the fields, but the essence of the sweet grass manure, filling the air with youthful memories of stall and stable.

I held onto my hat as I trotted across the parking lot, making for the double-front doors of the low brick building and the warmth of its environs. One of the aged custodians, sweeping the hard tile floor, pointed me in the direction of the auditorium, where another man with a broom was working to clear the stage of the leavings by the previous night's drama production. This second man showed me what they had for a sound system and lighting setup, and when I was satisfied that it all worked, I thanked him and headed back to my car, hoping to catch a short nap at the motel before the show.

Now and again, something is offered to me by life that is profoundly moving, a moment in time and place that, as an observer, I must try to understand for its meaning and its reason.

As I was leaving the building that afternoon, I followed three young high school girls, probably just out of a late class or activity, as they headed out through the front doors of the school. Approaching within ten feet of the doors, all three of them reached to the back of their necks and pulled up the hoods on their windbreakers until the fabric covered their heads. I couldn't help but notice this sudden action because it was done as if it were an orchestration written by the wind. Still behind them, and now a few yards out from the shelter of the building, I overheard one of the girls say as she lifted her face to the Kansas sun and sky, "You know, I really love that smell."

It was a tiny act, a simple statement by a young girl to her friends, but something went off inside of me and I was incredibly moved.

Why was this such an important moment? What was life trying to show me? I felt that I had observed something truly significant. A window had just opened and closed in front of me, and while it was open I had a chance to glimpse an essence, an essence that is an important part of all of us in this country. For months I searched for what it was that had moved me so deeply at that moment in Kansas. I asked friends for their opinions and none seemed to be able to pinpoint the answer, until one day someone answered me with another question.

"Bill, just before you get up onstage to play the music that you love, what is the last thing that you do?"

I responded, "I take a deep breath and make sure that my guitar is in tune."

That was it! It was all a matter of being in tune with what you love. What I had seen that afternoon in Kansas was three young Americans completely in touch with their world, their world that was a small town at a crossroads in the middle of a great country. What I had seen, in a way, was the essence of music—sweet, profound, and perfectly in tune, and I thanked life for showing me that moment.

How many of us are really in tune with our lives? I ask myself this as I approach the exit on Interstate 5 for Albany, Oregon. I have the whole day, and only an hour's drive to Portland. This morning might be a good time to stop and do a little housekeeping in the van—as well as find a Laundromat, considering the pile of dirty clothing that has been accumulating behind the back seat. This gala life as a traveling musician still has its menial responsibilities. Doing the laundry will also give me a little time to take care of some business along the road. There are always bills to be paid at home, so after making a few financial calculations and writing a short note to Karen, I seek out the nearest post office which, as it happens, is directly across the street from the laundry. There I can send off a letter or two and also mail a package home.

With my business at the post office completed, I walk back across the street, stop at the van, and carry my now nearly empty suitcase into the laundry where it is refilled with the clean and neatly folded clothes. All set for another two weeks, I tell myself as I pull away from the curb and into the traffic, which seems considerable for such a small town. My final stop is the local gas station.

Pumping gas into my vehicle is something that I have done hundreds of times in my travels, but as I begin the task today I am set upon by a large, lumbering gas station attendant who begins railing at me about some infraction that I have brought upon him and his world.

"I understand," I say. "I'm sorry, I just forgot."

I remember now that Oregon is one of the few places, if not the only place in this country, that does not allow customers to pump their own gas. Standing idly by as the attendant takes over, it strikes me as interesting how our habits have changed over time. I remember when self-service stations first came into existence and customers were expected to pump their own gas, and how it seemed so inconvenient. After all, service stations were not only supposed to sell gas, they were supposed to check the tires, wash the windows, and provide these services for the customer with a smile.

Why then am I now feeling put-upon by not being able to pump my own fuel? Why am I not able to remove the nozzle from the filler tube after the pump has shut off? Why am I standing here, shuffling around and waiting impatiently as he makes his rounds, taking care of the customers parked at the other pumps?

"Wait a minute," I think. "My sense of inconvenience sure has changed. Why am I in such a hurry to get back on the road?"

I open the door of the van and get back in behind the wheel, watching while the attendant collects money from the two cars ahead. I notice a blank postcard on the seat next to me. I bought the card to send home to my son, yet I have not had a chance to write any message on it. There is a pen next to the postcard on the seat, and now I have all the time in the world. I will take this time, while my windows are being washed and my charges are being rung up; in these minutes I will write my son a note—something far more important than pumping my own gas.

I know that it is probably a safety issue, or an environmental one, that is served by Oregon's reluctance to have people pump their own gas, but it was nice to be able to live again, if even for just a moment, as we did so many years ago when service stations provided service, and we had just a little more time to be in touch with each other.

* * *

Portland is a city on the way to somewhere. It is not only a city *of* passage, but also a city and a place *in* passage. It is a city of constantly changing contrasts, of old neighborhoods, beaten and weathered by the rainy climate of the Northwest, and of vibrant rebirth. Even though it is obviously on a much larger scale, it is not unlike Portsmouth, New Hampshire, so familiar to me now and yet so far away. Even though they are a continent apart, there is something very, "Portsmouth" to be found in Portland, Oregon, both towns once only stopovers for those headed up and down the great coastal arteries of Interstates 5 and 95. And within these towns abide the people who reflect these contrasts. There are the old "Portlanders," those who have lived along that wide bend in the Columbia their whole lives, and there are those who have recently come to settle, those who have moved out of southern California to find a less electric environment in which to raise their families.

There is the youth, the college students gathered in many of the bars along North West 21st Street or South East Hawthorne; there are the professionals, filling the restaurants in the Pearl District, where everyone seems to have their favorite hangouts. There are the migrant workers, following the harvest from the valleys of California to the apple orchards of Washington state; and there are the musicians, the artists, and the craftspeople, plying their talents to a society within a greater society always in motion, from the vagrants who seek refuge and food at Baloney Joe's on East Burnside to those fans who can afford front-row season tickets for the Trailblazers' games. They are all here, all side by side and each alone, onboard for the all-encompassing passage of time.

My first show in Portland, back in the late 1980s, was at a place called the East Avenue Tavern, an old pub on East Burnside.

Barbara Luscher, the woman who owned the place, called me at my home in New Hampshire and said that she had seen that I was going to be in the Northwest that year, and she wondered whether I might be interested in playing in Portland at the tavern. It was the beginning of a ten-year run of shows that I would do at the pub each fall. Barbara and her husband James eventually sold the pub in 1988 to Irishman and button accordion player Mike Beglan, who continued to offer music at the old place until the doors to the East Avenue Tavern finally closed. The spot in my fall tour was then picked up by the Portland Folklore Society, run at the time by Bill Murlin. The group continued to bring me into the area each year, and it is for this very folklore society that I am playing tonight.

The venue for my concert is the Multnomah Friends Meeting House, a building rented to the folklore society by the local Quakers. It is a space of simple yet elegant design, and a room perfectly suited for a small acoustic concert.

I have spent most of the day dawdling about town, checking out the music stores and old book emporiums, as well as doing a little writing in my journal. I have also booked a hotel room in Vancouver, just to the north and over the river from Portland. This will give me an easy exit out of the area the next day without having to deal much with any kind of traffic.

It is a warm late afternoon, and the sun is declining over the yellow, green, and orange tree colors of the town. I drop into a sandwich shop to pick up an easy meal to go on my way over to the hall. Arriving at the meeting house a little before 6:00, I tarry in the car a bit and open the fragrant package on the seat next to me. The hard-crusted bun is oozing with tuna, and I wash down each bite with a sip of clear, cold apple juice from the bottle at my side.

It strikes me that my van is not only my means of transportation on the tour, but also my security, privacy, and shelter. It is my world on four wheels, dogged in its determination to get me where I want to go, vigilant in its protection, and not a bad place for a picnic.

A car pulls up in front of me and parks. A few seconds later, another arrives and repeats the procedure. It is a little after 6:00. The driver of the first car is the sound man who unlocks the doors to the building and begins to unload his equipment. The driver of the second car is Bill Murlin, a tall, bearded, soft-spoken man sporting an Irish cap and smiling as he steps up to my driver's window.

"It's good to see you again."

"Well, it's nice to be back in town," I respond. "Have you had some calls for the show?"

"Oh yeah, we'll have a good crowd," he answers reassuringly.

Opening the back of the van, I unload my guitar and the box of CDs that will be for sale during the intermission.

Inside, the sound man is done setting up and just about ready for a sound check. How many times have I been through this routine over the years: 3,000? Maybe 4,000? I don't know. I've sound-checked so many times that nowadays it takes only five or ten minutes to get the equalization right and the balance between the vocal and the guitar sounding pretty good.

"It's straight acoustic," I offer, "nothing but vocal and guitar." I guess I'm still a part of the old school of music: no electronics other than the sound system, no talent enhancers, no tuners, no gadgets—just a voice and a guitar onstage, standing alone, for better or worse. I guess that sometimes I get a little arrogant about staying totally acoustic, but in the end I know that what it comes down to is an old folksy pride and a whole bunch of stubbornness.

I think back to the days when I ran the hoots at The Club 47, watching the Fariñas on stage with just an acoustic guitar and mountain dulcimer. I can still hear the vibrant sounds of the Mandrell Singers as they filled my heart and soul with music one night at The Unicorn. It was just two singers, their voices deep and resonant, leaping and somersaulting over each other in harmony, while the only backup they had, a big 12-string guitar played by John Nagy, hammered out the constant rhythm in a cadence that drew me into their songs so that I wanted to stamp my feet and shout for joy.

It is still there for me, all of the images, the quiet sounds of Mississippi John Hurt, of Ramblin' Jack Elliot and his version of "Don't Think Twice, It's Alright." They are all still with me.

Ramblin' Jack played that song in concert, opening for Judy Collins one night in 1964 at Rindge Tech in Cambridge, Massachusetts. He took off his finger picks to do the piece, maybe to feel the guitar better, or maybe because he knew that a soft voice could speak with great power. I still don't know why, but I do know that to this day, when I have an occasion to perform the piece, I play it without any picks. It just seems right to me.

There were so many others: Ray Pong, dressed neatly in new jeans and a blue work shirt, introducing a Tom Paxton song that no one had heard yet, a song called, "The Last Thing on My Mind." I believe that Ray went on to become a brain surgeon. I remember that his guitar playing was precise and oh so clean. I think now that if I ever had to have my scalp lifted, I would be sure to look him up to see if he was available for the job.

They all played simply, they all played acoustically, and to me it was magic.

There is a Vanguard recording from the early 1960s of Judy Collins and Theodore Bikel at the Newport Folk Festival performing the traditional song, "The Greenland Whale Fisheries." It is one of my all-time favorite recordings: one guitar, one harmonica, and two voices in rough and yet exquisite harmony. As the dying vibrations of the last notes fade away and the applause begins, one can hear a single voice in the audience utter, "Beautiful!".

Yes, it certainly is! How could this simple music not drive my life? How could all these people not become a part of me? They are with me always. Even as I take the stage tonight in Portland, on the 18th day of my tour, I am not alone; they are all with me: Dave Van Ronk, Jean Ritchie, Paul Siebel, Alan Damron, Mary McCaslin—they are all singing tonight. Paul Geremia, Chris Smither, Dayle Stanley, Liam Clancy, Tommy Makem—it is not just one voice that the audience hears when I sing out my music this evening, it is all of their voices, all of their rich and beautiful voices, and I know in my heart that I would have it no other way.

CHAPTER 39

The Little Cowboy's Lullaby

By January of 1988 I was doing 175 shows and driving nearly 65,000 miles a year. I had logged well over a million miles behind the wheel, and my life was as busy as I could stand it to be. During the first two weeks of February, I played 14 nights in a row from upstate New York to Charleston, West Virginia, where I appeared on Valentine's Day on the "Mountain Stage" radio show.

It was good to see the host of the show, Larry Groce, again. I had opened for him some years before at Passim and had always enjoyed his music. After the broadcast, a couple of members of the Mountain Stage Band and I headed a few miles out of town to catch a set of music at one of the local honky-tonks. The lead singer of the band was a spitting image of Willie Nelson—not only looking like Willie, but also sounding exactly like him as he covered Willie's tunes.

He invited Ron Sowell, the guitar player for Mountain Stage, and me up to sing. As I recall, I did a rather loose but roaring version of the old Johnny Horton classic, "Honkey Tonk Man." I also made a very late-night attempt at some yodeling. I may have missed the mark a bit with the yodeling, but I don't think that anyone at the bar really noticed, because they all got up to dance to my vocal acrobatics and then cheered when we were finished. It struck me that night that there must be some truth to the old line, "The drunker you are, the better I sound."

By spring I had completed another long Midwestern tour through Michigan, Wisconsin, and Minnesota, and in late June I was homeward bound from my annual trip to Kerrville, with stops in Houston and Austin.

While I was in Texas that year, I heard that Jerry Jeff Walker had been performing my song, "The Quiet Faith of Man." He would eventually record it on his "*Live at Gruene Hall*" album. This was a real treat, because Jerry Jeff had been one of my early influences. Even during the years when he sometimes seemed lost in the cosmic ozone onstage, I still felt that he had twice the soul and sincerity in his music than many of the performers who were riding high in the music world.

Also at Kerrville that June, I was approached by a fellow who was interested in booking me for a concert at a science conference that was being held in August at Brewster Academy, a prep school in New Hampshire, only 20 minutes from my home. He explained to me that this was one of the Gordon Conferences, a gathering of elite scientists from all over the world. This specific conference was to be on "Vibrational Spectroscopy," and many of the world's leading scientists in biophysics would be attending. He figured that having a little music after the Thursday night dinner would be a good way to break the tedium of straight science that could build up during the week-long conference. Of course, not everybody is admitted to these conferences, and I would have to have the proper credentials.

I was told by this fellow, who was the chairman of this specific conference, that I would receive some application forms and various letters of correspondence in the mail. I was to ignore them all until he called and notified me, late in July, that my final credentials were on the way. This I did, and when I attended the conference on that Thursday in August, I proudly presented my papers at the gate. I received a program with my name on it and a colorful ID badge that read:

Dr. Bill Staines
Non-Classical Transmission of Transverse Acoustic Modes

Of course, no one knew that there was going to be a folk music concert after the dinner that night, and it was all a great joke on the audience (which was wonderful and enthusiastic about the whole scheme).

I still have my "Dr. Bill Staines" button and occasionally get to impress a scientist when I tell them that once I gave a presentation at one of the Gordon Conferences.

* * *

I was gone again in the fall, making the usual stops across the country. During that tour of 1988, I played 24 out of the 38 nights. The Red Sox won the American League East that year, but by the time that I was out on the road a week, they were out of the running.

After concerts all through California, Oregon, and Washington, I returned to Alaska, where Doug Geeting again took me flying up onto Denali. For the first time, I drove up the Parks Highway, clear through to Fairbanks, marveling all the way at the brilliant snow-covered mountains and the immense spaces all around me. How very small I felt, how very fragile, and how so very insignificantly human.

At one point along the highway, I happened upon what appeared to be two large dogs happily sauntering down the center of the road in the same direction in which I was traveling. Looking back at me over their shoulders as I slowly approached them from behind, they looked totally unperturbed by my presence. As I drew closer, I realized that these were no ordinary dogs. In fact, they were two very large Alaskan wolves, magnificent in their size and superb in their color and markings. Slowly, I inched the four-wheel-drive rental car close by them, and once clear continued on my way north, gazing at the two animals in my rearview mirror, and wondering at the greatness of the beasts that have been put upon this earth.

I returned from the tour by way of Colorado, Nebraska, and Minnesota, just in time for the first snows of the season as they dusted their way across New England. One morning, after building a fire in the wood stove and staring out of my window at the wind-blown falling flakes, I picked up my guitar and wrote the song, "Winter." A week later, I wrote "Heart of Stone," and then one day, after looking in on my napping child and wondering what he might be dreaming about, I penned the song, "The Little Cowboy's Lullaby."

It was certainly a good time for songwriting, but with the cold breath of winter in the air, it was an even better time to be home.

A Minneapolis landmark, the Coffeehouse Extempore occupied this space on Cedar Avenue from 1970 until 1985, when it moved across the street and one block to the south. (Photo: B. Staines)

The "400" bar where we gathered after concerts at the Extempore for late-night music (Photo: B. Staines)

Anderson Fair, Houston, Texas (Photo: B. Staines)

Performing "Red River Valley" with David Amram onstage at the Kerrville Music Festival in 1984 (Photo: Unknown)

A weekend show at Passim in the fall of 1983 with Nanci Griffith and guitar player Brian Wood (Photo: Wayne Miller)

The George Parks Highway just south of Denali National Park. It was at this spot that I came upon two Alaskan wolves out for an autumn stroll. (Photo: B. Staines)

The Redbird of the song "Redbird's Wing"
(Photo: B. Staines)

"Your friendly Alaskan bush pilot," Doug Geeting
(Photo: B. Staines)

The Latitude 62 Motel and Lodge, Talkeetna, Alaska
(Photo: B. Staines)

Nancy and Mack, innkeepers extraordinaire
(Photo: B. Staines)

John Hill, Bill Staines, and Brian Wood at Loma Ranch Studio, 1993 (Photo: Mickie Merkens)

At the board, working on *Going to the West* at Loma Ranch Studio, Fredricksburg, Texas, 1993 (Photo: Mickie Merkens)

Two old friends, Jerry Rau and Jana Metge
(Photo: B. Staines)

CHAPTER 40

The Fall Tour, Day 19

My journey today takes me to Pendleton, Oregon, 210 miles east of Portland, and a concert sponsored there by the Blue Mountain Folklife Society. I leave the hotel around 10:00 in the morning, scoot over to Interstate 205, and head south, hooking up with Interstate 84 just outside of Portland for the trip east.

It is a cool fall day, the sky completely clear except for a few cotton-ball clouds off to the south. By noon, I am well up into the Columbia Gorge again, climbing the ladder of dams along the great river. I pass the Bonneville, the Dalles, and a little farther upstream, the John Day. It is these dams, along with others built to the north in Washington, that provide much of the hydropower that fires the Northwest.

> "*Your power is turning our darkness to dawn,*
> *Roll on Columbia, roll on.*"

So go the lyrics to Woody's tune, "Roll on Columbia," written in 1941 for the Bonneville Power Administration. Little did we know then the extent of our energy demands and how much we would thirst for that power in the years to come, that power that would light our cities until they glowed in the night sky as if lit by a billion campfires.

It is also these dams that have changed this rushing river of long ago into a series of wide water terraces, miles long and harnessed to the hilt by man's technology and ingenuity. Between the dams, the river is a favorite place for fishermen and wind surfers. The latter of these skim across the white-capped swells like some sort of colorful water bugs, barely touching the surface and looking as if they could be blown into distant Idaho by the canyon winds. With a little time to spare today, I turn into an overlook and watch as a pair frolic across the water. One of the bugs with a rainbow-colored sail goes over on its side, and then with a burst of spray and violent motion it is upright again, caught by the wind and driven on a collision course directly at the shore. It is only at the last moment that it escapes into a sheltering cove, and though it is still sought after by the wind, it is not found and soon settles peacefully on its side, exhausted and complete in its endeavors.

I am on my way once more, against the flow of the river and out of the upper end of the gorge and into the open country, the high desert, the treeless hills of central and eastern Oregon. I have been along this route many times before, and I laugh as I pass by Hermiston, home of the high school Bulldogs and the infamous "Praise the Lord!" haircut.

On one of my tours through the area, I found myself in dire need of a hair trim but sorely pressed for time. Approaching Hermiston, I figured that I would seek out the nearest barbershop to see if they would take me as a walk-in customer. The first place that I happened upon was a little shop that I will call Duffey's Hair Salon (I can't remember the real name).

When I opened the door to the little storefront operation, I was immediately greeted by a woman of middle age, about 5 feet tall and weighing what must have been at least 250 pounds, who guided me over to the only barber chair in the place and told me to sit down. She draped me with the customary plastic apron, secured it at the back of my neck, and positioned herself atop a stool next to my chair. Reaching for and turning on a nearby radio, she then took a pair of scissors and a plastic comb from a jar on a small table at her side, placed one in each hand, and closed her eyes as if she were about to embark upon a long journey or begin a feast.

In only a second or two, the shop was filled with the voice of what could only be called a real hellfire and brimstone preacher, reminding her of the power of the Lord and warning her that it was time to repent. She began to move about on the stool. I was feeling now like the sacrificial lamb. She positioned the scissors and the comb and sat poised until the preacher's voice reached a crescendo; then she screamed, "Praise the Lord!" and struck home. A huge tuft of hair cascaded down the front of my apron, leaving me dumbstruck. Before I could even gather my thoughts, the preacher laid it on again; there was another "Praise the Lord!" and repeat action with the scissors.

I tried rise up out of the chair but to no avail. The back of the apron that covered me was placed over the headrest of the chair and I was held in place, writhing and wriggling like a worm on a hook.

"So what brings you to our neck of the woods?"

I was about to answer when she struck again, this time on the very top of my head. Once more, a pile of lopped-off hair tumbled to my feet. Dismayed, I looked into the mirror at the crater that had been carved into my hairline and thought that by the end of the ordeal I was going to resemble Yul Brynner.

It was "Praise the Lord!" after "Praise the Lord!" until, with a look of pure ecstasy, my captor announced that she was done. She switched off the radio, silencing the preacher, and as soon as I was released and had paid my tithe, I scrambled out of the door, never to return, feeling lucky enough that I had escaped with my ears.

Farewell Duffey, I hope you make it into heaven. I would warn you, though, to be careful in life, for the devil needs a few good barbers too.

I laugh again, thinking of Hermiston and Duffey, and of all

the other stories given to me by the road. Sometimes I feel that my whole life is nothing more than a collection of these stories.

It is early afternoon when I arrive at the outskirts of Pendleton. In the distance, off to the east and the south, rise the heights of the Blue Mountains, one of the last high land barriers faced by those headed west along the Oregon Trail. Once over the Blue Mountains, emigrants were faced with the choice of either making the 230-mile trip on hastily built boats and rafts down the hazardous Columbia, or mounting a land assault over the Cascade Mountains and then down to their destinations in the Willamette Valley. With the white majestic cone of 11,239-foot Mount Hood standing silent and sentry-like, dominating their view of the western skies, it seems no wonder that so many opted for the water route, even with all of its dangers.

This show in Pendleton tonight will be my last performance for the next four days. Tomorrow, Monday, I drive to Seattle, and at 7:00 on Tuesday morning I will be on a plane to Alaska.

I book a hotel room in Pendleton adjacent to one of the exits on the interstate and spend the afternoon packing for my trip to the north. There is a large blue duffel bag in the van. I carry the bag with me each fall, and it is this duffel that I use as a "shuttle craft" during my week-long stint in Alaska. Packed with all of the warm clothes and boots that I have with me, there are also extra strings, CDs, books, my journal, a hunting knife, and all of the odds and ends that threaten to make my attempts at packing lightly nothing more than an impossible dream.

After the packing is complete and the duffel stuffed to the bursting point, I seek out some food and drive down the hill into Pendleton, wondering where I might find the woolen mills that produce the shirts that are so popular in New England when the winter winds blow in and the temperature drops into the basement of the thermometer. A good Pendleton shirt might last one a lifetime—provided he does not become bloated with old age or too many martinis. I have always loved those beautiful plaids, easy on the eye and warm against the wind.

And so it is with the music this night in Pendleton, as warm and as comfortable as an old shirt, as quiet as the subdued colors of the woven plaids. It is out of the mills of time that these songs have been spun, blue and green with life; orange, red, and yellow with the seasons; and then gray and black with the ages passing before me. They are all colors, these songs. They are the brown dust and the white snow, they are the golden of the grain, they are the bright, silver color of the waters that flow constantly down to the sea.

I have been a weaver in my life, a weaver of common threads into uncommon designs, passing the shuttle to and fro until the fabric of a song appears. And it is with this fabric that I can only hope to reach out and surround those in front of me tonight, deny the cold, and have them feel the warmth of that which is truly in my heart.

Shall I sing one more tune? It seems presumptuous to turn and take the stage again after only a few steps toward the exit door. But I have always said that I am easy. Let's call it energy conservation. Besides, it has been a wonderful audience, and I have absolutely no place else to go.

CHAPTER 41

The Long Trains

My winter tour in February and March of 1989 had me running a gauntlet of storms throughout the Midwest. It seemed that Mother Nature had it in her mind that I should have to prove my driving abilities that year. With concerts all over Ohio, Michigan, Wisconsin, and Minnesota, and a series of low-pressure systems that hovered over the area for weeks, I was always trying to get to my gigs in some sort of foul weather. One night in Chicago, I was blessed with a combination of snow, wind, thunder, lightning, and hail. It was not a pretty sight, and yet I was bound and determined to get to the gig, hoping in some way that there would be a few brave hearts there to make up an audience.

By the end of the tour, I was ready to sit my body down on a warm beach and lose myself somewhere, drinking bright blue concoctions with pieces of fruit and little umbrellas hanging out of them. At the beginning of April, a call from a travel agency in Massachusetts threatened to make my dream come true: how would I like to earn a fat paycheck performing a concert set during a barbecue for 200 award-winning diesel engine salesmen and their guests at a world-class resort in the Dominican Republic?

It seemed like a great deal to me. I would fly early on a Monday from Boston to Puerto Rico, catch a connecting flight, and be into the airfield at the resort by 2:00 in the afternoon. Airfare and accommodations at the resort were included in the deal, and my sole responsibility was to do a 45-minute set on Tuesday afternoon at the barbecue, as well as four songs with the local Dominican country-and-western band that was also playing the gig. If I sent charts to them early, they would know my music, and performing with the band would spice up my show with a bit of the local flavor. I would then fly out of the resort on Wednesday afternoon and be back in Boston that night. All of this meant that I would have Monday afternoon and evening to myself, and I could spend most of the day Tuesday at the beach.

I jumped at the chance to travel, little knowing that what I was about to experience was the classic "monster gig from hell."

On Monday, the first of May, I was up at 4:00 A.M. and driving to Logan airport for my 7:00 flight to the Caribbean. Over Boston Harbor, the early morning sun burst upon the world, flooding the airport with its warmth and washing the city skyline with a pink, golden hue. It was a good day to be alive, and dressed in my straw hat and light linen jacket, I was ready to make my mark upon the throngs of diesel engine salesmen.

Climbing out of Boston, we passed 10,000 feet, but as we approached cruising altitude some 20 minutes later, something went wrong. The cabin was becoming over-pressurized. People began holding their ears, and in only a few seconds the pilot was on the intercom. He explained to us that some sort of a valve was stuck open, and although it was not an emergency, we would have to make a rapid descent to 10,000 feet and return to Boston.

I knew that I was going to miss my connection in San Juan, so I was one-two-three on the air phone to the travel agency that had hired me, explaining the situation as the man next to me became violently ill.

So much for my Monday at the beach. The only other

connection in San Juan would put me into Santa Domingo, Dominican Republic, at 10:00 P.M., then I would have to catch a bus to the resort some 100 kilometers away. The travel agency would have someone waiting at the airport in Santa Domingo to make sure that I got on the right bus to the resort.

Twenty minutes after we had landed in Boston, we were told to get back on the plane, and once again we were off into the wild blue yonder, bound for paradise. I did miss my original connection in San Juan (but only by a few minutes), so there I sat at the airport bar, with a 7-hour layover, waiting for my 9:00 P.M. flight to the Dominican Republic.

"I'll have another rum and coke. No, make that a Mai Tai this time." So went the afternoon. "I'd like a double shrimp cocktail appetizer please, with a vodka and tonic." So went the dinner hour. "My German is not great," I respond to a couple from Bavaria, on their way home from the islands. Why did I say that? I don't know a single word of German! By the time I boarded the plane to the Dominican Republic that night, I might just as well have been on a flight to Borneo, and when I landed in Santa Domingo at 10:00, I felt as if I had just made it to the moon.

The sign with "MR STAINES" printed on it in bold letters was being pumped up and down by a mustachioed man named Charlie at the airport gate. When I raised my hand, he grabbed me by the arm and led me off in the direction of his friend the customs official. With two nods of the head and a flying stamp onto my passport, we careened around official barriers and tables, in front of everyone else, and out into the warm, humid tropical night. A single bus, parked with its engine running, spewed forth heavy fumes as it waited at the far end of the parking lot, and it was over to this bus that I was led.

Once I was literally signed aboard the bus, Charlie's duties were done, and as the door closed and we pulled away from the curb, he raised his hands in a farewell and scooted off across the parking lot and back into the terminal building.

I was the only passenger on the bus. I could only hope that the bus driver knew my destination, for although he motioned for me to take a seat near the front of the vehicle and offered me a cigarette, which I politely declined, he said absolutely nothing at all for the whole trip.

We wound our way through the darkened streets of Santa Domingo and out into the countryside, bouncing across the potholes and washouts, swerving to avoid various farm animals on the loose, and occasionally almost running off the road when a thin human figure ran out in front of us, waving his arms in the air to flag down a ride. Other than our own headlights, the only other lights visible were those of the occasional casita bars at the side of the road with four or five people gathered around the open-walled, thatched-roof structure, drinking beer and looking forlorn.

We approached a crossing, two highways converging in the night. The acrid smell of a small pile of burning tires, placed at the center of the intersection for light, and the smoky haze hanging in the night air, gave the scene an almost battlefield-like quality. There were dark rows of windowless, box-like single-room houses—how naïve I was to think that they were just storage sheds.

Now and then we came upon the iron entrance gates to some fortress-like structure surrounded by vine-carpeted walls and high manicured hedges. These were the compounds of the affluent, the lantern-lit courtyards of the unseen rich in a land where wealth and poverty stand as uneasy neighbors.

We bumped along now, picking up speed, as the highway widened into three lanes and the heavy tropical forest fell behind us. This was the south shore. Here, a few kilometers to the west, amidst the colorful lilies and bird-of-paradise gardens, was the 17,000-acre resort with its multiple golf courses, secure beaches, and world-class entertainment.

It was here that I had come to sing for the diesel engine salesmen, and at the stroke of midnight, after a 19-hour trip, I checked into my room, bought a vodka and tonic from the mini-bar in the corner, and opened a sliding-glass door onto a tiled patio.

The night was alive with the screeches of birds and the drone of tropical insects. A small green lizard scurried across the tile floor and into the low bushes, perhaps in search of some of those insects, or perhaps just out on the town for a little adventure. Who could know? I was so tired that it didn't matter in the least, just so long as he was happy and had all of the energy that I lacked as my head finally touched the three giant pillows at the top of the bed, and the Caribbean night faded into kind oblivion.

The next morning, Tuesday, I reported to the travel agent in charge of the whole shebang. He told me that the day was mine until 4:00 in the afternoon when I would have to show up at the resort's athletic fields for the barbecue and my gig with the band.

My dream of a few months before, when I was battling the Minnesota snows, had actually come true. I spent the morning and the early afternoon of that day sitting under the palms, staring out at the aqua Caribbean, sipping on a bright blue libation, and getting a kick out of watching two young boys who were hired to patrol the beach picking up any of the fallen leaves that might assault the pristine beauty of the sands after each gust of wind. Once that job was accomplished, they would return to their two chairs in the shade of a thatched shelter until the next breeze wreaked havoc upon the shore. They would jump up once again and repeat the gathering procedure, returning to their perches as proud as punch with the results of their police work.

There was a human being employed at the resort for just about every task imaginable. There were baggage handlers, door holders, golf cart drivers, shoe shiners—I wouldn't have been surprised if there were someone employed to tell you the time. Still, with an average annual income of just over $2,000, every person working is an admirable end, and I found myself doing all that I could to make use of the services.

I was enjoying the afternoon at the beach, but as the old saying goes, "Be careful what you wish for; it someday may come true."

At one point during the day, I wondered what the diesel engine salesmen might be doing, but quickly put the thought aside. As it turned out, the fates—Clothos, Lachesis, and Atropos—were cooking up something of a surprise for me.

While I was basking in the warm afternoon sun, my audience

for the barbecue was scheduled to participate in a three-hour-long "donkey polo" game. The game, of course, was out in the open, under the sun at the athletic field, with plenty of beer and liquor to stem the thirst and lubricate the action of the game.

When I arrived at the barbecue, there were 300 people who could barely tell a pork rib from a tennis racket milling around. While the Dominican country-and-western band was up onstage, immersed in a lethargic version of "Deep in the Heart of Texas," three people who had managed to find seats at the tables had actually collapsed, face first, into their beans and cornbread, arms splayed out to their sides, oblivious to everything around them.

In the midst of this scene, I could make out the form of the travel agent who had hired me. As an official for the polo game, he was dressed in a football referee's outfit, complete with black-and-white striped shirt and white shorts with red flags hanging out of the pockets.

What he was doing at this moment was a little beyond me, but he seemed to be running back and forth, either propping people up to keep them awake, or rescuing those who were now wandering off, bleary-eyed, into the nearby undergrowth. The whole crowd was as cooked as the steaks flaming up on the grills, and I was about to have them for an audience.

"Bill, oh, Bill!" came the call of the travel agent, running up to me with a distressed look. The band was in the middle of a plodding version of Jimmy Cliff's "I Can See Clearly Now."

"Nobody's listening to the band, and we need somebody who can bring some energy to these people. I think it was a bad idea to have booze at the game this afternoon."

"Right," I thought. It was now incumbent upon me, mister folkie balladeer, to get 300 snockered guests up on their feet, cheering for songs like "The Roseville Fair."

With red flags waving in his hands, the referee instructed the band to finish their set—which they did to sparse applause, because nobody in the audience had the ability at this point to find one hand to strike against the other—and my time had come.

"All right, everybody, here he is, direct from Nashville, country music star Bill Staines!"

"Just roll with the flow, Bill," I thought as I climbed up onto the stage and stared out at the sea of bodies sprawled this way and that—and also at the one microphone on the stand in front of me. There was no mike for the guitar. How was anyone going to hear what I was playing? I pointed this out to the travel agent, who was now pacing back and forth at the side of the stage. He assured me that if I could get through the first song, he would have a guitar mike for me right away.

I started with "Rodeo Rose." Another face fell into the chili. I finished the song. There was no response. One of the band members arrived with the other microphone. I began my second song as the new mike and stand were placed in front of the guitar and the switch was flipped. It was as if all hell had broken loose. It sounded like the finale at a heavy metal concert. The high-pitched squeals of the feedback, and the sonic explosions from the reverb unit, came flying out of the speaker columns. Assaulted by the sound, some members of the audience bolted upright and reached for their ears. All I could do was keep playing, leaving the sound problems to the bass player in the band who was now frantically spinning knobs on the console of the amplifier to no avail. I kept playing, but I soon found myself flooded with the overwhelming desire to laugh.

Then it came to me, the sharp repeating sound of a whistle raging in the air as the travel agent leapt to the stage, waving his flags. It was the first and only time in my career that I had ever had a song whistled dead, and I was expecting to be penalized five yards, when the referee grabbed the mike stand.

Whistles arose from the audience as the referee began to speak.

"Hold on, folks; we've got to stop and get the sound in order."

"How will you know if it's in order if he doesn't keep playing?" came the response from the crowd.

The squeals finally abated and the referee, leaving the stage, ordered me to play something that everybody knew. I began to play, "Take Me Home, Country Roads." I had not played that song in 12 years. I had no idea what the words were, or in what key I could sing the song, and my attempt brought more whistles and jeers from the crowd. I countered with "Wild, Wild Heart," one of my songs about truckers. I figured that the diesel engine salesmen could take this one to heart, but it was to no avail. I had only done four songs, and already I was dead meat onstage.

"Just keep on smiling and singing," I thought to myself as I secretly asked a greater power for deliverance. That deliverance came with another blast from the referee's whistle and his presence on stage. This time, he covered the mike and told me that I was excused. "These people will never listen to your type of music. Just do the four songs with the band and call it a day."

I thanked everyone for listening, and invited the band back up onstage with the charts for my songs. "All right, let's do "Border Blues." One, two, three, four, hit it!" Everyone began playing a different song. There was absolutely no rhyme nor reason to what was being played. I kept singing as the band limped along behind me. I started the second song.

"Close your eyes, Bill, and pretend that you are back in the snows of Minnesota."

Two songs later, my musical ordeal was over. I was feeling guilty that I had not played the whole hour that had been expected. The answer to this dilemma, however, was right in front of me. I simply got back up onstage and sat in as a rhythm guitar player for the band's second set.

We played "Deep in the Heart of Texas," "La Bamba," "San Antonio Rose," and a funky version of "Peggy Sue." Then we played the same songs over again. Someone brought out a broomstick and we did a 30-minute version of "The Limbo" while watching the gyrations of the crowd as the stick was lowered. A few of the women were drunk and limber enough to do a respectable performance, while others goaded them on with bawdy comments and cheers.

That was it for the barbecue, and although some people lingered in a stupor, I hopped on one of the nearby golf carts and headed for my room, avoiding contact with anybody. I was promised that my pay would be sent to me in a few days (which it was), and that I would be picked up at 10:00 in the morning and driven to the resort airstrip for my flight home. An hour later, I was sitting on the edge of my bed laughing uncontrollably and crying at the same time. What a life, I thought, what an incredible life!

Ten in the morning came with no ride for me to the airstrip, four miles away. I looked around for anyone that I might know, but they had all disappeared. "Was this a dream?" I thought. "Was this all just a dream?"

I began to get concerned about getting to the plane on time when I noticed that one of the resort golf carts was parked nearby. That was it! I was out of there, my guitar and bag hanging off the end of the cart as I bumped my way down the road to the airport. So long Dominica! Off to Las Vegas! Have a great day!

A lone figure with a banjo case stood at the other end of the loading area as I walked out onto the platform at Logan Airport in Boston later that night. It was where I would catch the shuttle bus to the north shore of Massachusetts, and continue to the seacoast of New Hampshire and my home. I stared at the figure until I recognized him as one of my Irish musician friends, Tom O'Carroll. Tom was waiting for the same bus, and as we climbed aboard I asked him what he was about nowadays. Sitting down on the seat next to me, he just shook his head, sighed, and began telling me a tale about the weekend he had just done in Atlanta. It was the story of the worst gig of his life. As I listened, I couldn't help but smile and be glad that, in all of this, I am not alone.

* * *

Late in the summer of 1989, I received a call from the head of the video production department at Burlington Northern Railroad. His name was Saxon Rumwell, and he was interested in having me do some voiceovers and simple incidental music for one of their video projects. I agreed, so they sent me a script for the voiceovers and some direction for the musical interludes. It was a video about shipping low sulfur coal out of Wyoming. I suppose that as a folk singer I was treading on thin ice, but the script concentrated on national energy independence, and I have always been in favor of that.

I played a few occasional notes on the banjo, played some simple guitar parts at the appropriate places in the film, and did the voiceovers, sending the finished product off to Burlington Northern, hoping that it was what they wanted. I also included a note suggesting that if they ever needed any other music for a film, I could provide it for them. A week later I received another call from Saxon.

Burlington Northern was initiating a quarterly video magazine entitled "BN on Camera." The magazine would include news items, as well as some history of the line, but the primary purpose was to tell the stories and pay tribute to the daily lives of its modern-day employees. The program wasn't just a quarterly industry film, it was to be a glimpse into the world of all of those people who made the railroad run.

Saxon told me that they loved the simple guitar and banjo parts for the coal video, but my first challenge for the new project would be to write and produce a musical theme for the series and make it sound large and exciting like the music heard on the network nightly news broadcasts. Was I up to the assignment? I assured Saxon that I was and hung up the phone, ready to go to work. There was one problem: I had no idea on God's good earth how to even begin to create music like that.

Once again, it was my old friend Mason Daring who saved my life. I called Mason, who was now doing music for major Hollywood films, and explained my situation. I had never done any arranging, I didn't have a studio, and I couldn't do string parts. I was, to say the least, in way over my head on this project, but at the same time always willing to learn something new.

Mason's response was simply, "No problem, man."

I already had a melody for the theme in mind. Why not take "Sandstone Cathedrals," the title instrumental on the 1983 album, and flesh the piece out with big brassy sounds and a driving back beat? It certainly was, musically, a western motif, and with a barrage of trumpets doing the melody and a big bass and percussion track, the piece might just work. What was this? I was beginning to sound like an arranger already.

I booked time at Mason's studio, and two days after we started the sessions, we had the theme for "BN on Camera" recorded and ready to send to the Fort Worth facility.

I expected that I would never hear from Burlington Northern again, but to my great surprise, Saxon called and informed me that everyone at the production facility thought that the theme was perfect. This, then, was the beginning of a three-year collaboration with Saxon Rumwell and his crew that would find me writing songs like "The Long Trains," "Winter on the Railroad," and "Buffy's Quality Café."

My musical life was expanding again. I was developing a feeling for string parts and orchestration. I bought a synthesizer so that I could arrange music at home, and it was often now that I thought of my friend Logan English, six years gone, and how he would always be willing to accept my failures, so long as he knew that I was venturing out onto uncharted waters.

CHAPTER 42

The Fall Tour, Day 20

It is Monday evening, the 20th night that I have been on the road. My drive from Pendleton, Oregon, to Seattle is picturesque but uneventful. I cross the high hills of eastern Washington, their names ringing in my mind: Horse Heaven, Rattlesnake, and Toppenish. I descend into Yakima and rise up again over Yakima Ridge and down into Ellensburg, where I pick up Interstate 90 west and begin the final leg of this part of the tour. Tomorrow morning I will be on my way to Alaska, but tonight I am alone in Seattle.

I have a reservation at a hotel just five minutes from the air terminal at Sea-Tac. By spending one night at this hotel, I receive eight days of free parking as well as a shuttle van to the terminal gate. It is a good deal.

I have left my Martin guitar with friends in town and am now on my way south to Sea-Tac, when I stop for a traditional round of drinks at the lounge of the University Plaza Hotel on 46th and Interstate 90. From the big picture windows of the bar, the lights of this beautiful city by the Sound twinkle and dance in the distance. The Space Needle, built for the 1962 World's Fair, is under attack by a giant inflatable red crab, clinging to the tower sides and ready to devour any tourist who should venture within its reach.

It is here at one of the marinas that the beautiful yacht "Denali" is moored. "Denali" was once owned by Al Capone, who outfitted the vessel with a grand piano, pewter and silver dinnerware, and such accoutrements as would be fitting for those of his perceived stature. When he was busted for tax evasion in 1931, the yacht was confiscated by the United States government and during World War II was used as a training and patrol vessel on Puget Sound. When it was acquired privately after the war, all of the contents, long in storage, were given to the new owners. It has changed hands a number of times. To stand in its presence as it shifts at its moorings, ever so slowly with the turning tides, one cannot help but see a portrait of elegance and experience the eloquent beauty of a bygone time.

I am asleep now at the airport hotel, dreaming of Indians and yachts, of treeless plains and wide rivers that cut great gorges into the high mountains. Now I am awake, only three hours before I need to get up for my flight. Now I am dreaming again, this time of caribou and little children, of songs and cheers, and of the great game of baseball.

CHAPTER 43

A Cowboy's Hard Times

"I never was a drunkard, but this I can say,
The taste of the whisky gets better each day.
The bartender scowls, 'Mack, you're drinkin' too slow,
And we close in ten minutes.' Now where shall I go?"

Early in 1990, I began to notice a subtle change in my attitudes. Perhaps to others it was not so subtle, but to me it was the shadowy revelation that I was drinking too much. Of course, it is not unusual for a musician who has spent a lot of time on the road to become a denizen of the taverns, but I was beginning to think that the time that I was spending in the bars was starting to have an effect on my output as a writer. I thought back to the revelations that came to me when I read David Amram's book *Vibrations*.

Revelation 2: It is amazing to me how much time we waste in our lives when we could be more productive with that time.

I remembered Mark Twain's comment: "How can one kill time without injuring eternity?" Was that what I was doing now, injuring eternity? I thought also of the balances that we strike within our lives, and it occurred to me that this musical existence was indeed a striking of balances.

It must be that when we are born, we are endowed with a certain finite quantity and quality of talent. For some, it may be writing songs. For others, it may be building houses. It is this endowment that is in balance with how we live our lives, and how we bring upon ourselves the forces that would sap that endowment.

Of course, there are those who would claim that it was only after drinking heavily or experiencing a time of pain in his or her life that a particular artist actually attained their full potential. Perhaps this is so, but at the same time, does it not hold that the life of that artist may have been shortened by those same forces? Perhaps the world was denied a great masterpiece by a single drink of absinthe that fired a chain reaction of cells that became the raging downfall of the body of a creative being. Facing this dilemma, it was Jack London who once stated something to the effect that he would rather burn out than rust out.

I suppose that it is then within us all to decide how we deal with the balances in our lives, but certainly it must be known that there *are* those balances, and it is only us as individuals who can decide the fate of our own potentials.

In June of 1990 I was back in Texas, performing at the Kerrville Folk Festival. One night, back at the performer's hotel, I participated in my first songwriting collaboration. I had always been more or less a lone wolf when it came to songwriting, but with a little of the festival mood in my veins I sat down with Fred Koller (who wrote many of the songs that were successful for Kathy Mattea), and we wrote, "I Never Got to Say Goodbye."

I was once again sitting on enough of my own material to do another album. Rounder was interested, so I contacted Mason to see if he would like to be on the project as producer. Mason agreed, although at the time he was also busy with new film projects in California.

In July of 1990, we began recording the *Tracks and Trails.* I have always been fond of the album, but in retrospect it was one of the most difficult recording projects I had experienced. The musicians all played well, but finding time to record, with Mason's movie work and my performing schedule, was nearly a nightmare.

After three months of occasional two—or three-hour sessions in the studio, the tracks were recorded but yet to be mixed. My 1990 fall tour was coming up, and that meant that the mixing would have to be done in the late fall when I returned, and all I could do while I was out on the tour was work on the liner notes and arrange the artwork for the cover. I sent a design concept to Rounder just before I left for the tour, and while I was gone they sent two artwork proposals to Karen at home. She liked both of the watercolor paintings and described them to me over the phone. I told her to pick the one that she liked the best and that would be just fine with me. I never did see the artwork before it became the cover for the CD. On the road that fall, I was feeling more and more divorced from the project. It wasn't until I began writing the liner notes that the connection to the recording returned. Perhaps it was just that a little bit of magic fell out of the sky and into my pen, but it was that magic that opened my eyes to the life that I was living, and it was that magic that had manifested itself in the songs of *Tracks and Trails.*

I was a traveler in a barren landscape, conversing with the road upon which I was traveling. We had spent much time together, that road and I. We had seen much of the ways of life, and now I asked the road what was beyond the next bend. The road answered with only two words, but they could not have been more.

"Trust me," sayeth the road, and with that I returned home that fall. In the first two weeks of December that year we finished *Tracks and Trails,* and I was home again for the winter.

"Winter, I heard it whispered on the wind this morning,
So I arose, put on my clothes and went out walking,
Along the hills around my home,
The naked trees tossed to and fro, and it was winter."

CHAPTER 44

The Fall Tour, Fourth Week

It is 11:00 A.M. Alaska time on Tuesday, the 21st day of the tour. After descending out of a cloud bank over the mountains southeast of Anchorage, we have made our turns above the mudflats and are on final approach. There is a loud crunch directly under my seat and the sudden rushing sound of air as the landing gear comes down. Tiny droplets of water race across the window at my left, and the bluffs at the end of Runway 6 rise to meet our descending wings. The power is throttled back, and the whine of the engine is gone until there is a subtle bump, and the engine once again roars to life, only this time as a braking mechanism. I am driven forward against my seatbelt, and then the forces subside as we turn from the active runway and begin our taxi to the terminal gate.

"Welcome to Anchorage, everybody. The local time is 11:02 and the temperature is 34 degrees."

We taxi past the cargo terminal, its gates busy with the loading and servicing of the big jets operated by Flying Tigers Freight, United Parcel Service, JAL Cargo, Federal Express, and others. The little freight carts whiz back and forth and seem to hover like tenders to the great queen bees as they release their egg-like pods of cargo.

And then, for just a fraction of a moment, we are still. No one is speaking. There is no sound at all until suddenly the clicking of seatbelt buckles, and the rustling of passengers as they stand to retrieve their belongings from the overhead bins, floods the cabin. We have officially arrived; I am once again in Alaska.

Out of the gate area, I sprint down the stairway to the left that leads to the baggage claim where I pick up my big blue duffel bag and wait for my guitar at the little stainless-steel chute where the off-size luggage arrives. It is there. No need to check its condition. The Guild, my flying guitar, must weigh 25 pounds and is nearly indestructible.

Down another set of stairs now to the car agencies, the blue and red neon tubes lighting the tiled tunnel until it opens up at the rental desks.

"Yes, this is my address. No, I don't need any insurance. Yes, I know my way around. No, I'll bring the car back with a full tank. Thank you, I *will* have a great day. Have one yourself."

I check the controls of the blue Chevy Blazer parked in space 49, and in 5 minutes I am out of the airport and headed for town. I turn left on the Old Seward Highway and travel north until it turns east for a block and intersects with the New Seward Highway. Damn, no left turn! I always get messed up at this intersection. Right turn now, to the next light; now a U turn and I am northbound again, straight for downtown. At Sixth Street I go right, where in a few blocks it becomes the Glen Highway, and I am gone from this place where the mountains meet the strip malls, and on my way to Talkeetna.

Thirty miles out of Anchorage, I take that old familiar left turn off the Glen Highway and onto the Parks Highway just south of Wasilla. I pass the Windbreak, where 13 years before I met Doug Geeting and because of him came to know Talkeetna. I am north of Wasilla now, and out into the black spruce and birch forest, where the road cuts a swath to Willow.

It is the time of year when the last loons leave Willow Lake before it freezes. They leave for warmer climates, and yet it is their memory of this place that brings them back each spring to raise their young, and to sing out loud in celebration of their northern home. I long to hear their call, but I find that this year they are gone early, and the lake is very silent. It is only the wind now in the spruces, the distant barking of an old brown dog, and the sound of a small, single-engine plane circling overhead that brings me back from my reverie and urges me back on down the road.

At Mile Marker 99, I turn right onto the Talkeetna spur road. It is the middle of the afternoon now, and the sun, burning through the thinning cloud cover, is beginning its daily descent over my right shoulder. During the Alaskan fall, the afternoons are short, and when I reach the crest of the hill just outside of Talkeetna, Mount McKinley, Denali, the Great One, is in front of me, fire orange in the afternoon light.

The massif is actually a trinity of mountains, with Mount McKinley flanked on one side by Mount Foraker and Mount Hunter. I stop at the viewing area along the road just outside of town and gaze for a moment at the scene before me. It is reminiscent of the grand old painting by Archibald Willard of "The Spirit of '76." In the painting, the three musicians—a fifer and two drummers—are marching on to grand and awaiting glory. Is the spirit of these three mountains so different than that of the three marchers? Do they not invite us to become more than ourselves? Do they not invite us to triumph over all that would hold us down?

On a late spring morning, when the great mountain looks down on those upon its heights, does it rear up and shake them off in disgust, or does it welcome those who triumph and with its spirit lift them far beyond its summit and rejoice that now it is in the presence of kindred souls? Do not get me wrong; I know that there are *great* spirits, but as it is with tradition, those spirits come in all shapes and sizes.

* * *

The parking lot at the Latitude 62 is empty except for a car, a truck, Nancy's Suburban, and a snow machine parked against the side of the log building. The sun is still up, but it offers only a cold light, and the temperature has dropped in the waning afternoon. A column of smoke rises from the chimney of the lodge, and as I open the front door of the place, I know that I will be greeted by the warmth from the fireplace next to the bar.

A couple of locals are sitting at one of the tables. I don't know their names, but recognize their faces, and we exchange nods as I pass. At the same time, Nancy Trump and her black Labrador, Forbes, enter through the back door. They have been out for a walk, and obviously Forbes is pleased with the exercise.

"Hey, we all figured that you'd be showing up sometime this afternoon. Welcome back to Talkeetna."

We cross the room toward each other and Nancy gives me a big bear hug.

"Doug was just around here about an hour ago. He's probably down at the Fairview. You've got the room at the top of the stairs. Nothing much has changed. It looks like a pretty good house on Saturday. Where else are you playing on this trip?"

"Oh, it's pretty much the same tour, Nancy. I'll be here until Friday morning, and then I'll head up to Fairbanks for a gig at the Crazy Loon Saloon, come back here for Saturday, and then do Sunday in Anchorage. After that I'm out of Alaska for another year. By the way, isn't there a game on the television this afternoon?"

"Yeah, people usually show up around 4:00. I think it starts at 4:30."

It is World Series time. This is one of the rituals that I look forward to each fall. For the past 13 years, I have always managed to arrive in Talkeetna in time for the annual event, and when the games are on one can always find me sitting at the Latitude 62 along with 20 other locals, hollering and cheering for the underdog.

This year the series pits the Yankees against the Braves, and after I haul my duffel bag and guitar in from the car and stash them in my room, I hang my vest over one of the bar stools downstairs in hopes that when I return from the Fairview, I'll still have a seat.

When I arrive at the Fairview Tavern, just down the road past the "Welcome to Beautiful Downtown Talkeetna" sign, Doug Geeting is there, having an animated conversation with the barmaid, a pretty young woman of about 25. As I enter, he looks around and breaks into a wide grin.

"Hellooo there, I figured you'd show your face in town sometime today."

It fascinates me that my routines have become so predictable. Here I have not spoken to Doug in six months, and he knows when it is exactly that I'll be getting to town. In a way, I am glad that there is no surprise, because then it really feels as if I have only been absent for a day.

Of all of the places that I know in this country, of all of the inns in which I have stayed, and of all of the bars which I have been known to frequent, the Fairview has got to be one of the funkiest and most interesting of them all. The downstairs bar and restaurant is the entire first floor of an old house. The second floor contains the rooms of the inn, and it was here one night in the summer of 1923 that history came to town.

On a visit to Alaska that summer, President Warren Harding fell ill. Too weak to travel, he was put up at the Fairview, which was deemed at the time to be the only place around suitable to provide for the president. Alas, it was to be Harding's last venture into the North, for shortly after returning to San Francisco, he died. Some claim that it was a stroke that did him in. Others claim that a coded message from Washington that was received while he was in Alaska alerted him to the fact that the corruption rampant in his administration was about to surface, and this message brought on a heart attack. Still another theory, that he was poisoned by his wife who was fed up with his political affairs, also remains. One thing is for sure, though, and that is that he died.

When one gazes at the walls in the bar of the Fairview, one is treated to a grand gallery of local color. Charcoal portraits of legendary characters like Don Sheldon and Cliff Hudson, old-school, seat-of-the-pants pilots, hang in places of honor. There are the faces of trappers and hunters, of musicians and odd-lot folks that were here and gone in a moment. There are memorials to the hikers that never returned from the mountains. In the corner, there is an antique slot machine that long ago spit out its last rewards into the hands of some sourdough gambler.

I look from the walls to the people sitting around the bar. They have not changed over the years. There are still those rugged smiles, those eyes that dart this way and that until they focus on the new presence that has invaded their space. There are the caps of all shapes and colors, set upon the shaggy heads, and there are the faces of all demeanors, sporting a heavy beard here or a goatee there. No, it seems that these people will not change. They will always be the characters they wish themselves to be, and it is with them that I will spend the next three days, until it is time to be on the road north to Fairbanks.

* * *

Time has passed like a quiet wind and it is Friday morning. The sun has not yet even considered rising but I am awakened by the rumbling sound and the flash of the yellow beacon lights atop the school buses outside my window at the Latitude as they pick up and haul the Talkeetna kiddies off to school. There is an easy snow falling, and I wonder about the road and the weather to the north. It is 275 miles from Talkeetna to Fairbanks, and although I have four-wheel drive on the Blazer and have driven New England winters all my life, there are still those hidden patches of ice below the snow cover that can surprise even the wariest traveler. The Talkeetna rescue squad is always on the road, responding to winter calamities that still befall the most experienced of the local drivers.

By 8:00 A.M. I am up, out of my room, and have all of my gear loaded into the Blazer. The Latitude is alive with the morning breakfast rush, and the kitchen crew is busy with orders for bacon and eggs, sourdough bread, cups of rich, freshly brewed coffee, and that spicy favorite, reindeer sausage. I opt for the reindeer sausage and eggs, sourdough toast, and a big glass of orange juice. With all of this under my belt, and a glimpse at the morning Anchorage paper, I leave a message for Nancy that I will be back the next afternoon and head out on the road, out on that stunning and beautiful highway that cuts its way north through the ridges and valleys of time. I feel as light as a spirit running along beside the shining mountains, where the winds sing out to the gods and the ghosts of those long gone answer with a howling that is echoed by the wolves and then fades, ever so sweetly, into the far and oh-so distant snowy hills.

I cross the bridge at Hurricane Gulch, 260 feet above the water, carving its way into the hard earth, and descend out of the hills into the broad valley of the Chulitna River, where years before I came upon the two Alaska timber wolves out for a stroll. Then there is the gentle climb out of the valley and over Broad Pass at 2,300 feet above sea level. It is the lowest traveled pass in the long Rocky Mountain Range that stretches from Alaska to Mexico. There is the town of Healy, named for Captain Michael Healy, commander of the Revenue Cutter *Corwin*. Healy plied the waters of the Arctic in the 1880s and 1890s, keeping a semblance of law and order in the area as he searched for illegal seal hunters and whalers.

I cross the Tenana River at Nenana and drive the last 50 miles over the high country just south of Fairbanks. The weather has held for my trip, but up on these ridges the sun is bright and cold, and the low scrubby trees are stiff and crystalline with ice. The glare makes me squint, even though I am wearing sunglasses. Off to either side of me, the vistas are of the great distances of forests, rivers, and mountains that remind me once again of my tiny insignificance.

It is the middle of the afternoon when I drive down out of the hills and reach the southern outskirts of Fairbanks. Off to my right, I pass a large metal Quonset hut. It is the Blue Loon Saloon, the venue for tonight's concert. Since it's still too early for a sound check, I continue up the road into town and book a room at the Captain Bartlett Inn.

The inn is a large sprawling wooden building that on the outside reminds me a bit of a northern log fortress. On the inside it is cozy and pleasant and offers its warmth against the cold temperatures of the Alaskan interior.

In the parking lot of the hotel, a number of local artists are busy with huge blocks of ice, sawing away at them and chiseling out intricate shapes that will ultimately come to represent the unmistakable symbols of the North. Out of one block will come the grizzly bear, out of another the wolf, out of a third the caribou, and then the eagle, with its wings outstretched, struggling for flight against the weight of the battling salmon imprisoned within its talons. The crystal chips fly into the air, and the spray of the icy dust brings forth miniature rainbows, flashing here and there in front of me as I watch, fascinated with the artists at their work.

Once in my room, I phone Trudy Heffernan, the woman who over the years has promoted almost all of my shows in Fairbanks, and we agree to meet around 6:00 at the Loon for a sound check. I lie down on the bed for a short nap, and when I am awake again I have just enough time to stop at the hotel saloon for a beer and a sandwich before I leave for the concert.

The Blue Loon is really nothing more than a giant steel Quonset hut, set a little back and separated from the road by a large parking lot. By the entrance to the lot, a small sign displays the names of the acts currently appearing. Once parked, one enters the Loon by a covered doorway at the side of the building.

Inside, the place is divided into two rooms: the smaller front room serving as the bar, and the larger back room serving as the performance space with seating for about 250 people.

In another time, the place was called the Crazy Loon, but either due to new management or in an attempt to upgrade its character, it was renamed the Blue Loon. I have seen it through both names and all of the changes, most of them good, but I will always have one fond memory of the place in its earlier days.

One might ask, "How do you heat a large steel Quonset hut through the winter in the middle of Alaska?" The answer, of course, is that you take a 14-foot-long discarded section of the Alaska

Pipeline, turn it up on end, attach a chimney to the top, cut a hole in the side, bolt a door to it, and create an Alaska-sized wood stove, insatiably hungry for 3-foot logs, that is capable of heating a city. It was a little smoky and perhaps not exactly up to code, but it did the trick, and I will never forget its warm towering presence when the nights were cold and great gusts of wind buffeted the Loon like they were dancers upon a giant steel drum.

The stove has long since been removed from the building, consigned to the back lot, lying on its side like some display rocket at Cape Canaveral. When I arrive this night for my concert, I can't help but walk to the back of the yard, place my hands upon its side, and still feel the warmth of its far-off fire.

It is later now, after the concert, and it has begun to snow. A few of us remain at the Loon, drinking and laughing about the state of the universe so far removed from this place. Some late-night revelers arrive, young and full of spirit. They stamp the snow from their heavy boots, emerge from layers of clothing, and claim a table at the corner of the bar. Their eyes are shining in the lantern light of the room, their voices are loud with the language of raging dreams. I wonder what they see when they look at me. I wonder if they can possibly see any trace of that same raging fire. It may be obscured by the mists of years, hidden by the silver beard that confronts their gaze, but it is still there, and I can feel it, just as I can feel the fire in that old stove, covered now with snow and lying alone out back in the emptiness of dark oblivion.

"I shall come to the land of the cold snows
And reach for the mountains, high.
I shall ride with the moon where the wind blows
And sing to the stars in the sky."

* * *

At 8:00 in the morning it is still dark. The snow has continued to fall through the night, and although it has only been flurries, the result has been an accumulation of five or six inches. As I am about to leave Fairbanks, I stop at a Tesoro station, make sure that my gas tank is filled to the brim, and take to the road provisioned with a large cup of coffee, two cinnamon buns, a bottle of water, and a bag of beef jerky, ready for the worst and hoping for an uneventful drive back to Talkeetna.

Twenty miles south of Fairbanks, I have already ascended out of the low-lying snow system that hovers over the town and once again enter a world of bright sunlight and ice-covered trees. I flick the scanner on the car radio, and after two circuits of the frequency range, the radio picks up the local public radio station out of the University of Alaska at Fairbanks. I tune in to a show covering the tribal affairs and cultural concerns of the northern people. Sipping on my coffee, I slow frequently to negotiate the dark ice patches on the highway, hidden and ready to surprise a traveler as he takes a downhill turn with no guardrail to save him from a nasty ditch or a tree if he breaks traction.

I am alone on the road this morning with no other cars in sight, and it is a good 45 minutes before I encounter another vehicle heading in the other direction. I stop and fill my gas tank again at Healy—not because I am short on fuel, but because it is the prudent thing to do this far north. Once again, I am over the bridge at Hurricane Gulch, and by early afternoon I am at the turn for Talkeetna. It is like coming home for me, those last 20 miles. I have often wondered why you can feel like you are home when you are actually so far away from your real home—and if it is wrong to feel that way. I suppose it always comes back to the people you know, and whether or not they make you feel wanted. Isn't it that we all need to feel wanted, and isn't it that need that drives us away from or roots us to a place? Once I wrote in a song called "Railroad Blues":

> *"Riding on the train, you know I may be back again,*
> *Or gone like the leather in my shoes,*
> *Never staying very long in a place I can't belong,*
> *And feeling restless when I get those railroad blues."*

By 4:14, a group of regulars has gathered at the Latitude to watch the World Series game and have something to eat before the show. Mack is sitting quietly at the end of the bar, nursing his Jack Daniels and water and staring intently at the television screen, his surveyor's eye about to analyze every play, while Nancy checks the liquor stock for the evening. A bunch of people have driven up from Willow and rented rooms for the night, and in the music area Doug is setting up the sound system.

By 6:30, the audience begins to arrive. It is not so much an audience as it is a gathering of friends. Time after time they are here. There is Myron "Ace" Ebling, who came to Alaska in 1966. Ace carves beautiful eagles out of moose hooves and once gave me one. It still hangs from the rearview mirror of my van. He tells me that he carves two kinds of eagles, the male and the female.

"How can you tell the difference, Ace?" I once asked.

"The females are the ones with their mouths open."

Jim Okonek, another of the famed Talkeetna glacier pilots, is here for a meal and the show. As the room fills, a plain and simple desire to play music wells up within me. It is not to perform, but simply to play the songs that mean so much to me to the people that mean so much to me. These, I think, are the realest of people, the true souls, without pretense, and with nothing to prove to others save that they are capable of living out their lives in a way that demands so little of everyone else, and everything of themselves. How could I perform for these people? Performing is an act. No, I shall only play, but I shall play with all of my heart, sharing the music and all that is true to me on this night in "Beautiful Downtown Talkeetna."

* * *

It is late now—or early, depending upon how one looks at life. The concert is long over and a few of us are left, picking out tunes at the Latitude. I have a favorite. It is a little piece written by a group of Talkeetna characters including Pam Rannals, John Wallace, and Mike Folkerth one night around the bar. Doug Geeting first sang it for me, and now we sing it out loud again tonight, all of us, on this little spot of earth so far away from it all.

"We all are not there, because we're right here,
Somehow we all missed the flight,
So here we all are in beautiful downtown
Talkeetna, Alaska, tonight."

Tomorrow evening, Sunday, I will play a show in Anchorage, and then on Monday I take the brief but very long flight back to Seattle. It will be another year before I come back to Alaska, but she will remain with me throughout the coming months, a place of solace, cold winds, and the warmest of souls.

"Mama moose and grizzly bear,
With finned and feathered they do share
That wild country lying there,
Beneath this Redbird's Wing."

CHAPTER 45

Crossing the Water

In January of 1991, we went to war in the Middle East. Fortunately, by March the fighting was pretty much over, but in the initial stages of the troop deployment, with forecasts of a long bloody affair and rumors of thousands of body bags ordered by the government, daily news images of family farewells and poignant partings made little else seem important. Life, though, always manages to carry on, and time still slips away, thumbing its nose at us as it passes, laughing at our endeavors as if they could possibly mean anything to the great forever of things.

It is different, though, with the human heart. With as little of itself that time *does* share with us on this Earth, these endeavors *do* mean something. They should be, and are, important. What we do with our lives is ultimately the only power that we have over time. Waste and war leave us nothing but an empty hole to occupy the space that was once opportunity. When we are remembered for the good that we have done in our lives, for the enlightenment that we have brought into being, then in a sense we have held time for a brief moment, bent it to our will, and quietly laughed back in its jesting face.

One day while I was home that January and watching the television images of so many interrupted futures, I sat down at the piano and wrote "Crossing the Water." As the lyrics evolved, I knew exactly what I wanted the song to be. I wanted it to be a simple flower of hope springing from the seeds of an uncertain time, and an anthem for all of those who would ultimately prevail. It would be two years before the song was recorded, but on that day in January something within me flowed out onto the music paper, and I could not rest until it was finished.

I was out on tour when the war ended that March, playing at my usual haunts in the Midwest, as well as a number of places in the South. While I was in Kentucky, I spent a day at the University of Kentucky Library, dropping about $50 in dimes into the Xerox machine to make copies of Logan English's poetry, plays, and short stories. The library had accepted all of Logan's writings as a collection, and although I knew they were safe there, I also knew that the boxes of manuscripts would probably end up on a dusty back shelf, out of sight and out of mind. I have always had it in mind to someday publish his works, but for the time being his poems and stories have an honored place in my home, standing beside the books and writings that have always been special to me.

That spring *Tracks and Trails* was released, and I spent most of my time performing close to home. Close to home, of course, was anywhere east of Buffalo, New York, and north of Washington, D.C. I was also working hard on the projects that Burlington Northern was sending my way. One of these was a training film concerning customer relations and working well with people. It was filmed at a restaurant on the north side of Fort Worth called Buffy's, but Burlington Northern changed the name to Buffy's Quality Café and wanted a theme song for the video. That was my job.

I called Buffy's, told the woman who answered the phone what I was up to, and asked her to describe the place and what she saw around her. The picture was enough. It sounded like an old time

Texas roadhouse, and with that image in mind I wrote "Buffy's Quality Café." The song was really a piece of fluff, but it was fun and just what Burlington Northern wanted for the video.

There were two other projects, far more moving in their scope, to be done for the railroad that spring. The first of these was a video tribute to one of their employees, a Marine who was killed in the Gulf War. I was to sing an *a cappella* version of the "Marine's Hymn," and although I felt a little uncomfortable singing it, having never been in the military, it was an emotional and powerful experience.

The second of these projects involved writing a theme song for a video dedicated to the anti-drug program "Parent to Parent." The program, making its way around the country at the time, offered guidance and the opportunity for parents to get together and talk to each other about getting their children off drugs, or keeping them off drugs. Burlington Northern was considering adopting the program into their system as an in-house resource for their employees, and the video presentation was an introduction to the program. My direction for the project was simple: write a song about how parents feel, or should feel, about their kids. The song I wrote was, "Child of Mine."

* * *

In September of 1991, I was invited to the Walnut Valley Music Festival in Winfield, Kansas. Not only was I to be a performer at the festival, but also one of the judges for the National Finger-Style Guitar Picking Contest, and the Songwriting Competition. My old Texas friends, Aileen and Elkin Fowler, were the coordinators for the songwriting contest and had just arrived in Winfield after a tour through California in their bus, the "Prairie Eagle." I flew in from Boston, and another of my music friends, Brian Wood, drove up from Austin to play guitar behind me for the weekend.

I had come to know Brian through his work with Nanci Griffith when they toured together in the 1980s. These days, when I traveled to Texas, Brian would sit in with me as my backup guitar player.

As judges for the songwriting competition, Aileen, Elkin, and I spent most of a day at Winfield holed up in the Prairie Eagle, listening to demo tapes of the song entries and sampling the wine selection that they had brought back from the West Coast. By evening, we had narrowed the entries down to three songs, the problem being that each of us favored a different song and nobody was willing to give up on their choice.

As the wine flowed and the hour got later and later, Elkin and I began to point out to each other the shortcomings of the other's choices: the melody was not as strong in his, the lyrics did flow as well in mine. Back and forth we bantered while Aileen, with all of her wisdom, sat there and said absolutely nothing. Then, at the appropriate moment, after Elkin and I had sufficiently condemned each other's pick for a winner, she piped up with, "Well then, it's obvious that the winner is my choice."

Feeling rather foolish, Elkin and I had to concede that Aileen had a point, and that is how the winning entry prevailed and the songwriting competition was decided.

At the close of the festival in Winfield, I flew back home, but within two weeks I was out on the road again for the long fall tour.

That year, I opted not to return to Alaska, but instead booked a week of concerts all around Montana. Even with the foul weather that I had experienced the year before in the Midwest, nothing could have prepared me for the driving challenge that was about to befall me on that 1991 tour.

The first two weeks on the road were rather pleasant, with the traditional stops in Ohio, Michigan, Wisconsin, and Wyoming. Likewise all went well with the concerts in California. It wasn't until I reached Kennewick, Washington, that an incessant wind began blowing out of the north. It originated in Alaska, howled across western Canada, and generated, with its 60-mile-per-hour force, about every kind of weather condition imaginable.

In eastern Washington, clouds of choking, dark brown dust were carried across the highways, settling in the low areas and making visibility and travel nearly impossible.

The wind continued, buffeting the entire western part of the country, reaching as far south as Arizona. I began to move east, but the storm followed, dumping snows on Montana, where they were especially heavy in the mountains. The concert dates survived, but I was beginning to get the ominous feeling that I was driving just ahead of a huge wave spawned by Mother Nature, and that that wave was about to break over me.

I headed south for a show in Durango, Colorado. The snow followed, blanketing the passes between Salt Lake City and Moab. It was the night of Tuesday, the 29th of October. It continued to snow. All the next day I struggled to get to Durango, sometimes in white-out conditions, pulling ahead of the storm briefly when I turned east again at Cortez. Late that afternoon, I arrived in Durango, tired and barely ahead of the storm.

The concert was a great success, but uneasy about getting over the mountain passes to Denver, I slept little that night. At 3:00 A.M., I left Durango to tackle 10,857-foot Wolf Creek Pass in the snow that had already begun to fall.

As I climbed the steep 8-mile road to the summit in the dark, wind, and snow, all I could think about was getting the next 100 feet of pavement behind me, and that above all I must not stop. I slipped a cassette tape into the stereo of the van. It was *December* by George Winston. The music eased the stress a bit, but humming along to "The Holly and the Ivy" did not alter the fact that when I reached the summit of the pass, I was still faced with the downhill side, and that was going to be winding and very, very slippery. Hour after hour, the wind howled outside my van. I was over the summit! Mile after mile and slowly, ever so slowly, I made the descent out of the high peaks of the San Juan mountains and onto the south central plateaus of Colorado.

At Monte Vista, I had the option of turning due north through South Park or continuing to the east on Route 160 until I reached Interstate 25. The latter seemed the safest route, for now the snow had increased in intensity and the driving was miserable.

Near Alamosa, I fell in behind a camper. Following the camper that day became one of the lighter moments of the trip, for roped to the roof of the vehicle was a Weber charcoal barbecue grill.

There it was, standing on its tripod magnificently above all else, appearing now and again to me like a beacon through the clouds of kicked-up and wind-blown snow. A thought occurred to me, and I began to laugh. For a time afterwards, when I told this story to people, I would refer to it as the time that I found myself on a quest for the "Holy Grill."

By Thursday night, the 31st of October, I had made it to Denver, but with no concert in town that year, I did not stop. The storm was now raging across the entire western half of the country, and the authorities began closing the interstates. Idaho and Montana were closed. Interstate 80 in Wyoming was closed. Interstate 70 in Colorado was closed. Minneapolis, over this 24-hour period, received 34 inches of snow. The Dakotas were now closed. On Friday night, I was scheduled to do a show in Lincoln, Nebraska, but at 10:00 that morning, after I had made it to Grand Island, Interstate 80 in Nebraska was shut down, and all of the trucks and cars on the road were ushered off into a huge travel plaza. I phoned the folks in Lincoln and told them that I couldn't make it. They understood and told me that no one else could possibly make it either.

I phoned Austin, Minnesota, where I was scheduled to play on Saturday. They informed me that all of the power in the area was down and that we should reschedule. I called Minneapolis. They had pre-sold 400 tickets, the city was dug out, and they were ready for me on Sunday evening. I had to make it to the show. It was Friday morning. I had all that day, as well as Saturday and most of Sunday to make the 550 miles to the Twin Cities.

With all of the interstates closed from Denver to Kansas City, and from Helena to Des Moines, I had only one option, and that was to take the state highways and back roads. It was a crazy choice, but I decided to do it. The first leg of the odyssey was from Grand Island to O'Neill, about 115 miles. The road ran almost due north, and with the wind blowing out of that direction, it struck the van head on, blowing the snow into my face but leaving little accumulation on the road surface. It was when I got to O'Neill at

2:45 P.M. and turned east toward Sioux City that the real problems began. I recorded the events in my journal.

"I then headed east toward Sioux City, not knowing that all of the interstates there were also closed. When I reached Plainview, Nebraska, I was told that eight—to ten-foot snowdrifts blocked the road ahead and that I would have to stay put. I instead opted to drive southeast to Pierce, arriving there at 6:00 P.M., once again in white-out conditions. Turning north on Nebraska Route 81, now in the dark, and bucking snowdrifts of two to three feet at forty miles per hour, I pushed on for three hours until I arrived in Yankton, South Dakota, at 9:00 P.M., and spent the night in one of the local hotels with a dozen stranded truckers."

The next day, Saturday, I was up early and started east, but had to return to Yankton because of road closings. I then drove north to Salem, South Dakota, only to find that Interstate 90 was closed eastbound, and that I would have to continue northeast to Madison.

By noon on Saturday, the snow had stopped falling, but now I was about to experience another prairie phenomenon—the ground blizzard.

The ground blizzard is simple. It is wind driven, and though there may be blue skies overhead, within 50 feet of the ground the driving snow, whipped up off of the surface of the prairie by the wind, is blinding and almost impossible to navigate.

I was now eastbound through Pipestone and Florence, Minnesota. Near Lamberton a huge snowdrift blocked the entire road. Knowing that a snow blower with a maw the size of Rhode Island was on its way to clear away the snow (I had passed it only moments before), I waited, talking to the backed-up truckers on my CB radio.

It took the highway crew close to three hours to complete the removal, and it took me another two hours to get to the junction of Routes 14 and 71, where I turned north in a whiteout and started for Redwood Falls. By the time I arrived in Redwood Falls, the local armory had been opened for people stranded by the storm. Still I decided to push on. It was only 22 miles to Olivia, and there I would turn east again for the final push to the Twin Cities.

This was a decision that I almost came to regret, for just outside of Redwood Falls, the wind picked up even more, and in the dark I had no sense of where I was on the road. Over the radio in the van, the local weather spots had the wind blowing at close to 60 miles per hour, and the wind-chill factor at 59 degrees below zero.

I had no choice but to keep going, mile after agonizing mile. I listened to the George Winston tape again, over and over; 10 miles gone, looking for the road; 11, 15, there was no place to stop. Tire tracks appeared in front of me, and then the two faint taillights of a van trying, as I was, to make headway in the storm; 17 miles, 20, and then the lights of Olivia. The wind died, its force buffered by the buildings in the town. I followed the van into a service station and after filling my tank went inside, tired, grateful to see another human being, and very thankful to be off the dark, snowy, road.

The driver of the van was a young kid who was trying to make Minneapolis as soon as possible to tend to his ailing mother who, given his sense of urgency, I suspected had little time left in this world.

By now I was ready to get a hotel room, if there were any available in Olivia, but the kid, after talking with the service station attendant, decided to keep going. It was 90 miles to Minneapolis. I guess his doggedness inspired me, so I suggested that the two of us caravan. If something happened to one of our vehicles, the other would come to the rescue.

At 1:00 in the morning on Sunday, November 3rd, I checked into the Days Inn on University Avenue in Minneapolis, took a shower, and thanked the spirits of the road that I had finally made it to town. I also thanked George Winston for recording the *December* album. There could have been no better music with which to face what became to be known as the Halloween Blizzard of 1991.

CHAPTER 46

The Fall Tour, Day 28

I am on my way home. It is the last leg of the tour. At 2:00 in the afternoon, my flight from Anchorage to Seattle touches down at Sea-Tac, and I phone Karen and leave a message telling her that I am still alive. There is yet another week of concerts to do, but now I am eastbound. I will now know the sunrise on the road instead of the sunset.

I retrieve my duffel bag and guitar from the baggage claim at the airport and catch a shuttle bus back to the hotel parking lot where my van waits patiently, that old horse tethered to the hitch rail.

"It is good to see you, amigo. I have been far."

A line from an old film comes to mind and my van asks, "Were it worth the trouble?"

"Heh, what trouble?"

Sure it is a long road, and there are times when I wonder whether I will die alone in a hotel room some night far from home, but I am playing music, and what more could one ask out of life than to know their own song, to live it, to sing it out loud for all to hear, and then to have it return to them, rich with the essence of all that is?

My concert tonight in Seattle is at a large home on Lake Washington where the driveway is lined with carved jack o' lanterns, and the stage is set with bales of hay, dry stalks of corn, orange pumpkins, and the tangled reds and yellows of the bittersweet vine.

CHAPTER 47

The Happy Wanderer

In the summer of 1992, I received a phone call from Bob Feldman at Red House Records in St. Paul, Minnesota, asking if I would be interested in doing a children's album for the label. With the exception of *Bridges,* which Red House re-released after the Coffeehouse Extempore closed, and *Sandstone Cathedrals* on Mineral River, I had done all of my recordings in the 1980s for the Rounder/ Philo label. I was good friends with one of the owners, Bill Nowlin. Bill was also from Lexington and was a part of that same neighborhood crowd which included the Curtis brothers. Growing up, I could frequently be found spending afternoons at the Nowlin's house, listening to Bill's Buddy Holly records or to old Spike Jones recordings. Bill had quite a record collection back then, and 35 years later I would kid him about how large that collection had become.

When the call came from Bob Feldman, my first thought was that I should ask Rounder how they felt about me doing an album for Red House. My agreements with Rounder were always for single projects, so I was not legally under contract to them, but I felt that it was the right thing to do to get their okay for the Red House project. Rounder responded that they were fine with the switch, so in September of 1992 I went to work on *The Happy Wanderer.*

I had never considered myself a "children's performer," but I gathered together a half dozen of my own songs, went searching through the *Sing Out!* songbook *Rise Up Singing*, as well as every other campfire book of songs that I could find, and recorded *The Happy Wanderer* in three days.

The album had a simple folksy charm about it. It was not really a children's recording, but more of a family project, and to this day it is one of my favorites. Among the songs that were not originals, two had always been dear to me. "Little Brown Dog" I learned from my early days in folk music, listening to Jackie Washington and his recordings. "The Happy Wanderer" was well known to most everybody, but still a song that I always loved to sing to myself when I was very young.

Some three years later, Charles Kuralt, on one of his many trips to northern Minnesota, heard my version of "The Happy Wanderer" being played on a radio station out of Ely. He phoned the station, asked who was singing the song, and dropped by to pick up an extra CD that they had of the album. I had always been an admirer of Kuralt's work and often thought that I should send him some of my songs, just to make a connection with him as another kindred spirit of the road. This, of course, I never did, and when he died in 1997 I felt badly that I had never made that connection. Six months after his death, however, I received a phone call from the radio station (which, coincidentally, Kuralt ended up buying), and they told me the story of that first encounter when he dropped in to pick up the extra CD.

So there it was: in spite of myself, the connection was still made. Perhaps in that place beyond us all, Charles Kuralt and I will someday meet, swap some stories, and travel a few miles together, two happy wanderers on a single road that will never be lost for adventure.

* * *

That fall when I was back in Alaska, Doug Geeting gave me my first flying lesson. It wasn't an official logged lesson, but he let me take the controls of his plane and make some climbs and turns through the mountains not far from Talkeetna. As we cut through the passes and the mountain valleys, brilliant and white with pure, freshly fallen snow, Doug said, "You know, Bill, there are pilots who have flown for years who have never ventured into places like this."

We circled for an hour or so and then I flew the plane back to Talkeetna where, with a lot of guidance from Doug, I managed to line the thing up with the airport runway for a landing approach. As the plane settled, Doug once again took the controls and brought us the rest of the way down. It was then that I knew that I was going to learn how to fly. It was then that I decided that someday I would take Doug flying upon my own wings.

On the plane back to Seattle, I made an entry into my journal. It was a note to my young son.

"Someday you will stand on a high peak and look down upon your dreams. These dreams will never fail you. They are the lights of all the runways on which you will land. They are the forces that will guide you through life. Keep your dreams in sight and be strong; your wings will carry you to them."

* * *

I had a busy performance schedule during the rest of that year, 1992, but the driving was easy, the weather held, and for as long and as endless as it sometimes felt, the road was kind.

CHAPTER 48

The Fall Tour, Day 29

Snow covers the high peaks standing guard over Snoqualmie Pass. The sky is deep blue this Tuesday morning, and the long, low climb over the Cascades offers a magnificent panorama of gray granite rock walls and tall, stiff, dark spruces. In just a few weeks, the ski areas at the summit of the pass will be in full swing, and already preparations for the season are underway.

I have four concerts left to do on the tour. The first is on Thursday in Colorado Springs for my good friend Gary Knighting, cowboy singer and poet. The second is in Denver for the Swallow Hill folks on Friday. The third concert is on Sunday in St. Paul for the New Folk Collective, and the last performance is a house concert on Monday in Milwaukee. Then there is the two-day drive back home to all of the beginnings once again.

I stop for lunch at the Cottage Café in Cle Elum. The faint scent of wood smoke hangs over the town, and the surrounding hills are still alive with tamarack golds, aspen yellows, and the rusts of the beautiful mountain oaks. I bring my road atlas in with me from the van and pull up a chair at one of the tables by the white-curtained windows. The sun is warm on my shoulders. When the waitress hands me a menu, I decline and order my usual BLT, with a cup of chili and a glass of orange juice.

I have a little over two days to get to Colorado Springs, so I open the atlas and begin to examine the options for the routes and roads over which to travel. By now it seems that I must have driven most every road in this country—but then there are so many roads, so many different roads. In the atlas, I see the wide, dark blue lines bordered in red of the interstates—the fast, safe roads with little to offer except chain restaurants and a speedy way through life. I spend too much time on the interstates and not enough time anymore on the blue and red roads, the roads less traveled, the Charles Kuralt roads, the William Least Heat Moon roads. I knew them once, those passages, when life was much slower and each day came equipped with enough time to accomplish what needed to be done. I can't remember a time now that I did not know and love those byways, those paths through the haunted hills where I played banjo and autoharp in local barbershops or bought used tires from men with no teeth. Their breaths smelled of apple-flavored tobacco when they spoke, and they were hard to understand. It was mostly with their eyes that they communicated, and it was mostly through those eyes that you could see into their souls.

Once an 18-year-old boy replaced a timing belt in the van for $100 and a handful of my cassette tapes. I tried to pay him more, but he would have none of it. As I was about to leave the garage, I stopped in the men's room. When I returned, my songs were playing on the tiny tape deck that was plugged in between the old grease drums and the boxes of oil cans stacked against the back wall of the service bay. My presence would remain there after I left, just as the memory of that salvaged, broke-down afternoon remains with me after all of these years.

I move my fingers over the pages of the atlas. There are a number of routes that I can take to Colorado, but the atlas has become like a Ouija Board; beyond my control, my fingers opt to travel the long, slow roads. I will journey south, past Moscow and

Lewiston, Idaho, through Grangeville, and over spectacular White Bird Pass where nearby, on June 17, 1877, Chief Joseph and his band of Nez Perce, pursued by a much larger cavalry force, turned and routed the pursuers. This victory for the Nez Perce at White Bird Hill gained them much needed time in their attempt to reach sanctuary in Canada.

I will continue on through Boise and pick up Interstate 84 east, but only as far as Twin Falls, where I will turn south on U.S. Route 93 and traverse the desert country into Nevada at Jackpot. From Jackpot and its glowing casinos it is 68 miles to Wells, where another stint on the interstate will take me across the Salt Flats to Salt Lake City.

My fingers move over the atlas with a mind of their own as the truck drivers enter and leave the café, and my late breakfast arrives with a smile from the waitress.

"Goin' far?" she asks, glancing at the open pages before me.

"Goin' far and been far," I answer. As she walks away, I follow her form, thinking about all of the songs that tell the stories of the lonely truck stop waitresses longing to see the rest of the world, just beyond the parking lot and yet so far away.

I guess that I will never know her mind. She is only one of those shadows that move about me on the road. Yet I know that she is real, and that deep inside she is passionate about her own life and dreams. Perhaps she is someone's lover. She wears no wedding ring. Perhaps she is content with her life in Cle Elum, or maybe, just maybe, she is one of those souls of such songs who is willing to leave all behind when opportunity calls and fly away to unknown places and unknown things. She smiles lightly and strikes up a conversation with another customer at the counter. My thoughts return to the atlas and the roads east out of Salt Lake City.

I decide to take U.S. Route 40 across northeast Utah to Vernal and then continue through the vermilion sandstone country east to the mountains of northern Colorado. This part of the journey will take me through the land of the dinosaurs where, at Dinosaur National Monument, surrounded by sheer cliffs and bright red escarpments, the fossilized bones of these wondrous creatures were first discovered by Earl Douglass in 1909.

Douglass, a paleontologist for the Carnegie Museum in Pittsburgh, sensed, because of the geology and topography of the land, that dinosaurs may have wandered about this area millions of years ago, and that their fossilized remains might very well be found imbedded in the gravel and sandstone of these ancient river beds. His quest proved fruitful on August 17, 1909, when he spotted eight tailbones of a *Brontosaurus* in perfect order protruding from a sandstone bluff. This find led to subsequent exploration and the unearthing of well over 1,500 fossils of these ancient giants. In 1915, President Woodrow Wilson had the site preserved as Dinosaur National Monument, and so it remains today, one of the profound treasures along the many roads less traveled.

I trace the red line in the atlas representing Route 40 eastward, past Craig and Steamboat Springs, where the road rises and winds up the western slopes of the Rockies to 11,315-foot Berthoud Pass, and then descends to Interstate 70 near Georgetown. From Georgetown, it will be an easy drive to Denver and the highway south to Colorado Springs.

I have driven these roads before, and perhaps it is this energy of memory that guides my fingers as they travel along the colored veins of the road atlas, determining the route that I will travel today. Am I not now finally like the spider, crisscrossing the horizontal paths I have traveled with those of the vertical, stopping at the crossing points to anchor my trailings and to remember my last time through when the direction was different but the goal was the same? If I were to examine a map of this country and trace my passages, would they not confirm a web of perpendiculars and angles that have sustained me all of my life? Was there ever a road that did not bring me some sort of adventure?

I lift and fold away the pages of the atlas, pay my bill at the counter, and with one last glance at the waitress exit the front door of the Cottage, entering again the clear, bright world of the northwestern autumn. I have always been intrigued by the name,

Cle Elum. I have no idea where its origin might lie, but it has come to my mind that if one were to spell the name backwards, it would unfold as Mule Elc—a sketchy spelling at least for "Mule Elk," but still intriguing in its similarity.

I have a long drive today and tomorrow on the roads less traveled, but I am confident that these will be the paths along which I will ultimately find the simplest, and yet the greatest, of all God-given treasures.

CHAPTER 49

Going to the West

The first two months of 1993 brought with them a dark spirit. I shall not delve into or dwell upon the rhymes and reasons of this time, but its effect left me as senseless as a tiny leaf tossed upon a fickle wind. Nothing seemed to matter to me anymore, and my world began to fall in upon itself and then fly apart in different directions. It was a hard time—no more or less of a hard time than could happen to anyone else in their lives. It was during this period that I came to understand and appreciate the true uplifting power of music.

That spring I became involved with two projects. The first of these would ultimately manifest itself as a 34-minute symphonic piece entitled, *The Alaska Suite.* The second project was the album, *Going to the West.*

The Alaska Suite began one afternoon in April as a melodic doodle that I had composed and recorded as a violin sound on my synthesizer. After listening to the playback, I wrote and recorded a corresponding bass part. I repeated this procedure a number of times, using the sounds of the string and brass instruments of an orchestra, until nine hours later I had what sounded to me like the music to some sort of old western movie. I glanced over at my desk, and a book that I was reading about the Alaskan Gold Rush caught my eye. The book was opened to one of the classic photographs of the line of prospectors climbing the ice steps at Chilkoot Pass, and the concept for *The Alaska Suite* struck home. The first piece for the suite was already completed, and I called it "Nome 1901" after another of the photographs in the book.

I would compose 15 pieces for *The Alaska Suite* over the next 9 months, and I would produce an 86-page handwritten score for the project. At times, it seemed that I would never finish the project. I put my other songwriting on hold. Occasionally, as the suite progressed, I sent tapes of it to a few of my dearest friends and they prodded me on, urging me to find the strength to finish the project. I had no musical education, no theory, no fundamentals other than my instincts. I did not even know what note the low string on a violin sounded. I read books. I found that some of the parts that I had written for the violin were actually too low for the instrument to play, so I changed the designation and the scales and made it a viola part. I had no experience writing for brass instruments, so I went to Bob Cohan in Saratoga Springs for help. In his earlier life, Bob had been a band director before opening The Parting Glass, and he showed me how to write for French horn and trumpet.

While I was in town that weekend, Bob introduced me to Phil, a retired music professor at Skidmore College, and it was Phil, a quiet man of few words, who closed the door on my doubts about *The Alaska Suite.*

On a Sunday morning, over breakfast at Bob's house, Phil listened to it in its entirety while doing the *New York Times* crossword puzzle. He said nothing to me while the suite was playing, but when it was done he smiled and spoke. His words were not concerned so much with the quality of the music that I had written, but instead were directed toward the creative process, and to a kindred musical soul. His words were an admission on his part, but an inspiration to me.

"Bill, I have taught music for a good deal of my life, and if you were to go to my home, you would find my compositions lying all over the place. If you were to look closely at that music, what you would find is a lot of beginnings, a lot of middles, and a lot of ends. What you would not find, though, are many pieces that are all of the above, together and finished. What you have here in *The Alaska Suite* is a beginning, a middle, and an end, all together, and done. I wish you well with it. It is perhaps too long, but then I suppose that Alaska is a big place."

I think of Phil now whenever I begin a project, and I quietly thank him for instilling in me a sense of doggedness and an appreciation of what it really means to finish something. A CD of *The Alaska Suite* was released that winter on Mineral River. It was unlike anything else I had ever recorded.

During 1993, while I was working on the suite, the only time other than concert tours that I took from the project was the time that I spent in the south recording *Going to the West.*

* * *

I was ready to do another album, but when Brian Woods called me and suggested that I come to Texas to record, I had second thoughts about the venture. It wasn't that I didn't trust Brian—he was one of my best friends and a phenomenal musician—it was just that I would be going to a strange studio and recording with other musicians that I had never met before. What would they think of my music? How would we relate to each other during a recording session? On top of that, my life at home was under a lot of stress, and I was afraid more time away would not help matters any.

I felt free of my responsibilities to Rounder and was still on good terms with everyone there, so with a little urging from Brian, I called Red House to see if they would be interested in releasing the project. Bob Feldman welcomed the idea, and that May I was off to Texas for the Kerrville Folk Festival and ten days in the hill country, recording a new album.

* * *

On Sunday, the 30th of May, 1993, I pulled into the dirt and flint-gravel driveway of Loma Ranch Studios, just east of Fredericksburg. The mile-long driveway dipped and rose, bisecting a large field where huge rolls of freshly cut hay sat out in the open under the hot Texas sun. In the distance, under a grove of trees, I could make out the form of a large, two-story stone farmhouse, a wooden barn, and a low, single-story building of corrugated metal. It was in this tin wonder that John and Laurie Hill did their recording, and it was this house, barn, and studio that would become my home for the next ten days.

It was noon when I took the last left bend in the driveway, drove past the multilevel starling house perched atop a 15-foot iron pole, and parked my car at the grassy area alongside the barn. Noon was the appointed time for arrival, and as I got out of the van and looked back down across the field toward the main road, I could see a caravan of three or four cars coming up the drive, all of them kicking up dust, and all looking as if they had some important place to go. I could make out Brian's silver-blue station wagon at the head of the pack.

Brian had lined up all of the musicians for the sessions, done all the scheduling, and taken care of the financial arrangements for the project, and so it was really his baby. Because we made the musical decisions together, I got a co-production credit on the album, but it was really Brian who had done all of the footwork.

The cars pulled into the parking area, lined up neatly in a row like some returning squadron of fighter planes, and in a few minutes Brian was making introductions all around.

John Hill was a wide-eyed soul, with a heart as big as one of his hay rolls and a mind for engineering that was genius in its scope. When he got excited about something, he had the habit of wandering off in Spanish. One minute you could understand what he was saying, and the next, well, he was gone, the mariachi music in his mind having taken over and led him off somewhere to grand fiestas of sound specifications and track assignments. John became a dear friend over the next ten days and was always there when I got a bit down or was unsure about what we were doing. He could also sing high tenor, which helped us immensely when it came to some of the harmonies. Already he had spent most of that morning running mike cables and firing up his equipment, so that when we all arrived he was ready to go.

I met Ron Irwin, a fabulous drummer, and bassist Randy Glines, who had played for most everybody in the Austin music scene. A little later that day, we were expecting my old friends Bill and Bonnie Hearne, who had just finished their gig at Kerrville, to drop by and play on a cut or two. The recording began as soon as Ron had set up his gear, and by supper break, when Bill and Bonnie arrived, we had already knocked down a few of the basic tracks.

Bill and Bonnie were scheduled to play and sing on the title cut, "Going to the West." Neither Brian nor I were fancy flat pickers on the guitar, and I was a little concerned about doing the song in a fast bluegrass style until Brian suggested Bill and Bonnie. Bill was one of the finest flat pickers I had ever met, and immediately my trepidation went away, knowing that the song would be right down their alley.

And so it went for seven days of recording and three days of mixing. Paul Pearcy, the percussionist for Jerry Jeff Walker and Tish Hinojosa, dropped by to play. Gene Elders, on leave from George Strait's band, played the violin, while David Webb played the piano. Mickie Merkins, Brian's wife, came in with Melissa Javors to sing harmonies, and Melissa sang the mother's verse on my song, "Child of Mine." Paul Sweeney played the mandolin, and by now I wondered how I could have ever thought that coming to Texas to record was not a good idea.

Only once did the dark spirit overtake me, and that was one night after everyone had gone to bed and I had had a few shots of tequila. I sat alone at the big, round, antique enameled gas station sign that John and Laurie had fashioned as a table for their patio, stared out at the stars and the full Texas moon, listened to the soft sounds of cattle on a nearby ranch, and wept out loud until I could weep no more.

I can still remember those days at Loma Ranch, but more than remembering them, I can still feel them. I can feel the mild evening breeze picking up and blowing across my skin. I can still hear the chirping of the hummingbirds as they flitted about the feeders overhead on the patio. I can still feel the heat of the morning when I walked the length of the driveway and back to pick up John and Laurie's mail, and I can still feel the magic of what it was to play music with so many new and wonderful friends.

* * *

I spent most of the summer that year at home, working on *The Alaska Suite* and doing outdoor parks concerts around the Northeast. That August, my family and I managed some time together on Prince Edward Island in Canada. Prince Edward Island had become a favorite vacation spot for us, and it was good to stand once more on those beautiful red cliffs overlooking the Gulf of St. Lawrence.

I wished that we had had more time together over the years. My son was now seven years old, and every time I returned from a tour, he was a different person. It seemed that I was always trying to catch up with him and never quite making it.

At the end of August, I flew to Omaha, Nebraska, for the Festival at the Fort weekend put together by Tom May, the host of the public radio show, "River City Folk." Returning home to a busy September schedule, I found myself constantly up late at night, working on *The Alaska Suite.* On September 9th, *The Alaska Suite* was completed, with only the score left to write out by hand. When the last part of the final section, "Hymn for the Wilderness," was done, I just sat back in my chair and cried.

I dedicated the suite to my father, the violin player who I had never gotten to know as an adult, and I sent a tape of the composition to David Amram, hoping that he would listen to it. Some weeks later, I received a phone call from David. He told me that he liked the piece a lot and that he listened to it in his barn whenever he was out milking his cows. I thanked him in the album credits for teaching me not to think more of myself than my music.

As the days and weeks of that September slipped away, I once again began to examine my life and exactly who I was as a person. I was quite comfortable with the idea that I had been placed upon this earth to create music; my creative self was being cataloged at home in the form of "my cabinet." And yet I was beginning to wonder who I was as a man, as a human being, as a spiritual entity. From whom and what did I draw the life force? What were the truly important things in life that kept me going?

For some time, I had been amassing a tiny collection of items from the places I had traveled to and the friends that I had known: a limestone pebble from Kerrville, a shard of flint from John and Laurie's studio, a pinch of earth from Minnesota, a spruce sprig from Alaska. All of these bits, all of these items, had now become very important to me. They were the tangible symbols of my life, and from each of these I could draw strength, hope, and the will to carry on. I mixed them together: the sacred tobacco, the sand, the clay, the hair—and I began to carry them with me on my travels in a small plastic bag. On my trip to Alaska that year, I spoke of this to a young woman who understood, and before I left she gave me a small, fringed leather bag in which to carry these things. It is my medicine bag, and I keep it close now, for within are the symbols of my life, and most of that which has made me who I am.

CHAPTER 50

The Fall Tour, Day 31

It is morning in Georgetown, Colorado. My hotel on the north side is just a few blocks from the downtown area, so before getting on the road to Colorado Springs, I walk the short distance into town and order breakfast at one of the restaurants along Sixth Street.

Georgetown is one of the old mining towns in Colorado. It was first settled in the summer of 1859 by George and David Griffith, two brothers who had discovered gold along Clear Creek. By early 1860, subsequent incoming mining operations had already created the need for the establishment of a mining district, so the Griffith Mining District was formed. In just two years the gold played out, but in 1864, rich deposits of silver were found in the area and the valley villages of Georgetown and Elizabeth Town experienced a revival.

Looking up into the red, rocky hills around Georgetown, one might still see the evidence of those early operations. A rock wall, once wounded, is slow to hide its scars, and there are many of these in the West. It is a living history, and it is all around me.

How often have I stood in the shadows of a ghost town and listened as the wind sang through the cracks of the shriveled boards that define the skeletons of the buildings? How often have I stared at the flowery, brittle wallpaper on the walls of the empty rooms and wondered what kind of a day it was in the life of the person who hung that paper? Perhaps it was ordered by catalog from Chicago, or from some merchant back east, and shipped to Denver, where it was brought by horseback or mule up the slopes of the mountains to the mining camps. How many days or months or years did the inhabitants of that room enjoy the paper's intricate patterns before it was time to move out, or move on to the promise of richer horizons? And what of the memories of these people? Did they at some time in their lives look back and think about the folly of their mining experience, or laugh out loud at the night the fiddle player about town got drunk, climbed a tree, and played on the instrument until he passed out and dropped to the ground? The fiddle got caught in the branches and was saved, but the miner broke his leg, and from then on walked with a limp.

"Husband," or "Wife," they would ask, "I wonder what ever happened to those extra rolls of wallpaper?"

And the other would laugh and answer, "That was long ago and far away, my dear. It seems to me now like another lifetime."

I am staring at what remains of my breakfast when the muted chime of an antique clock in the corner of the restaurant brings me back to the present. While musing about wallpaper and ghost towns, the crisp piece of sourdough toast I have been holding down on the plate has become soggy with the golden yolk of the eggs, and it tastes good as I wash it down with the last sip of the orange juice in my glass. Another morning on the road, another day of promise in my life, another cup of coffee to go.

I step out into the cool, clear mountain air and walk back to the hotel. The van is already packed and I am checked out of the room, so with a quick stop at the local post office to mail some letters, I am once again back on the long ribbon of highway that is carrying commuters to Denver, and commerce across the nation.

I am scheduled to hook up with Gary Knighting late in the afternoon, so it will be an easy drive to Colorado Springs, with maybe a stop or two along the way to catch up with my journal entries.

I first met Gary in the late 1970s when he lived in Fulton, New York. Every once in a while, he would invite me up to play a private party at his home, and we would swap stories about life and music long after the party was over and everyone had left. He moved around quite a bit after that, to Boston and then Chagrin Falls, Ohio, where occasionally I would stop by to play for a small gathering at his place on my way west in the fall. We lost touch for a number of years, until one day he sent me a volume of cowboy poetry he had written entitled, *As True As Anything I Ever Told You*, and I found that he had moved west and was living in Colorado Springs, pursuing a life as a cowboy poet. When we next spoke, he suggested that if I were coming through Colorado, he would be glad to promote a concert for me. The only stipulation, he said tongue-in-cheek, was that he got to be the opening act and would read some of his poetry. This all agreed to, he booked a space in one of the small local arts centers. That space, once one of the last Kaiser car dealerships, is the setting for tonight's concert.

I am almost down out of the Rockies now, the hazy skyline of Denver before me, and beyond that, to the east, the broad expanse of high plains that reaches all the way to Nebraska and Kansas, where there it becomes the great central prairie. Taking the exit for Colorado Springs, I turn onto the beltway that circles the city and head south for my afternoon rendezvous with Gary.

He has written a poem called, "Tagalong." The poem is about an old cowboy and one of his horses. Although the horse has been devoted to the cowboy since it was just a foal, it has always shied at the idea of being ridden. Rather than forcing the issue, the cowboy instead allows the horse to work happily over the years as a pack animal, and this mutual respect has always been a great bond between them.

The wisdom in this harmony between two living things, the wisdom that offers respect rather than submission, strikes me as I listen to Gary, dressed in his cowboy hat and bandana, recite the stories and poems during his set this evening.

I have always been an admirer of the cowboy poets. Perhaps it is this subtle wisdom that abounds within their work that draws me to them. From where does this wisdom spring? It springs from their everyday living, and the trials and tribulations that come with that life. It is not an easy life, that of a cowboy, but it is a life rich with the opportunity to understand the simple things that surround us all: life, death, and a strong cup of coffee to see you through to the next stop along the trail; an old hat, an old shirt, and the notes of an old guitar strummed by the fire beneath a golden October moon.

Some say that children are wise. I do not believe that children are wise; they are innocent, and out of this innocence they occasionally speak to that which *is* wise. I believe instead that wisdom is how one deals with the lack of this innocence. As we grow and emerge from the oblivious veil of youth, it is then that we are struck, unsheltered, by what can be cold and hard in the life before us. It is how we deal with the tough reality of this life that fosters the wisdom within us. Wisdom is patience and understanding, humor and perspective. We all have it within ourselves to be wise. We also have it within ourselves to be blind to that which would make us wise.

Many times in my life, I have been blind. Many times I have walked in darkness and not seen the light of the stars, even though they were shining brilliantly just above my head. Tonight, listening to Gary, I have it in my mind that I will strive to be a wiser man and understand not only the melody which is my life, but also those things which bring with them the most cherished of harmonies.

It is Colorado Springs, on the 31st day of my tour, and I am about to take the stage. I think that I will begin the show tonight with an old western ballad, for in the back of my mind I can still see those two old friends, the cowboy and the horse, buried now together in the familiar soil of the high plains, and remembered always in the loving lines of a cowboy poem set to music:

> *"Oh say, little dogies, when you goin' to lay down,*
> *And quit this forever shiftin' around,*
> *My limbs are weary, my seat is sore,*
> *Lay down little dogies, like you've done before."*

CHAPTER 51

Ceiling Unlimited

In the spring of 1994, I returned to Key West with my family. It was on this vacation that the seed of desire within me to learn how to fly took hold.

One of the local flying services had in its stable of aircraft three 1941 Waco biplanes, two of them scarlet red, and the third jet black. One had only to look upward at any time during the day to see them in flight, their powerful radial engines droning overhead as they circled the city or ventured out over the islands nearby. I became fascinated with these planes, and each time I saw them they became more and more beautiful to me. I called the flying service and found that it was $150 for a flight in one of these planes, but that the front cockpit was wide enough to carry two people.

"What if it were just me going up?" I asked. "Could you put a control stick in the front cockpit and let me fly it for awhile?"

"Sure thing!" came the reply. "Of course you can't take off or land the aircraft, but we can let you play around with it once it's up in the air for a little bit. You won't have any rudder up front, but the pilot can take care of that from the rear cockpit."

My time had come. I drove over to the airport. Standing there, just outside the door of the flight service, was one of the bright red Wacos, poised, elegant, and leaking a little oil.

"They all do that," I reminded myself. "Any vintage plane in the book worth its wings leaks a little oil."

It took just a minute to install the control stick. I was given a leather flight helmet with an intercom mike so that I could speak with the pilot behind me, we climbed in, and within just a few seconds, we were airborne and climbing out over Key West.

"Okay, it's yours." I heard over the intercom in my helmet.

"So soon?"

"Sure, you wanted to fly didn't you? Just keep the nose lined up with the horizon and have a good time."

"Where should we go?" I asked.

"Anywhere you want," came the reply. "Let's have a look at some of the backwaters north of town."

I moved the stick to the right and the plane responded, although the nose dropped a bit.

"Pull back on the stick as you turn and that will keep us from dropping." came the instructions over the headset.

Of course! I thought. When you bank the plane, you lose lifting area over the wings and you start to lose altitude.

The wind whistled through the cables between the wings and it was like a song to me. Shall I sing too? What? "Wild Blue Yonder"? No way! I did not know a song—yes, I did.

> *"I have left the ground behind,*
> *On windy whispers I am climbing . . ."*

I was lost in the skies over Key West, lost for just a little while in a world of long ago, a world of Jennys and Newports, of Spads and Fokkers, of every biplane model I had ever built, and I was flying them all now between the endless sky above and the deep blue waters below. When we landed and I touched the earth again, I was not the same.

Later that night, as we celebrated the sunset on Mallory Pier with the rest of the daily revelers at the occasion, a flight of the three Wacos appeared overhead, the black one in the lead, and the two red ones on each side and a little behind. As I watched, one of the red ones peeled out of the formation, circled the pier, and rocked its wings. I had no idea what was really in the pilot's mind at that moment, but I do know that I found myself standing on my tiptoes and lifting my hand into the air as far as I could reach.

Three weeks later, I took my first flying lesson in Lynchburg, Virginia.

For the remainder of the summer and the fall, I flew whenever I could afford it. I began taking flight instructions at a flight school in Nashua, New Hampshire. My instructor was a young Italian woman named Natalie, and she must have had the patience of Job's mother. I became what amounted to something just short of the "touch-and-go king" of Boire Field.

Up and down, over and over.

"Let's do it again," I raved to Natalie after we fell the last ten feet out of the air to the runway.

"Hold it off, hold it off!" became her patient mantra as we slammed the ground again, eliciting a moan from the control tower.

"What is with this last ten feet?" I thought to myself as I thanked Natalie and told her that I would see her again in a week.

"Be patient," she would say. "For some, all it takes is one good landing, and it all comes together after that."

I worked on my ground school courses and scored a 96 on the written exam, but still the landings evaded me.

In the fall, I was back on the road and flew very little, only occasional flights with an instructor at one of the local airports along the way when I had the opportunity and could afford it. I was busy again with concerts all over the country, but by November of 1994, when I returned home from the fall tour, I had a concept for a new album.

Even though I was far from my goal, all of that year I had been living in the middle of one of my dearest dreams, that of learning how to fly. My idea was to do an album of songs about people living their dreams, whether they be lives of adventure or simply making a living off the land.

I took to rereading some of Anne Morrow Lindbergh's books, two of which had a profound effect on me. The first was *North to the Orient*, and the second was *Listen, the Wind*, both books about the flights that she took with her husband, Charles Lindbergh, in the early 1930s over some of the most remote parts of the world. Her two chronicles of these flights struck me, not only for her incredible insights into the human spirit, but also for the fact that it was just the two of them, and that their fame would have no bearing on the outcome of a situation if they developed engine trouble along the far northern shores of Canada, or at night over the middle of the South Atlantic. Their plane, a Lockheed Sirius model, was dubbed *Tingmissartoq*, or "one that flies like a big bird," by a young Eskimo boy who painted the name on the cowling of the airplane.

The story of these flights became music to me. As a tribute to their spirit of adventure, I wrote "Song for Tingmissartoq" and an instrumental entitled, "Ceiling Unlimited." These pieces certainly would go on the album.

I learned Archie Fisher's song, "Bill Hosie," a tribute by Archie to a man who rebuilds a replica of a 1930s seaplane racer and loses his life to his dreams. I selected a tune by Ann Reed, a songwriter from Minnesota, called, "Every Long Journey." This was Ann's tribute to explorer Anne Bancroft, who was the first woman to reach the North Pole by dogsled.

These were among the songs that would make up the album, *Looking for the Wind*, and in the spring of 1995, during a year that would see me doing more than concerts, I was off to the hill country of Texas once again to do a new album at Loma Hill Studios and to renew my friendship with many of the musicians who had played on *Going to the West*.

It was good to see John and Laurie Hill again, as well as Brian

Wood, who had agreed to produce the project, but because of everybody's schedules, we would only have about nine days to finish the recording.

All went well until bad weather moved into the area, and we lost precious time because of electrical storms and rain delays. This often forced us to record to the point of exhaustion, well into the wee hours of the morning. There was actually an episode when I fell asleep as I was overdubbing a guitar rhythm track. Awakened by the laughter in the control booth, I was told that after nodding off, I just kept playing until I slowed down to a stop and then just sat there, holding my guitar, with my chin down on my chest. They figured that it was time to quit for the night.

During the day, we lived on beer and jalapeño poppers. At night, when the recording was done, we would often fire up John's barbecue pit and dive into ribs or steaks, Texas style. In rare quiet moments, I would sit out in the shade of the trees next to the house and read books about flying, sometimes aloud just to hear the language of the skies.

When *Looking for the Wind* was finished, I returned home, playing shows in Houston, Dallas, South Carolina, and Washington, D.C., along the way. That summer, between concerts all over New England and festivals in Ohio and Wisconsin, I also returned to my old routine at Boire Field in Nashua, falling that last ten feet out of the air on my landings, with Natalie urging me to hold it off, hold it off! I was convinced that I would never learn to land a plane without the result looking or sounding like some sort of a controlled crash. Still, Natalie insisted that "sometimes it only takes one good landing."

* * *

The leaves of the New England oaks and maples began to turn early that September, and once again with the fall I began preparing for my extended time on the road. My son was now nine years old and about to enter the fourth grade. He now considered among his friends a large tarantula named Melvin that lived in his room and kept him company, crawling up onto his shoulders as the two of them sat in front of our television screen and watched the film *Arachnophobia.* I wasn't much for the film, but they seemed to enjoy it.

It was always hard to leave in the fall, and it struck me years later that I never got to see my son dressed in a Halloween costume. Of course I had talked with him on the phone as he was about to go out on the town and had seen pictures of him later, but I never got to see him with the costume on. I realized this one night at a motel in the middle of Wyoming. I was the only one staying at the motel, and as the dust and the tumbleweeds blew through the parking lot and I sat in the darkened room staring out of the window at the dim lights of the bar across the street, I felt very, very alone.

I left on October 4th that year and once again played the usual haunts on my way across the country, with new stops in Schroeder, Minnesota; Logan, Utah; and Bellingham, Washington. When I returned to Alaska, I also played a concert in Juneau. I had not been back to Juneau in more than ten years, and I could see the changes in the town. The airport terminal looked like that of any large city in the "lower 48." The back country was filling with homes and condos. What got to me the most was that the Red Dog Saloon had moved from its original site to a larger building across the street with a real floor. This meant that they could serve a full menu to twice as many tourists. In all fairness, I supposed that this was a good thing for the owners, but still I missed sitting at my traditional place at the bar and after a few shots communing with the spirits of all of those who had gone before.

When I arrived in Talkeetna, I met up with Doug, and he asked me how the flying lessons were coming along.

"I don't know, Doug," I answered. "I've got everything down but the landings, and I guess those are pretty important to the daily affairs of a pilot."

"Yeah, I guess they are. Look, why don't you try taking a lesson from one of our local pilots? I know a woman who is a flight instructor. Maybe she'll take you up. Her name is Andrea. I'll write it down for you. She pronounces it Ann-dray-a."

I called Andrea and made an appointment to go flying the following day, which dawned over Talkeetna crisp and as clear as a fine jewel. Andrea had borrowed a Cessna 172 from the air freight service where she worked, and at 1:00 in the afternoon we were airborne over the little airstrip. We went through a few basic maneuvers, and then she suggested that we do some landings. I told her about my landing skills, or lack of them, and she proposed that I leave the first landing to her and just watch what she did. I could then tell her what I thought of her landing—which was a bit bumpy, but made with all the confidence that I expected she would have.

"If I could land like that, I'd be very happy," I told her.

"Well, it wasn't pretty, but let's see what you can do."

We took off again, circled the field, and I lined up my approach. It was as if everything were happening in slow motion, as if the plane were buoyed by some invisible flying carpet. I lowered the flaps. We slowed and settled. I kicked the rudder to line the plane up with the runway, adjusted the trim, and when that final ten feet came at me, I could hear Natalie telling me to hold it off. I held it, and held it, and we touched the ground as if some great hand had just released us gently upon the earth. We rolled easily to a stop at the end of the runway.

"Well, there was nothing wrong with that," Andrea smiled. "You don't hear anybody in here screaming do you?"

"No, and I think I'll just call it a day with this one," I answered.

"Oh, no you don't," Andrea countered. "We're going up, and you're going to do it again." And so we did, over and over, and the landings were all the same. When my time with her that afternoon was over, I felt as if I were standing atop that great mountain in front of me, shining now, coral in the late-day sun, and I heard myself saying, "For some, it just takes one good landing, and then it all comes together after that."

I soloed on December 5th, 1995, at Nashua, New Hampshire, when Natalie unexpectedly got out of the plane as we were about to taxi, told me that it was mine, and said that I should remember that flying was meant to be fun. They say that one never forgets their first solo. I taxied to the run-up area, completed my procedures, approached the runway, and radioed the tower that I was ready.

"Taxi into position and hold," came the reply from the tower.

I moved to the end of the runway, turned along the center line, and waited. I thought of my family. I thought of Doug and the Doug Geeting Aviation cap I was wearing. I thought of my father and the squadrons of F-86s that flew over our house so many years ago. I thought of the B-17s and the B-24s and the P-51s, and the young people that flew them, and I thought of the words to the old hymn that I had just recently recorded in Texas:

> *"Up and away, like the dew in the morning,*
> *Soaring from Earth to our home in the sun,*
> *Thus would we leave from the world and its toiling . . ."*

"Cessna 61765, you are cleared for takeoff." And I did, and when the wheels left the pavement I thought to myself, "Bill, you'd better damn well know what you're doing." And I did, and all went well, and when I came down after finishing my takeoffs and landings, and had flown around for a little bit, Natalie was there to take my picture for the wall of the flight school. Subsequently I received a certificate stating that I had successfully completed my first solo. I wondered what they gave to anyone who was not successful at the attempt.

That night I called Doug Geeting to give him the news, and he asked me if anyone had cut my shirttail off, as this was a tradition among pilots when someone completes their first solo. I told him that my picture had been taken, but that no one had cut off my shirttail. True to the Alaskan style of doing things, some ten months later, on a Saturday night while I was up onstage at the Latitude 62, Doug and some of his cronies came marching up the aisle to carry out the tradition. I finished the show that night with only the front half of my shirt hanging from my shoulders—the back half finding its way now up onto the wall of the place that I had come to hold so dear.

Shortly after the release of *Looking for the Wind* in the spring of 1996, I received a note in the mail from Reeve Lindbergh, the youngest daughter of Charles and Anne Lindbergh. She had heard my "Song for Tingmissartoq" and had played it for her mother, who picked up her pen and began to write something down on a scrap of paper, something that Reeve had not seen her do in some time. I could only hope that the song in some way may have rekindled in Anne just a little bit of the spirit that had carried her and her husband aloft, so far above us, in such a long ago and different time.

CHAPTER 52

The Fall Tour, Day 32

I have been on the road now for more than a month. Tonight's show in Denver for Swallow Hill will be the 20th concert of the tour, but my energy is holding, and the bright sunshine of the new day is good for the spirit. In the mountains to the west, thick white clouds sit like dollops of whipped cream over the high peaks. Where the wind has ushered the clouds away, one can see the fresh autumn snow cover and sense that the year is growing older now, quickly and without regret.

After checking into my hotel, I drive over to the old church on East Yale, which is now the new home for Swallow Hill, to let them know that I'm in town and to find out how the ticket sales are going for the night. They tell me that the phone has been busy all day with calls about the show, and that we should have a good turnout.

My friends Jacquie Manning and Rich Prezioso (also known as Small Potatoes) will be doing the opening set, and Rosalie Sorrels, who will be in concert the next night, is in town a day early and plans to drop by the show.

With some time to spare for the rest of the afternoon, I drive over to the Denver Folklore Center to buy some guitar strings, sit around to play a tune or two, and catch up on the news from Harry Tufts. Being an old folkie like myself, Harry is always willing to put up with my ravings about the state of folk music and the music scene in general. Why do people feel the need to use two capos on their guitar necks? What's the deal with these tuners that do everything but cook breakfast for you? Can't anybody tune from an A note anymore? Where's the depth of spirit in the songs?

Harry nods and quietly smiles as he waits on another customer. Let's sing us a tune together, Harry, maybe "Blue Mountain" or "The Colorado Trail." I'll play the autoharp, you play the guitar, and maybe the wind blowing off the mountains will hear us and carry the music upon its back until it is spent and the easy notes of the songs once again fall gently back into their own good earth.

At the hotel bar after the concert, there is a table of friends: Jacquie, Rich, Rosalie, and I. We are telling stories about other friends—Bruce Phillips, Malvina Reynolds, Bob Gibson—and about the road, or shows gone by, or what is in the future for us. We talk about poetry and books, authors and style, and what life is all about and where it might lead. And then we order another round, and we drink a toast to all of those who have ever felt the same.

CHAPTER 53

Dear Friend

I was feeling pretty good about myself and the fact that I had learned how to fly. I did not have my license, but I had accomplished what I had set out to do and knew that now and again I could hire a flight instructor as a human insurance policy and take a friend up with me to get away from it all. I was passionate about flying, and it was the only thing that seemed to be able to clear my mind of the other pressures and turmoil that surrounded me.

In the summer of 1996, when I was in Minnesota for a gig at the state fair, I invited Jerry Rau to go up with me for a flight out of Flying Cloud Airport near Minneapolis. Not being one for small airplanes, Jerry reluctantly agreed, and we made an appointment at one of the flying services for the flight. I, of course, was eager to show off my newly acquired skills to my friend, and we arrived at the airport almost two hours early.

When we checked in at the receptionist's desk, we were told that we were very early, and that our plane, a Cessna 172, and the instructor were not yet available. No problem, there was a wonderful little air museum at the airport, so Jerry and I spent the next hour and a half touring the adjacent hangers amid restorations of some of the classic aircraft that saw the country through two world wars.

When our tour was over, Jerry and I headed back toward the flight service hanger. In the distance, on the other side of the building, I could hear the din of what I knew to be a 172 engine.

"That must be our plane," I told Jerry. "I can recognize the sound of a 172 engine anywhere."

God has a funny way of dealing with egos and people who think that they know more than they do, and this day was no different. As we rounded the corner of the building, we came face-to-face with, indeed, a parked airplane, a twin-engine Cessna—but the engines were not running. The roar that I was certain was being made by a 172 was actually someone using a powered buffing machine to polish the surface of the wings.

Jerry looked at me and started to laugh. What was I to say? "Hey look, it sounded like a 172 engine."

Jerry laughed again. "At least if we go down, the obit will be great."

"Thanks, brother. You know, there is something to be learned from this."

If Jerry was like a brother to me, then Jana Metge was like a sister. Jana had wandered onto the stage of things during the closing scene of the Coffeehouse Extempore years, and the three of us had become close friends. Whenever I was in the Twin Cities, Jerry, Jana, and I always spent time together, and it was this special friendship, surviving the years, that was one of the foundations of my life on the road. Through the musical and personal ups and downs, they were always there to make me laugh to the point of tears when sometimes tears no longer seemed possible.

My touring schedule for 1996 was as busy as usual with spring concerts in the Midwest, concerts coinciding with Kerrville during May and June in the South, festivals in the summer, and the long tour to the West in the fall, when I returned to Alaska and my friends at the Latitude 62.

The days now seemed to have been reduced to 18 hours, the

months to 3 weeks, and the years to 9 months. Where was the time going?

In November of 1996, Karen's father passed away after a long illness, and just a short time later, our dog Hallie left us. It was a sad time. I was beginning to feel a little worn. It was as if I closed my eyes one night, and when I opened them again, it was a year later and I was 50 years old, half a century, first of the baby boomers, a child of the Sixties.

I decided that I would go on a quest, much as an Indian youth would do to seek a vision as to the purpose and reason for their being. In my case, I would seek out and write down the words to a prayer that when spoken would bring me some sort of inner peace. It would not be an easy quest, for the words would have to be chosen for their precise value and meaning, and it would take time, for to write such a verse might require my entire life. My thoughts again turned to Logan and the times that I watched him struggling to find the perfect word or phrase for one of his poems. I knew that I would wait until the right words came, and that I would not abandon this quest until it was complete. I must search within my own soul and find the path to that peace, for to do anything less would simply be a betrayal to my own conscience.

Fall turned to winter, winter to spring, and with the magnificent unfurling of the pubescent green leaves of the oaks, birches, and maples, I was writing again. It was only a single song, but when I was finished I cried, and that was always a good sign. It was a song about how much music meant to me, and how much it had an effect upon my life. The song was entitled, "When I Hear the Music Play," and I thought that it was one of my best songs. I had not been writing much in recent months—only two tunes, "On the Road Again" and "Dear Friend"—but I was happy with how the songs had turned out, and that was all that really mattered.

In August of 1997, I was invited by the Lindbergh Foundation to Little Falls, Minnesota, for the 70th anniversary of Charles' flight to Paris. I would be performing at an arts evening, and Reeve Lindbergh would be there to read from some of her works. I was honored to be invited to the event and felt as if once again my music had provided that means by which I could feel closer to those who have shaped the history of this country.

On that same trip to the Midwest, I also did a number of shows in Wisconsin, with stops in Rhinelander, Fond Du Lac, and Milwaukee.

During September of 1997, I recorded my 21st album, a family album for Red House called, *One More River.*

The Happy Wanderer had been a steady seller, and Bob Feldman was keen to do another recording in the same vein. *The Happy Wanderer* was labeled an album for "Kids, Cars, and Campfires," so we subtitled *One More River* as "More Songs for Kids, Cars, and Campfires."

For the recording, I returned to the little studio in Arlington, Massachusetts, where I had recorded *The Happy Wanderer* and also done much of my work for Burlington Northern. The studio, called Straight Up Music, was operated by Larry Luddecke, who was not only a fine engineer, but also a talented keyboard player who had worked with the likes of John Hammond, Tom Rush, Laverne Baker, and Buddy Guy.

We recorded *One More River* in eight days, using many of the same musical friends that I had known for years, those who had played on so many of my albums and had played so well. Again the guitar player was Guy Van Duser; the bass player, Mike Walsh. Stuart Schulman was the violinist, and Billy Novick played clarinet as well as saxophone.

I also brought in a new voice to help out with the vocals. My son Bowen, who had just turned 11 and was now playing the guitar, came by the session to watch, but was pressed into service to sing on one of the choruses. He was reluctant at first, but my offer to pay him $20 changed his mind in an instant—a true studio player in the making.

With the completion of *One More River,* I was back on the road for my 18th fall tour, the familiar routine almost second nature to me. Inasmuch as I was making a living on the road, it was often suggested that I vary the tour a little to broaden my audience. Perhaps I should skip Alaska for a year and spend the time performing in the South. Perhaps I should pass on playing San Francisco, and play Phoenix or Taos instead. It seemed like good advice, but then what of my friends?

For 18 years, I had played in San Francisco on the second Sunday of October. It was a part of my nature to be there, a constant in the changing lives of others. And for me, it was the people, the familiar faces, that were so much a part of my life on the road. One night stand after one night stand, town after strange town, would have brought nothing to me, except perhaps a little more fame or fortune, and how could that compare with once again seeing the smile of a good and dear friend?

The old months of the year slipped away, with the words and the music of a new song rising within me and the snows of New England falling gently through the wind-blown and bare branches of the shivering trees.

"Dear friend, we have carried life within us like a fire,
A hot and burning fire, running on and leaping higher,
And though we've danced within the flames,
We will always be the same, my friend . . ."

CHAPTER 54

The Fall Tour, Day 33

The mountains are gone now behind me, the last image of their rocky, snow-capped majesty resembling low-lying white clouds in the far distance. I shall not see them again for perhaps another year, or perhaps another eternity. One never knows. Life offers us nothing as a promise, only an opportunity to run with the years that we have as far as we can go, and with them to do what we will with our lives, to be what we can be, and to hopefully contribute something, no matter how insignificant, to the great passing of time.

It is the last Saturday in October. It is also an important game day. It is the day each year that I drive east along Interstate 80 across the broad expanse that is Nebraska, and I share the road with the fanatical fans that are rooting for either the Colorado Buffaloes or the Nebraska Cornhuskers in their annual gridiron rivalry.

This year the game is in Boulder, so my side of the interstate is relatively vacant. It is the westbound side that early this morning is resplendent with scarlet banners and flags streaming from the trucks and cars of the Cornhusker fans as they head west for the yearly classic. Rumor has it that the teams are pretty evenly matched, but the odds makers are with Nebraska as the slight favorite.

This is a travel day for me, so I can take my time driving, knowing that it is only about 450 miles to Omaha, and that I will arrive easily in St. Paul by tomorrow afternoon for my show in the evening at the University of Minnesota.

By late this morning, I am at Julesburg, on the Colorado-Nebraska border, and by noon I am at the junction of the North Platte and South Platte rivers at Ogallala. The long straight stretches of the interstate and the warm sun in my face make it difficult to stay awake, so I stop for coffee and turn on the radio, only to catch the pre-game interviews with the coaches of both teams, each with their predictions of a tough game and of victory for their side.

At North Platte, where the settlers heading west to Oregon took that fork of the river northwest toward Chimney Rock and Scott's Bluff, I hear the roar of the crowd over the radio as the game gets underway. I pass the Pony Express Station at Gothenburg, feeling a little uneasy about driving east when so much of the history around me deals with those headed in the opposite direction. But then I have already been to the West this year, and now it is time for me to return home.

The first quarter of the game winds down through the last few seconds, and with the sound of the referee's whistle, the teams also reverse directions. It is all again a matter of balance, the gaining and losing of yardage, the breathing in and the breathing out, the great circle of time and seasons arcing back upon itself until it becomes complete, only to then unravel and begin again and again and again.

By the end of the first half, Nebraska has chalked up a considerable lead, and the flow of the gridiron tide is with Big Red. This lead, however, is not to last, for by the time I reach Kearney, the Colorado team has rallied and made it a game once more.

I stop for gas just west of Grand Island, and as I enter the mini-mart to pay for the fuel, I am just in time to hear a collective groan from the customers gathered in front of the small television behind the counter. Colorado has tied the score, and the game will go into overtime.

It will be Nebraska that prevails this afternoon, but barely. With a final push into the Colorado end zone, the Cornhuskers, in overtime, come away with a 33-30 win, and the celebrating begins on the streets of Lincoln, just an hour down the road to the east.

And then Lincoln is behind me and now it is Omaha, and soon it will be Des Moines, where I spend the night at a small trucker's motel just off the interstate. The roof of the motel is outlined in yellow neon lamps that hum like bees around a new hive, and the headlights from the inbound and outbound semis fire the room with flashing luminescence—dark, then bright, dark, then bright again, until it makes no difference anymore, and the flashes become a rhythm to me, and the hum of the lamps becomes a one-note lullaby, soothing and leading me away from the road and the roaring football fans into a space that is deep and dark and ever so delirious with dreams.

CHAPTER 55

Changes

In January of 1998, Rounder released the second volume of *The First Million Miles,* the first having been released in 1989. The songs for the two-CD series were all original and taken from recordings that I had done for the label throughout the 1980s. The one exception was the traditional song, "Sweet Sunny South" that I recorded as a duet with Jeanie Stahl for a CD to benefit Club Passim in Cambridge. The club had fallen on hard times in the early 1990s, with Bob and RaeAnne Donlin struggling to keep the doors open in the face of dwindling attendance and changing demographics.

When the news of the club's impending demise reached the folk music community in and around Cambridge, a host of concerned characters charged in to the rescue. This group was led by Steve Baird, organizer, street singer, and one of the founders of the New England Folk Arts Network. With help from Rounder, various folkie attorneys and accountants, and a bunch of musicians, the wolf at the door was temporarily held at bay while the Donlins gracefully gave over the reins to Passim to a new order of management and a promising but uncertain future. For nearly 25 years, Bob and RaeAnne had been the heart and soul of Passim, and had kept the music alive in that little space at the upper end of Palmer Street that had always been so special to me.

Club Passim would survive, eventually operating as a nonprofit organization, recapturing in many ways the spirit of the original Club 47. Sadly, though, within a year Bob Donlin passed away, leaving a hole in the hearts of so many of us who missed his antics in the back of the room and his hand signals to the musicians onstage when it came time for "one more song." RaeAnne remained on the scene for a while, occasionally dropping by the club, but eventually she moved on to travel other paths in her life.

I had seen so many changes over the years. I had known the passing of friends, the openings and closings of countless coffeehouses, and the comings and goings of entire music scenes. I had seen the development of nearly two subsequent generations of singer-songwriters and even watched as a few of them became stars. In the summer of 1998, while browsing through a bookstore in Saratoga, New York, I came upon a volume of single-page biographies recounting who was who in the contemporary folk music scene. Curious as to whether I may have been mentioned, I started thumbing my way from the back cover to the front of the book. The last section in the volume was the bluegrass section. The next-to-last chapter was the blues section with Bonnie Raitt, Rory Block, and Lightning Hopkins. I knew that I would not be there. The third-from-the-last was the singer-songwriters. Perhaps I was here, along with Nanci Griffith, Suzanne Vega, and John Gorka. No mention. What would be the last section?

I turned to the front of the book. The very first section was labeled "The Old School." On the last page of the section, I came face-to-face with a photo of a grizzled Bill Staines. There I was. I continued to thumb through the chapter and the lives of those in "the Old School." Here were the stories of Pete Seeger, Joan Baez, Tom Paxton, Dave Van Ronk, Judy Collins, and so many others. I realized then that I had been included within the section that represented those who had been the real inspirations in my life of music. Here were my heroes. I might never be a star, I thought, but I was a part of "the Old School." As I left the bookstore that sunny day in Saratoga, that was quite enough for me.

CHAPTER 56

The Road Home, The Last Day

"Here's to the rainbow that's followed me here,
Here's to the friends that I know,
Here's to the song that's within me now,
I will sing it where ere I go."

The final two stops of the tour are in St. Paul and Milwaukee. It is good to see Jerry, Jana, and my friends at the New Folk Collective again. When the concert in St. Paul is over, we all head down the street to a local bar and talk until late, the bartender finally telling us that it is really time to go, but in the same breath offering us another beer if someone will just sing a song. How many years have I known these friends? How many beers have we shared together? The hour may be late, but it does not feel late. Only in the morning, when it is time to get back on the road, will the toll have to be paid and the piper compensated.

The miles roll away beneath me now: Minnesota, Wisconsin, Illinois, Indiana, Ohio, with my future always over the rise of the next distant hill, and my heart wondering what that future will bring. Will there be another generation of troubadours, or will these paved highways that have carried the music for so long be replaced by the digital highways of the internet, offering the option of downloading music and concerts direct to the listener without them ever having to leave home? I hope that this will not be the case, for life is more than that, and music is more than that. Life is the vast story that is told to us by ourselves, and within that story dwells a song which is ours alone, the flowing notes playing to the cadence of the passing years, and the lyrics to the contents of those years.

I retrace the miles across the northwest corner of Pennsylvania and into New York state, the waters of Lake Erie visible as a gray-blue ribbon off to my left, and beyond them to the north the hairline distant shores of Canada.

I now have to constantly check my speed, for the distances and the vistas of the open road have tricked my senses into believing that 80 miles per hour is just a ramble, and getting stopped by a state trooper on the last leg of the tour is an experience that I would like to forego.

I pass Buffalo and Rochester, then Albany and the toll booths at the entrance to the Massachusetts Turnpike. I am only four hours from home, but they seem like the longest four hours of the tour.

The November sun is low now as I make the right turn onto my road and am greeted once more by those majestic pines that are so familiar to me and so dear. It is hard to believe that 30 years have gone by since I took the step to become a full-time musician. It is hard to believe that it has been 40 years since I started to play those first chords on a guitar. I still think of my old friends often, of Roger and Jesse, and of the blonde-haired Cynthia in her great black coat and winter hat, strolling the streets of Beacon Hill, looking like some beautiful Russian princess. I think of Doc Cummins and of Mark Edwards, of Jim Rooney, and all of the people who knew me as a musical upstart singing for five dollars a night in the coffeehouses of Boston. They are all here, safe within these pages.

It is but a half-mile to my driveway, the brown fields around my home now gone into dormancy for the winter. It is hunting season for those who care. I do not. The tour is done for another year. My son, the musician, opens the door. Our young dog, Andie, bounds down the front steps, doing her best impression of a wolf, with her head turned to the sky and a long howl rising from deep within. It is her welcome song. My wife is also there, although a little behind the rest. I can only tell them that I love them all, that I love life and the living of it, and that I love the immense sound of the music that is all about me.

Once I was a child; somewhere along the way, I grew up and became a man. But if I have become a man, I must also realize that with each new dawn I will become a child again, and where this all shall lead I do not know. But that is okay, for I have never been a person with great lifelong goals. Perhaps that is a bad thing. I don't think so.

EPILOGUE

Great God of all things, spirit of my own wings,
Teach me to soar far above that which would bring me down,
And if I should come to fear and question the heights,
Remind me that I am in your arms, and that I am with the eagles.